BLUES FOR CANNIBALS

BLUES FOR CANNIBALS

THE NOTES FROM UNDERGROUND

Charles Bowden

NORTH POINT PRESS

A division of Farrar, Straus and Giroux

New York

North Point Press
A division of Farrar, Straus and Giroux
19 Union Square West, New York 10003

Copyright © 2002 by Charles Bowden
All rights reserved
Distributed in Canada by Douglas & McIntyre Ltd.
Printed in the United States of America
First edition, 2002

Library of Congress Cataloging-in-Publication Data
Bowden, Charles
Blues for cannibals : the notes from underground / Charles Bowden — 1st ed.
p. cm.
ISBN 0-86547-624-1 (alk. paper)
1. United States — Description and travel.   2. United States — Social conditions —
1980–   3. United States — Moral conditions.   4. National characteristics, American.
5. Bowden, Charles — Journeys — United States.   6. Mesquite — folklore.   7. Cannibalism — Folklore.   8. Bowden, Charles.   9. Authors, American — Biography.
10. Bowden, Charles — Political and social views.   I. Title.

E169.04 .B667 2002
973.92 — dc21

2001031721

Designed by Jonathan D. Lippincott

www.fsgbooks.com

1   2   3   4   5   6   7   8   9   10

For my *compañeros*
Arturo Carrillo Strong and Chris Clarke,
who showed me the way to go home
after midnight.
They will never leave my side
so long as I stand my ground.
And I know no way to leave.

Look harder! After all we don't even know where "real life" is lived nowadays, or what it is, and what name it goes by. Leave us to ourselves, without our books, and at once we get into a muddle and lose our way—we don't even know whose side to be on or where to give our allegiance, what to love and what to hate, what to respect and what to despise. We even find it difficult to be human beings, men with real flesh and blood of *our own*; we are ashamed of it, we think it a disgrace, and we are always striving to be some unprecedented kind of generalized human being. We are born dead, and moreover we have long ceased to be the sons of living fathers; we become more and more contented with our condition. We are acquiring a taste for it. Soon we shall invent a method of being born from an idea.

—Fyodor Dostoyevsky, *Notes from Underground*, 1864

BLUES FOR CANNIBALS

Cultural Instructions:
Prosopis juliflora, velutina,
glandulosa, pubescens

No more silence. Do not be confused by the simple words. The dust is now being blown from the throats, the sap rises in the gorge. There is nothing to be done about these matters since the seed has been cast, the moist earth licks the pods, and now the life comes on. The parts that seem familiar will turn out not to be familiar. Things have changed under the hand and grown new branches in their new settings. The stem lurks underground. Cut it down to a stump and it multiplies trunks. Cut a branch and gain twenty more. The pod of the seed lacks a suture and must rot off. The tree is made for hard times. The entire thing is rooted and now lives with deep hungers. The tempo has changed also.

As the tree grows, the roots sink deeper into the ground and the bone people are sucked to the surface, dead presidents, living dead artists, dead friends and men made newly dead by the force of law. Naturally, a living tree has a rhythm, the thing we call seasons, and this too is present and uncontrollable.

All this leads to an inevitable place, just as a seed contains within it the ancient tree with vast limbs.

Weather will be a factor. Watch for blue mists. Expect drought. Know the flood is coming. Read menus carefully. Open your mouth.

And be warned: "Mesquite is yet the most feared and hated tree that grows, a menace that is every year extending its ravages, spreading desolation where once was wealth."

Entrance Wound

Come with me and we will sink into our pleasures. No, we won't do a line or have a toke or open that bottle. Those things are nice but they never go far enough. The nose goes, the weed takes too long and the liver must be considered, don't you agree? This time we will get ripped and it will not be an idiom or a metaphor. This time we will take a harder drug, one denounced by the authorities.

I have deliberately picked a room for our work. The room is very small and American sterile, it is the perfect room for exploring our secret places and stirring the strong juices that lurk in our bodies. Edward Hopper lived trapped in this room and painted it again and again. When I was a child in the years just after World War II, special years when people were grateful to have survived and yet wounded and numb, I lived in rooms like Edward Hopper painted, sterile, lonely rooms where silence reigned and yet an explosion of violence was always close by, perhaps lurking in that closet or crouched behind the sofa. My father took me one day to the Chicago Art Institute and I saw Hopper's paintings, or so I remember, and they were among the first paintings I understood and felt. They were my world and my terrors and my loneliness.

So these matters go back a long ways with me, as I'm sure they do with you. And I am talking about the senses, about feelings, about the joy of song and the punch of death. Not certain types of feelings but being able to feel, and more important, being willing. I have been under siege, yes, I admit it, things have at times overwhelmed me. And you cannot deny that this has also happened to you. The sex crimes took their toll, so did the dying. We fled to the country and that was good but never enough. Besides, we could not stay. Country living is behind us, we can only visit or remember that part. The war came also. We felt love, we fell into the cooking, we worked very hard in the garden where we created a lover that rubbed us raw and drowned us in perfume. These things are only part of why I am talking to you from this small room with a cable television and fifty-five identical channels. The rates are posted on the door, plus the essential directions for escape when the fire comes to char our bodies. In this room, I can finally remember that it started with a tree. Come, we will go into the wood.

I met the tree long ago and have remained a slave to its song. And now it is bringing me back from the dead. My life is within the wood. Against the grain, but within the wood. I am an agnostic about God. I can believe in God but I can never trust Him. I waste no time on prayers, not a single moment do I spare for such a thing. It is not that I think prayers go unanswered, I actually have no idea. It is that I refuse to listen to such answers. They cannot be enough to explain what I see. I will not be cajoled into accepting the hurt. I refuse such blandishments. The hurt is real, and the answered prayers are not enough, not nearly enough. I can live the sin, aspire to the virtue, lust for grace. I am a fallen man and I know it, and I accept the torture of living this fact. But I will be damned—and they say I surely will be damned—if I will accept God's answer. So I do not pray. Nor do I worship. I can love, I can comfort. I am the tree struggling in the hot ground of my desert. No bended knee and please no messages from on high. The messages must come from here, from the ground itself or away with them. That is what I learn from the mesquite, my brother-in-arms.

Do not be confused. We are not druids here or pantheists or fairies in a sylvan whirl of velvet and chimes. True, we sing, we have our song. But no chants, never chants. Or ceremonies. We believe in cells and protoplasm and sex, a great deal of sex, and stench and dirt and slime and screams in the night. We are not of the peaceable kingdom here, and we have little peace. We contain a great deal of anger and even more of violence, the hand reaches out at all hours for the throat. We wait for the moment to strike back and yet we struggle, struggle each and every second, to still that hand, to open that fist into a warm palm and caress the face. To not reach for that gun, cool, black, the barrel short, the action fully automatic, the rounds—nine millimeter—resting in a banana clip like so many fangs anxious to tear flesh asunder. We are not sinners in the hands of an angry god since we do not have that trust and do not pray, and when we see a burning bush, we put out the fire. But we can accept the storm, the pitiless sun, the rot and then the dust. And we don't ask why, that is our wisdom, or at least the wisdom of my brother the mesquite and the one I reach toward every dusk and every dawn and sometimes in the blink of midnight.

Imagine this: a world of tongues and caresses, a constant touching of the genitals, a world hidden like the planet Venus from common view by the clouds of scents steaming off our desires, a world obscene with appetite and orgasm and strong spices and drenched in chilies. That is the world of mesquite. And it follows me everywhere because I am of the wood.

Recently I was in the city of New York to talk of the pope. They say he is senile now, but this I do not know. Anyway, I was not to speak to his mental acuity in his dotage but to his encyclical on the Culture of Death. This felt odd. I sat there in the Church of the Incarnation while the cameras rolled and a woman outside the eye of the lens asked me question after question about this pope and his fury about the Culture of Death. She was very quick with her tongue, a woman rich in agendas and welded to her cell phone.

The day before I had been hanging out with a United States senator as he wrestled with the wisdom of some war in the Balkans. I had followed him like a shadow for vote after vote, committee meeting after committee meeting, been allowed into the tent as it were while the elect, the hundred solons of Senate, kicked the matter of war and peace around like a soccer ball and hoped for a goal. At night I stayed in a very good Washington hotel, one rich with old woods and marble surfaces, a place expensive and generous with fine meats and vintage wines. One evening I drank with a Frenchman, an oil executive actually, who had a grandfather driven from Belgium by the

German onslaught of World War I, a father born as a refugee on the march as his grandmother fled the armies during the gore of August 1914, and this Frenchman, a Catholic naturally, believed two things absolutely: that this Balkan war must be fought lest the demons of European history break loose and run amok once again as they had in 1914 and that this pope was obviously senile. This second point he would give no ground on, no matter how long we talked, no matter how many fine bottles of cabernet we drank. And as we talked and settled gratefully into our drunkenness, images of that Balkan war played across the television screen like a sporting event.

Finally, after three hours, the Frenchman caved in, caved in I believe to the wisdom of mesquite, and talked of his chief passion in life, cooking. Like myself, he falls asleep at night reading cookbooks—that tongue wet with hunger again, always that tongue. He had just been out to Texas on oil matters and bought some fine chilies to take home to his kitchen in the south of France. He said I must come see him and his family, we would cook and let the world drift away into its madness.

The next day I left him and the senator and went to that church in New York for my meeting with the Culture of Death. They taped me for two hours as a gentle rain fell on Manhattan. I struggled to find words to connect the pope's Culture of Death with the world as I know it and finally, just before we ended the session, I lost my temper and said that any fool can see what the Culture of Death means, see it in our uncaring faces, see it in the gluttony of our markets, see it in our denial of how most of the earth's billions live or barely live, see it in our chemically charged and neurotic stabs at peace. I said it is not my fault that this demented old man in a dress sees this clearly, that this medieval mind grasps the true emptiness moderns ignore. Afterward I walked thirty blocks in the rain, workers hurrying past me on their way to dreams of a Friday night, and finally surrendered to a bar and wound up drinking until two in the morning. A few days later, the producers called and said the last few minutes of my taping were strong and fine and just what they needed for, well, maybe thirty seconds of airtime.

My best friend's ashes lie underneath the shade of two mesquites in my backyard. He was a drinking man and, in his cups, a terrible thing to behold, a brilliant mind reduced by the bottle to rage and idiocy. He would in his moments of darkness lose a weekend to two or three quarts of cheap vodka a day, the body steeled to the work by grams of fine cocaine. Years ago, when he had gotten out of detox yet again, I threw him into my truck and drove for hours across the desert and plunged into a volcanic wilderness in Mexico before we came to rest. We camped by a water hole named Tinaja Emilia, the naming happening long ago when a strange Norwegian wanderer passed through and thought to honor some woman he knew back in the United States. The ground was studded with ironwood, paloverde and mesquite. Sleeping circles left by some ancient folk lay close by and the litter of thousands of years—stone implements, charcoal from long-dead fires—was scattered about. My friend began to breathe again, and when night fell he called out the constellations like a schoolboy. At dawn the brittlebush was in bloom and the black volcanic slopes were ablaze with yellow flowers. We started up the cinder slopes, very slowly since my friend was weak. Halfway up, we came upon I'itoi's cave, his western house where he keeps one of his wives since she loves the sea and the Gulf of California swells nearby.

I'itoi is a largely retired god who was once quite popular in this area. His wife continues to live in the cave—after all, where is she to go with the old man now largely out of work—and thanks to the volcanic tubes left by some eruption, she can hear the beating of the waves as she goes about her household tasks. A giant honeycomb hung from the walls, and the roar of the insects was horrible as we dropped down into the god's dwelling. Prayer sticks left by the ancients peeked from cracks in the walls. My friend left a Marlboro Light as an offering. But then he was a praying man. We continued up, slipping and sliding, to the peak, and we stood there and could see across the gulf to the mountains of Baja. The change was electric, the life pulsed in him. Then we dropped down into the camp at Tinaja Emilia and the thorny embrace of the mesquite. He never went back. I think the singing was too much for him. He chose a different path and I could not stop him in his errand. I had done all I knew how to do.

Recently, I had four biopsies in an hour. The doctors were determined to discover what was wrong with me. I could not explain the deep sickness to them, any more than I could tell them of the cure, of the wood against my face. There had been a massive and sudden swelling on my neck, my fever rose, and I went to bed and waited for death. They thought cancer, since they are reasonable people. They also had me sign a form so that they could test me for AIDS. I did not agree with what I saw in their anxious eyes. I knew I had a soul sickness like the savages we watch on television documentaries and I knew the savages were not exotic or a distant and irrelevant part of my past as a homo sapiens but flesh of my flesh and that I was paying a blood price for what I had seen and felt and devoured like red meat. I knew the sickness was within me and so was the cure. I only had to remember. And so I did. And the swelling went away. I remember the first thing I did. I cooked and then I ate. Tongues.

They say mesquite will float but I do not believe this claim. I have seen it struggle in a desert storm, the waters coming angry out of a narrow canyon, then spreading against the soft banks of the arroyo snaking across the *bajada*, the air electric with energy and the light rich with a green cast of violence. I have stood right there as it came like a wall—the dreaded flash flood of our nightmares but a dream too often denied our waking hours—the waters four or five feet high, the brown face roiling and foaming, a sentence garbled by the fury of the statement, and the wind is down, almost a sick stillness in the summer afternoon, the core of the downpour is miles away on the sacred peak, one called Baboquivari, another place where I'itoi lives, the god of the people who knew the ground before my kind came, and I looked up at the rock tower now hidden in clouds and darkness, a blackness only broken by the jagged teeth of lightning, stood there staring: the foaming, licking the sentence fragments moving like a wall down the arroyo, the dirt banks here and there collapsing, falling with a roar like icebergs calving off a glacier, the hair on the back of my neck tingling from the currents of energy exploding off the peak and as I stared, I fell into the scene, lost all fear and succumbed to appetite. It took all of my will not to walk into that wall of water and merge with it and ride away with the flood. Then I saw it, a full-grown mesquite, one of the ancients that cling up above, a work requiring centuries of patience and sun and storms, saw it bobbing like a toy, totally uprooted now, a thing tired of waiting, weary of being rooted and now free to move and course hither and yon about the land.

I travel a lot, and when I travel I tell people it is for a story, but what I am really looking for is love. Not a woman for myself, but love on the faces of people and in their gait and in the smooth joy of their speech. I travel in the true desert. The Sahara, I believe, has more water than the modern world has love. I cannot easily explain this fact. Fornication seems to be operating at reasonable volume. But I sense this reality everywhere. I am in Washington having coffee with a Senate aide, an old hand who has spent decades on the hill and came to town as a youngster, and I look at all the young women in the cafeteria. Washington is a city of people barely past their teens clowning around in suits, and I tell the woman, this old Washington hand, that they all look cold and empty, and I know this is not a nice thing to say of strangers but I tell her I am the true stranger here. And she says, "Everyone here is lonely, this is a very lonely city."

Later I tell an editor in New York that I do not like the capital. He says he does not either. I jump on his statement and offer that if I lived there I would wind up killing someone. He says no, no, he would kill himself. But I want to make this clear: I don't know if Washington is natural or unnatural. I am not a poster boy for the Pleistocene. The city is cold, the modern world is cold, the flesh is there but people find it easier to hit than to touch, and the easiest thing of all is not to make a move, to sit and watch until your shift is over.

There is something missing, some vivid touch that the cool computer screens we now all stare into at work and at home cannot deliver. The last common feeling we have left is depression, and it is so common, we only notice it when we cannot bear any longer to go on. We can grow hair on our heads and stuff new breasts in our chests and suck fat from our hides but we cannot seem to paste a smile on our faces. We are not the people who will die of laughter.

The mesquite lives for centuries and we come and go with our cigarettes and coffee, and the mesquite rolls on and on as we pass through from womb to grave. The tree is stark, all bent and gnarly, and fails to make good wood for lumber. There is no straight to it, just this twisting and turning as it roasts under the sun. The grain is close and dark and runs to rich reds that rouge our eyes and make us envy. When burnt, the smoke is acrid, yet sweet, and hangs over our lives as incense for a church we cannot name and a faith we cannot fathom.

South of my town lie the brutal holes of open pit mines, giant eyes carved in the earth that stare dumbly at the sky. Once, years ago, the huge machines that carved these holes hit a living mesquite root at one hundred and seventy-eight feet, a finger of life and lust probing the hard rock seeking water. The flower of the tree is a five- or six-inch cylinder covered with tiny yellow florets. The pollen is heavy when the flowers open in the spring and bees forage furiously. The honey is dark and has a musky quality. The wood burns like a rock, shoots out no sparks, and goes for hours and hours, a glowing mass of red coals. The fire requires no screen.

Mesquite belongs to our world because we have unleashed its hungers. Once in that long ago believed by children and scholars, the grasslands lapped the desert's edge and splotched favored portions of its interior, and the mesquite huddled and reached for more ground, only to be beaten back by the fires that periodically walk across all grasslands. The mesquite has a seed that is hard and thick and I had a friend who once had this seed sneak up on his life. He kept finding a strange kind of hollowed-out grinding stone in my desert and in the bowl of each was a perfect hole. No one could explain these objects. My friend built a wooden staff with odd bulges to fit the cone and its hole and dropped in mesquite beans and then explained to the world the latest stone-age technology, the gyratory crusher, a prehistoric Cuisinart suited to breaking apart this fierce seed.

The bean is rich in protein, richer than beef itself, a thing on the level of, say, tofu in its nutritive powers. And the perfect way, it turns out, to break the coating on this seed so that it germinates and grows into a tree is to run it through a cow's mouth and stomachs and then cast it out in a pile of hot dung. With fire checked and the cattle fashioning themselves into horticulturists, the mesquite spread and engorged large tracts of land and when I was a boy was widely seen as a plague, something to be bulldozed, then piled in heaps and burned.

This sad era of mesquite murder is over and now the tree is valued for what it is: our brother, the better part of our desert nature, the way to belong here, the way to probe deeply and suck the healing earth.

Love, I know, is essential if death is to be put in its place, and it has a place, but love is essential even if I do not know the words that give it flesh and scent. That is why we find it so difficult to write about sex. Not because we are so inhibited and prudish but because when we write about sex, we get acts and organs, a breast, a vagina, a cock, juices, tongues and thrusts—and wind up with recipes but no food. Orgasm is just a word. We have a hunger and love fills it, however briefly, and our accounts of having sex do not catch what drives us into the night seeking light.

For the mesquite the rains come slowly, a foreplay in white light as the rage of June melts into July and the clouds, big white cumulus clouds, come floating like a flotilla from the sea. The clouds collect after noon around the mountain peaks that tower over the desert floor and become black, angry fists with thunder and lightning, but the mesquite crouched on the burning *bajadas* gets no relief, the leaves hang limp in the sun, and this goes on day after day after day as the monsoon builds its power. The meteorologists explain it all by dew-point, that this dewpoint must hit a certain number before the rains can fall. The mesquite believes none of this and knows deep in its hard wood that the waiting is part of the wooing and that rains cannot come on command or by the numbers or they will not truly be rains at all. The dry heat of June and much or all of July is part of the rain.

When I was twenty a woman looked into my eyes with an invitation and she was not innocent. She drove a Thunderbird convertible and I had never been in such an automobile. It had four seats and she kept a pint of whiskey under the driver's side. Her lover had been a musician and she had followed him around the country as he played and she went down on club owners to get gigs and after each gig he sodomized her. She still loved him, and I loved her. She lived alone in a rented house and had a lot of money. She came from Kansas and was the product of some fortune fashioned out of wheat and oil. She was tall and carried her height with ease, chin up, back straight. Long brown hair hung down her back and her body was firm and abundant. When she smoked, she left a delicious ring of lipstick on each butt. Her eyes were also brown and very quick, as were her words. She fought her demons by pouring herself into late medieval philosophy, the strange yearnings of all those womanless saints.

We would make love on the floor and the couch and the car seats, everywhere but the bed. This was obviously important to her but I never asked why. I did not care, I was so hungry for her flesh. She told me she had picked me out because I was bright, and she had done the picking. I was too uncertain of myself to make any kind of move. We did nothing but drink and drive and fuck and stop now and then in the dark of night at cheap fast-food joints. We ordered from the car and seemed hardly ever to leave it. The night air streamed across us, the summer air of heat and dryness as everything waited for the teasing rain.

One day she told me she was pregnant and I said nothing. I was not concerned, I did not care about anything but her and the scent that came off her skin. And then she cut me dead. Not because I failed to speak to the matter of her pregnancy but because I seemed to no longer matter. My part was done. She vanished, just like that, overnight, the house emptied, the Thunderbird nowhere to be seen, the classes at the university all dropped like toys that no longer amused. For decades I have wondered if she was truly pregnant and some odd nights, as I sat out in the August heat waiting for the first drops of rain in months and months, wondered if I had a child trapped in the golden wilderness of Kansas. Or maybe the musician has a stepchild and they are traipsing across the country from gig to gig, blow job to blow job, and then after midnight she is ritually sodomized. And all the while she is thinking of those flagellating saints seeking love without women, the Christian dharma bums we studied together in college, and their frantic efforts to escape death by clawing a way into the arms of God.

You have to understand the rain and the mesquite. The clouds come on slowly and torture the drooping leaves with the promise of rain and this goes on day after day, week after week, and sometimes, not often, but sometimes the rain never comes at all, the monsoon skips, and still the tree stands and believes and waits. But when the rain comes, and most years it does come, the feel in the desert is love. Not the word, the thing beyond the word, the rush of life pouring from the sky, the scent of that Kansas woman floating in the air without reason or explanation, the cells, millions and billions of cells drinking deeply and feeling lush with life and asking no questions, not a single one.

Spring finally came for me this year. The mesquite suddenly leafed out and blazed with a fresh lime color, and then as the days passed, the color deepened and sucked hungrily off the sun. My yard smelled ripe and clean and my friend's ashes sank into the ground and mingled with the hungers. Then the tortoise emerged, actually he came up twice. The first time was near Easter and he basked a few days, and I went out and leaned over him and told him of the Balkan war. I was careful to not tell him of the pope and his Culture of Death because I sensed he would have no truck with such talk. Then a freak snow swept down onto the desert and he disappeared for weeks until he regained his confidence in the sun. One day I saw a lone duck flying over the desert.

I felt the death leaving me, the cavalcade of dying that had poisoned me. I can still feel it, but I know it is leaving now. I did physical things for days. I pruned trees, put in banks of flowers, planted herbs, six kinds of basil, two of thyme, two of tarragon, some chervil, a splash of mint. The mesquite bloomed and suddenly the tree was alive with foraging bees. As the days grew longer, I entered back into life.

I felt enriched by the dying. This was not an abstraction. I lost four people and their passing took up most of a year and a half and the tending and caring was suffused with love. But still it had a price and the price was sorrow, and the sorrow was a poison. I would wake in the night for months and the time would be glowing in red demonic numbers on the clock, and for reasons I do not know, the numbers usually said 3:18. I would lie there awake on the edge of the grave, an anonymous hole in the ground and it was rank with rot and I would be poised on its edge. There was no terror. That was not the force of the grave. There was a choice, to go on or stop. The hole yawned before me and I could hear voices, muffled voices as if people were speaking in the next room. I could not make out what they were saying, nor did I care.

They were the voices of my dead friends and I respected their privacy and in all honesty, I only half listened. They had taught me not to fear death, nor to seek it.

I live in a time when death is off the table, the thing unsaid. We wish to live forever and because of this desire, we hardly live at all. I am trapped in the great age of caution, of watch out, of fear. But I was blooded in the age of desire and lust and love. I will always be a mesquite waiting for the rain and knowing it is coming even during those summers when it never comes at all. So when I came awake at 3:18 a.m. in the silence of those lonely hours when life waits for the sun, I was not afraid or in pain. I was indifferent and that was my sin and why I saw the grave lying open at my feet. Death is always right there in a slender wineglass, sparkling just within reach should we choose to drink it. The pope, that crazy old man, knows at least that much.

I bought new cookbooks, two on the food of the French, one on the proper way to cook fish, another based solely on the use of herbs. I made a rare steak of pepper-encrusted tuna and served the slices under a chutney sauce, I sautéed chicken in red wine vinegar. I grew lavish in the use of tarragon and cooked one fowl with forty cloves of garlic, *poulet en crapaudine*, chicken in the style of the toad, and dusted my creation with oil and bread crumbs and a mince of French tarragon, basil, rosemary and chives. My senses drank deeply and as the mesquite came on and flooded the desert with pollen, I felt like a beast beset with new and wondrous appetites.

The house became a cloud of scents and I bought new flavored oils and explored the world of shallots. I converted to free-range chicken and paid a premium for fresh fish. I eyed mussels, clams, and scallops, I wrapped shrimp in pancetta and sage and grilled them for two minutes a side over the coals. Butter lettuce seduced me, as did vine-ripened tomatoes hauled in from Mexico, and my salads were dressed with Dijon mustard, red wine vinegar, olive oil, pepper and salt, sometimes a dollop of mesquite honey. I made a pork roast and inserted garlic cloves and rosemary into the meat and served it with the *mostarda de Cremona*. Risotto returned to my life and I procured carnaroli rice and made a dish of salmon, cream, mushrooms and stock. The stock became blood for my soul and I simmered celery, old bones, an onion, a carrot and some pepper and salt for hours. One day I got a shank of veal and made *ossobuco*, the iron pot simmering for three hours until the flesh fell from the bone. I became quite mad with cooking and brooked no interruptions in the kitchen. Pork chops I preferred thick and center cut from the loin, browned briefly in oil, then simmered in tomato paste, wine and fennel seeds. I became ravenous for meat and made whole meals from flesh and a salad on the side. I drank red wine big and surly with the grape. This was my alchemy.

I did not wonder if there was life after death, but marveled that life was again possible before death. One day a turtle dove fluttered down into the yard, a species that accidentally occurs in the Los Angeles area and belongs nowhere in my nation. The bird was hand tame, evidently an escapee from some cage, and stayed several days before pressing on. Each day it became more cautious around humans and each day it became more like a wild bird. I would watch it studying the other birds and slowly learning the habits of its future life. I dreamed of a new grill so that I could burn flesh and salt the fire with the taste of mesquite.

I feel the wood now. I have always been of the ground and yet estranged from the ground by my ways and my hungers. The phone rings and I am off into the world toting up the carnage. I have lost, and lost willingly, years of my life to the various ways human beings can hurt each other. I have drunk alone and wept alone, two things they warn us to avoid. I have gone days without speaking and spent weeks at a time shut of all human contact. I have strayed from what is good for me in order to do what I knew must be done. But always the ground has pulled me back, sometimes from the very edge of some unnamed abyss, pulled me back and healed me and filled my belly with the fire to go on. Without mesquite I am nothing, nothing but one more man wailing at his fate in a bar at closing time.

If I had my life to live over, I would live very, very little of it the same. When people say they would change nothing in their life, I think they are either liars or fools. Life is about learning, and if you respect life and learn from it, you would of course not do things the same way. To start with, if I had my life to live over, I would never say no to a woman. And I would never skip a meal, not a single one. I would always eat the best food and price be damned. Just as I would drink good wines or do without. And no spring would pass without a planting, no fall without fat fires, no winter without black coffee in a dark room during the wait for the endless night to give way to dawn. To sleep in is a grievous sin. Also, I would do nothing purely for money, because every time I have done such a thing, I have failed myself. Nor would I throw a single stone, or sight down on a deer. I accept my hunger for the flesh but will take no joy in the killing. I would never raise my voice except in song and there would be no hurry, that word would be abolished. I would never think that wars are events recorded in the book of history but realize they are actual and always take my hands from my ears and hear the cries of the slain. I would live inside the wood, always waiting for rain, always receiving the rain regardless of the drought. And I would ask that woman about that baby.

I remember sitting with a man after his woman had died. I had taken him off to get him away from his sorrow. We were in a hotel room in a Mexican mountain town and he was drinking a liter of whiskey and drinking it damned hard. Outside tropical flowers bloomed and two macaws cried with their raucous voices. He held up the almost empty bottle and looked at it with disgust.

"She never would have let me drink like this," he said.

And then he fell into a silence and went on with his drinking. I said nothing, I lacked the words to vanquish his naked loathing of himself. He eventually found another woman and the drinking dwindled. But the moment never left for him or for me.

These moments belong to all of us, including those who deny them. She is sitting right across from me, the smile wide, the cheekbones high, the lips painted red. It is the crack that she remembers, that one time with the crack pipe. She is in Los Angeles for a visit, the why is unsaid. And they are at an apartment when the pipe is passed. The guy next to her is some kind of street person, a black man with dreadlocks. She takes a deep hit. Then the guy turns to her and puts his tongue in her mouth. That is all she remembers about crack, the hit, the tongue and the sense that she was no longer who she thought she was. Her voice falls as she tells this to me, becomes almost a whisper. She reached an edge and it frightened her.

She is not a woman who frightens easily. Her frame is slight, she is delicate. One night the blackness came and she got drunk and drove her car right across the median blowing all four ties. But her real thing is magic, the vague thing that hangs over her life and directs it and saves it from crack pipes and exploding tires. She studies Indian ways, burns sacred bundles of dried plants, collects the skulls of beasts and has a closet of teddies. She will never leave the desert, this is not thinkable. But as it is for me, she must struggle to stay true, to live the discipline of the mesquite and tame the dangerous impulses of the body. She remembers when she took confirmation and the priest tried to put moves on her, ah, she knows about those priests. She asks me if she will always meet worthless men who will betray her and I say no, she will not. But she must keep up the hunt, never forsake it. Her nostrils must suck in the breeze searching for scent, her hips must swing, and the dawn work is important also, I insist to her about the dawn.

Morning has come and I am on the edge of my world in a border town where the rain is maybe eight inches a year and the mesquite grows low and is viciously beaten down by the sun. I have been up most of the night, I watched the gray light come on. I am in that sterile tiny motel room by a freeway. There is coffee downstairs. The television sits silent, I want none of its flood of images. Across the river, there have been more murders. A woman paid two men about an ounce of heroin to murder a major drug dealer. One of the killers was a lover. She regrets this now but these things happen. She has been charged with being "the intellectual author" of the slaying. Another woman was a worker in a border factory earning a few dollars a day. She caught the bus home from work when her shift ended at midnight. Finally, she was the only remaining passenger as the bus ground through the soft soil down a desert lane leading to her *colonia* of cardboard shacks. The driver stopped, took her off and raped her. Then he carried her body to a brick oven and burned it. This was in the heart of April, when the mesquite bloom surged. Two guards at a mall were also slaughtered and the police say they are looking. One saw a drug execution and told his superior. The next day he was cut down and his colleague went with him. On this side of the river, a high school football star was arrested for the drive-by killing of someone from a different high school. The word is out, according to students, that there will be a payback, and they are afraid to go to school. Only the woman in the brick oven really gives me pause. She is too close to the bone, too close to the things I want to forget, too close to the cost of knowing.

The vacuum is howling in the motel hall like a forlorn wind on the Great Plains, the room smells sterile. I sit here worn and yet electric. Sleep is not likely and soon I will go into the streets and roam until the next dawn. These days and nights still come, I fight them, I try to keep regular hours and drink only decaffeinated coffee, but still they come. They are the fist of the knowing, they are what I must fight with the mesquite. There are too many voices in the room for sleeping, the muffled, half-heard words of the dead in the next room, that small talk of friends, the voice of the Kansas woman as she goes about her necessary errands, the cries I can never escape, it seems, of all the ladies in the brick ovens. And also, the woman with flat tires, bad men and a taste of the crack pipe. Her voice is always perky, I don't know how she does it, but it is perky and clean and innocent. Nothing seems to mark her.

They are all part of the reason I do not talk to God or listen to Him. I will be ready to listen when He is ready to answer for what he has done here. But now I can smell perfume. Sometimes it is of a woman, sometimes the thick scent coming off the mesquite in bloom. In the wood, her legs are spreading, there is that smile. I think of food. I have no bottle nor wish for one. It would do no good. I drank last night with a Mexican man who had been wounded in love. I told him I was not an intellectual and did not want to be. I do not want to kill things with ideas. I want to remain an animal. I want to want.

The flowers call me. The petals white, and then bristling below the sepals, smaller petals testing the air, inside the cup are sexual apparatus, things called pistils and stamens, everything on the come, the stars wheeling overhead, the flower open and breathless as it waits for a caress in the night. The bloom erupts from the slender body of a tree-climbing cactus native to southern Mexico, a snake hunting for light in the cool limbs of a tree. I am forced to look south by the flowers that yearn amid the disorder of a brown world. Mexico makes me human and rubs my nose in it and my eye. There is a kind of knowing based on notes and events and statistics that I crave. And then there is another knowing, trivial and discounted, that runs beneath this official knowing, and it is in the flower in Mexico, the big white flower bursting from a slender green cactus that climbs a tree. This insistence of the bloom always stops me in my tracks. I gather with friends, dusk turns to night, a drink is in my hand, the flower opens under the stars and a waxing moon, always waxing when the flower opens. The same deep chords rumbling through the earth that move the oceans in tides, the same invisible but strong force that hides from my understanding in words like gravity, suddenly this power is overhead with petals and yearning and it is white in the night, my friends are laughing, the drink in my hand feels good going down my throat and I can stay here, stay with the numbers and the facts and the studies and bad deaths, all because of a flower that will live only six or seven hours and then be no more. Forever.

I must have these eddies, pockets of dead water on the edge of the stream, or I will die. I must cook, touch a woman, look up in the tree at the flower. I know this, and I gather these moments diligently and with a desperate search. I can never be tougher than a delicate flower blooming briefly in the night as a tree-climbing cactus high in the tree decides to bet on the future, legs open and mouth wet with desire.

I am run off the road, five men approach with AK-47s on a Mexican road. And I am not tough and I do not swagger and I do not think. Not of them. These things happen, and they are never adventures. Nor are they ever moments of bravery. They are accidents in the pursuit of some sort of fact and linear order. They are superficial. The flower is not. There is this level, at least for me, and it is always delicate and unimportant, usually ignored, and the flower opens high in the tree, the voices of friends laughing surround me, a drink is in the hand, the very air relaxes as the flower strains and opens and yearns, and this is the deeper level where some kind of moral statement is made and it does not matter if anyone listens. It simply must be made. At those moments, I can handle the rest of my baggage. And those moments increasingly spell some shard of Mexico in my life, because when I look south I see the answers have not strangled speech and the questions are still in the night air right over my head as the stars wheel. I'll tell myself that these moments do not matter, that there are cannibals on the loose devouring life itself. I'll tell myself these are soft things and do not register in a hard world. But they do register and they cut through the hard and go to some level the brittle facts cannot imagine. And so often, here or there, they seem to make me look south, even when I am standing in my own backyard. At those moments I can still feel the blues and sing them and know them but I have touched a music underneath the insistent chords of the bloody work going on around me. Always the night before, a Mexican and I have drinks and he tells me about love.

Or a scene snags the corner of my eye as I roll by in my truck. This time the other life is in a small park on a side street. They are gathered at the swing set. The man is about thirty, soft around the belly and has the look of someone who will never be hard in body or in speech. He wears dark slacks, a blue shirt, glasses with black frames. She sits on the swing with short brown hair, a gingham jumper, and on her lap a child of about three. She is very pregnant and has a glow about her. It is about nine in the morning and the light still has the golden quality of spring. It is the week of one of those slaughters that now visit our schools, those killings we do not foresee, cannot explain and forget as soon as a decent burial has been performed. She swings slowly, the child leaning back against her swollen belly, the man gently providing a push. Her smile is serene and he is unhurried. I suspect that soon he will be off to work. I see them now in my mind, a scene of peace glimpsed on some distant unreachable shore that I will never reach. I go elsewhere.

I am standing on a street corner in Juárez, Mexico, at midday, and a grizzled man in his sixties is shucking green corn for sale. He wears a black cap that says NO FEAR. He has on a black T-shirt that announces LAST ACTION HERO. He laughs as he works. His skin is very dark, he has a sound beer belly, and he has the quick eyes that selling on the street gives a man. The wind blew through last night, howled for hours, and now the normally brown air over the city is crystalline and light falls down and washes every single thing, including the old man shucking green corn. I look at him and realize he is wearing my costume, that I must call the wardrobe department and get properly attired for my role.

I want something very simple: to be that mesquite root found alive at one hundred and seventy-eight feet in hard rock, a root shaped like a cock and probing for a wet place, or shaped like a finger on a mother's hand and reaching out to touch the face of love, a throbbing hungry thing pulsing and coursing onward without a care but with a purpose and that purpose may be no more than its own appetite but still that is something, an appetite, and it is greater than words like *consumption* or *bonds and stocks* or *pensions and retirement communities* or *credit cards* or *cruise lines* or *home entertainment centers*, it is something breaking through barriers, something propelled by desire and facing terrible odds and yet persisting, yes, not giving in, not thinking of surrender or safety, just plowing into the wilderness of dreams. I explain myself to others by saying I really just want a quiet home surrounded by a white picket fence with lilacs blooming by the door. I explain myself to others by saying I am really a hermit who just happens to like being with lots of people. But I explain myself to myself by thinking of things like that mesquite root searching almost sixty yards under the earth.

You have caught me in fine humor at the moment. I am in mid-flight in this cell of one of our anonymous motels, those places where we briefly warehouse all our lonely selves. My motel is incapable of hosting a wild fling on Saturday night where the clothes are torn off willy-nilly to haunt and almost puzzle the lovers when dawn comes and glows off the disarray. We have all been in that room or want to be. The window is open, the city sounds pour in, the curtain flaps out into space and licks against the exterior brick wall as we sink into our yearning. The woman always smells fresh, she has that magical female ability to smell fresh under any circumstances, and you press her to you and say, "Please hold me, hold me," and you finally mean what you say. Or it is out on the land and the moon plays on the ground, and the woman discards her clothing with smooth catlike strokes and says, "I knew you really cared for me, I knew it," and she is of course right and you kiss her tears and the breeze pours through the mouth of summer. Yes, we have all been in that room on lucky nights.

In this particular bleak cell, I live in the past, the present and the future. The clock on my laptop computer is set to my home, which lies west of here because I am an American and for Americans home is always and forever to the west. The town itself has yet another time, the present. But someone, some earlier inmate of my room I assume, has set the glowing digital clock by the bed an hour ahead and I left it that way.

I have made my choice or my choice has made me. Mesquite, a tree almost unnoticed with its low scraggly form, a kind of derelict tree sitting on the curb of our world clutching a brown paper bag and a bottle. A tree of alarming vigor, of rampant fertility, and doing the dark work in places we cannot see and seldom imagine. I am on a mission and I do not question it, nor do I fully understand it. That is why I am out here in this cell by the roar of one of our freeways. Soon I will leave and go on into this looking and probing and seeking. I will be gone for hours and return deep in the night. I will be weary and fall into bed. Then I will rise and continue on this way. I am reconciled. I will taste the other shores and wander far below the surfaces. I will be tempted by edges and fight mightily to keep my feet.

Like all of us now, I get messages, strange apparitions that in our era now appear on computer and television screens. I am lying on the bed in my cell doing punishing work with the remote control when suddenly the images are black and white and ancient and there is no sound. It is Al Jolson in *The Jazz Singer*, that first talking film made in the late twenties. At the moment, the film clings to its silence. Jolson is the Jew, the son of the cantor at the synagogue, and he is the son struggling with an awful fact: he does not want to sing the sacred songs of his father, he wants to sing jazz. The bulk of the movie is about this struggle, the basic struggle for most Americans between the culture they came from and the culture that America fashions them into being. The old man has a long beard and is clearly the old country. Jolson finally prevails—a fantasy ending we always promise ourselves but never taste. And yet the movie has a hold on us because we are all now immigrants cast on some cold and lonely shore we cannot name. We fumble to explain this place—postmodern? postcolonial? post cold war? post something?—but we cannot find the right name. Jolson does this: he puts on black makeup and paints his lips large in that caricature of black people called a minstrel show and gets up on a Broadway stage. His mother and father are in the audience wearing modern dress and smiling and beaming and he sings "Mammy," sings it loud and clear, and now we suddenly hear and need no subtitles, and sound has come to the movies, and we have for the short duration of the film triumphed over the immigrant state and truly come to our senses. And this is all a lie, of course, a smoothing of the rough edges, a denial of the edge at all, an insistence on smooth sailing across a calm ocean. But the ocean is not calm and the edge is always there.

There is an edge and we all must feel that edge or we will die. We may keep on eating and sleeping and voting and shopping but we will surely die if we do not feel that edge and admit its existence. I know I must. But we must respect that edge or we do not deserve to live. To topple off it and into the void is to become monsters. Women are found charred in brick ovens. The crazy pope returns and talks endlessly of a Culture of Death. So we must seek the edge but respect it. I am not a man of the center. I am from somewhere else.

In the wood.

Feel my face.

The bark has rubbed the skin raw and sap flows out of me, a sap dark and rich and intoxicating.

L
ove coated the walls last night. Faces I knew but had never met, smiles I believed but was certain were feigned, glamour I felt attracted to but could never trust. Movie stars, executives with casting-couch faces, starlets with the blank eyes of fawns and the hearts of great white sharks, all these faces staring down from the walls. Love. But not romantic love, not even the presence of love, but the yearning, the absolute emptiness that drives us all to be cruel and hungry and savage and suicidal and murderous. Of course, we try not to speak of these matters in our dances, we try to mask everything, we shout, "Action!" and do yet another take in our effort to get it all the way we think it should be and to blot out the way we know it is. All this trapped in celluloid and stored in canisters and occasionally projected on blank walls.

I sat drinking with a producer in an ancient hotel, neatly framed photographs of Academy Award dinners from the iron days of the thirties watching as we spoke. At the bar, a man dressed head to toe in navy blue was winning with a blonde and you could all but smell the sweaty sheets that would soon grace a room upstairs. They both had the look of hunger without any excuses or apologies. The producer himself was heavily into a hard love. His father still had some years to do in prison and he visited every few months and it was very hard. I could tell his father had never been his love until the blows rained down and destroyed him but that now, beneath all the quick words and unsmiling statements, love had flamed up and warmed the son's soul. He drank hard liquor, I inhaled wine. We were all about love. Something I had written intrigued him and I scrambled to return to the place I'd been when I wrote the piece in a three-day fury. I became a visitor to some wounded part of myself.

But the images caged on the wall, faces and bodies from a black and white world where men combed their hair and slapped it down against their skulls, where women swelled inside tight sequined dresses that advertised their hips but barely whispered their breasts, a lost world of double features, fan clubs, perfect marriages and scandals just slightly off camera, and every single soul is white, at least on the outside. As I listened to the bar buzz and the soft voice of the producer, a voice not harsh but driven with a rhythmic beat under the white noise of the saloon that sounded like the clickety-clack of the rails as a midnight express shot through a sleeping town, as I listened the photographs kept pulling me away to their places on the walls, and there I saw a world of smiles and love and romance and sweethearts, she-done-him-wrong, the strong, silent types, debonair dancing at the ballroom, and we-were-meant-for-each-other. But of course, this was the fiction of the screen, and blood actually drooled from their mouths as the stars devoured each other and then devoured us as we sat in the audience, and finally we were all devoured together as we became one big movie and stopped fussing with our dull, unscripted lives. We broke free of the flesh and the soil and then we simply broke.

We are cannibals now. We can devour and take but cannot give.

The *Cereus peruvianus* begs from the planter outside the building in downtown Los Angeles. The columns of tissue stare out at me with yellow skin from some kind of neglect. The flutes are tight and hungry for love and water. I hurry past. It cannot be rescued. In its native Peru, it has ceased to exist in the wild and lives solely in gardens and as living fence rows. This is the terrible fact of my time.

We cannot all be saved. Still, I want to rip the cactus from its planter, put my arms around it and flee into the soft deserts of desire. I will dig a hole, speak to the cactus as I sink it into the flesh of the ground. I will do this absolutely. It is a matter of roots, of severed things. I am about roots, the snakes of hunger that glide through the dark earth, yearning probes of lust and chemically driven dreams, tearing at the sediments of past lives, and bursting into zones where deep appetites may be fed. Sucking greedily at lost ones, the rot of other living things. Lips opening, ah, painted ever so brightly, but opening into what looks like a smile. And then the sucking, and I am gone into a void of some other existence, consumed and translated, slain and born.

I hurry past. There is not time for this adventure. The flowers open large, white and lush, tulip-type flowers but drenched in something banned from the very idea of tulips, no, these flowers are wet and all tongue and they come in the night and wear nothing but the insistence of their white flesh, and moths, big moths, flutter and wander deep within these blossoms, insect tongues sucking and lapping, and for that instant, in that blackness of the night, there is the soft warm air, the feeling that all is possible but everything must be now, right now and no excuses or delays, yes, that headlong plunge into the vulva of the flower and all around the city traffic is buzzing and hurrying and notices not at all the flower and moth and the carnal roar of the sucking and licking, truly just an instant, and with the light of morning the flower closes and it will never open again, not for God almighty, it must be now. Or never.

I cannot bear to look any longer and snap my head forward and march down the sidewalk toward the union convention. That's the trick, blocking things out, eye on the prize, now march and do not, I repeat, do not listen to the flowers.

Because he is hanging. I know the light. It is not north light but it feels like north light. He was a master of that kind of trick and understanding. I know the color of the pipe with the rope caressing its firm metal. He is hanging. The message posted on the wall nearby as he swings, ah, so softly and peacefully, says GET HOME. He is thirty-five there swaying at the end of his rope from that stout pipe, and I knew him from the time he was six and glowing with blond hair and fresh eyes.

The light softens everything, an artist's light, never so bold as to bleed the color of things, never so dim as to blind the eye. In my mind, he has been swaying a long time and I blot him out at all occasions. And then she calls. I'm lying in my hotel bed, up there twenty stories in downtown L.A., just sprawled there looking at the dresser, the chair, the table, the dead television, the ashtray, the barrenness of the walls with their mirrors and blank prints of someplace that is no place. Out the window is an office tower and I can see that early secretary puttering at her desk, and all the men in suits, young men, faces grim and joyless, voyaging toward the heart attack of their dreams. I'm sucking on a cigarette, taking this in, when the phone rings, and my heart melts at her voice.

"It's Barb," the voice says from Michigan. And then she sails off into the scheduling of the opening at an art gallery in New York, into the minutiae of conflicting dates and people.

I tell her what I have told her for a month or two: I will be there, just give me warning.

Her son has been taken down from the rope. His life's work has been warehoused. A book has been cobbled together. I will be there. The gallery is going to call it a book opening. Fine.

He killed himself. Now I must make sure he does not kill her. So I will be there.

Her handwriting always slants backward and is large and loopy. I fear her hand. When the envelopes fall through the mail slot, I recognize them immediately and always set them aside until I am ready.

I am never ready.

Past the words, brother! sister! past the words, deep into the things, blind like a root, grubbing out the meaning, deep, past, go. The union makes me deaf. The producer blinds me with images. Paul, in my head, Paul is always in that old factory he remade into a studio, a mill he forged into a tool to explore a word, *art*, and then to pull that word apart, *a-r-t*, and then to go beneath the word or beyond the word, to disappear into the materials, the metal, the plastic, the canvas, the color, streaking out there into inner space and outer space, his lips a hard line, his hands nimble and quick, his steps light, going out there into a place I can barely imagine, a place past art, curators, museums, past even form, a place he seeks because for some reason I do not understand or question, he has to know what is beneath the word *art* and what is inside the materials used to make art and what is directing the play of light and form. I think this is why he gave up painting. I think, and here I am guessing, he grew to hate rectangles and their safe corners and sure boundaries. I'll have to ask Barbara someday. She'll hesitate for just a moment but she'll tell me. She is sitting in Michigan now, going through the bones of his work and his letters and his sketches, holding them up to a light and searching for a clue. She has become Paul's lab assistant.

I want to touch things, to rub my fingers against surfaces and then tear at the surfaces and watch wads of stuffing pop out and springs leap into view, peer within these new holes and glimpse inner workings. Normally, I stay reasonably numb and such desires do not stir me. I let the words keep things corralled and under control. The union movement. The movies. The periods of art. Sculpture, painting, music, books. Life can be pretty calm with a card catalog and a SILENCE sign. Drink helps also, for a while. But eventually the sense of confinement grows and I feel the shackles and I can't maintain. That is when I hear the screams from the leaves, feel the tug of a plant as I try to hurry past, oh so faintly, the sucking sounds.

I am of two parts. One is the conservator, who wants to pick up a phone and call Paul and say, hey, lighten up, back off, get a handle on things. And the other says, let's jump. Let's break through, tear through, whatever it takes, get through. Find what is . . . beneath the skin, what is going on inside, what is within the *is*. Then I become the enemy of all the economies and governments and centers of learning and galleries, of all but the world spreading out in the hills and mountains and forests and deserts and seas. I believe it is a management problem, a trick of simply fixing the arrangements. I become the appetite, and the hunger sweeps through me, and I fear I will burn and become ash.

Paul is in his studio, reaching for one more object to install in the work. I can see him clearly, the light seeping in from the south.

I hear the cannibals, the chords of the blues.

For years there have been murmurs among the archaeologists in the Southwest. The murmurs are about the Anasazi, the Navajo word for whoever the hell left all those big ruins. The Navajo themselves have always scorned them as the places of the dead. Chaco Canyon, Mesa Verde, Keet Seel, Betatakin, a long roll of dwellings to be avoided because there is some kind of stench in the air. The murmurs among the bone diggers, the scholars, all fester on a couple of dozen sites where human remains, the bones of course, show a smashing and tearing, bold marks of dismemberment that could only be caused by cannibalism. Somewhere back in the dreamtime of the thirteenth century, during the dry years when rains failed for fifty years, the eating occurred. Men, women, children. Sucked empty. But such talk is dangerous, it implies barbarism, it fails to concur with our hopes of a lost Eden. It comes so close to our palate that we shudder and close our eyes.

There is a famous point in the secret debate over the meaning of these ancient bones. The evidence of cannibalism had been dismissed as religious sacrifice, as a kind of aberrant peripheral matter. One scholar insisted he would never believe actual cannibalism had occurred until someone found a piece of human shit with the remains of human meat in the stool. And then they found it. A ritual pile of dung plopped into the hearth of a consumed family that perished long ago.

Her voice is very warm as she talks about the opening, about this fete we will hold to make sure her dead son lives. I cradle the phone and stare out the window into the muted light of Los Angeles, where the sun must beat a way through smog and sea vapors. I can feel the tug of her grief and I resist. As she speaks, I can see her years ago in her kitchen by Lake Michigan, the golden light pouring through the west windows. She is spending the day on a Greek dinner, the lamb, the salad with feta cheese, the grape leaves wrapped around rice and meat. The old stove, a monster from early in the century, is chock-a-block with kettles. Bread cools on the sideboard and Barbara is all bustle and smiles and laughter. I sit there and drink a beer, intoxicated by the whirl of aroma. Paul is maybe ten and dashing around outside with other kids. It is spring in my mind regardless of the actual season. And we do not yet know our true diet. We are sharing, giving to each other, filling our mouths with love and fresh herbs.

1

I can't tell much from the back of her head. She's sitting up there toward the front, her shoulders hunched and a few rows further on is the box with the teddy bears. Or at least I think they're teddy bears. It's been years and years and I've avoided thinking about it because I did not want to know what I eventually knew. There are some things that float pretty free of time, chronology, the book of history and the lies of the experts. I remember I went to a funeral as part of my entry into a world, a kind of border crossing. It began for me when the breast and the mouth, the curve of the hip, the toss of the hair, the heat coming off the world, all these crossed over from the newsprint and the smell of morning coffee and came at my flesh.

It started as the golden light of afternoon poured through the high slit windows of the newsroom. I had no background in the business and I'd lied to get the job. I was the fluff writer, the guy brought on to spin something out of nothing for the soft features and the easy pages about how people fucked up their marriages or made a quiche or found the strength to go on with their lives because of God, diet or a new self-help book. Sometimes they wrote the book, sometimes they just believed the book. I interviewed Santa Claus, also, and he told me of the pain and awkwardness of once holding a child on his fat lap in Florida as ants crawled up his legs and bit him. That afternoon the newsroom was empty and the city desk looked out and beckoned me. I was told to go to a motel and see if I could find anything to say.

The rooms faced a courtyard on the old highway that came into town and were part of a strip of unhappy inns left to die or find new lives after the interstate lanced against the city's flank. When I was twelve this belt still flourished, and my first night in this city was spent in a neighboring motel with a small pool. I remember swimming until late at night, intoxicated with the idea of warm air, cool water and palm trees. My sister was fourteen, and the son of the owners, a couple from the East with the whiff of Mafia about them, dated her. Later, I read a newspaper story that cited him as a local purveyor of pornography. Now the row of motels had lost prosperous travelers to other venues and drifted into new gambits, most featuring rent by the day, week or month, as old cars full of unemployed people lurched into town and parked next to sad rooms where the adults scanned the classifieds for a hint of employment. The children always had dirty faces and anxious eyes. The motel I was sent to was a hot sheet joint, with rooms by the hour or day and featured water beds (WA WA BEDS, in the language of the sign), in-room pornographic movies and a flock of men and women jousting through nooners.

The man at the desk had a weasel face and the small frame of the angry smiling rats that inhabit the byways of America, the wife was a woman of some heft with polyester pants and short cropped hair. They seemed almost delighted to have a reporter descend and, after a few murmured words in the office where I took in the posters for the featured films of cock sucking, butt fucking and love, ushered me across the courtyard with its unkempt grass to the room. As we entered, she apologized and said she was still cleaning up. The linoleum looked cool, and the small chamber offered a tiny kitchenette and then a small lavatory with shower, the old curtain of plastic stained by years of hard water. The walls were block. The water bed stripped of its sheets bulged like a blue whale and as the woman and I talked—*he was quiet, she seemed nice, they didn't cause any fuss, the kid was a charmer*—a dirty movie played soundlessly on the screen hanging off the wall and confronting the bed. I seem to remember a mirror of cheap streaked tiles on the ceiling.

I walked around aimlessly and popped open the door of the old refrigerator—shelves empty—and then the little door to the freezer where a bottle of Budweiser, frozen solid, nestled as if someone with a powerful thirst had placed it to chill in a hurry and then been distracted. I heard the woman's voice in my ear explaining how the mother had gone to work—she danced at a strip joint, one of the new gentleman's clubs that featured college-looking girls instead of aging women with bad habits—for a few hours and so was gone when it happened. I nodded, purred soothing words, closed the freezer door and strolled back by the water bed, where the blue of its plastic had the gaiety of a flower in the tired room. I looked at the big splotch on the block wall and she said, "I haven't had time to clean that off yet."

That's where the head hit, the skull of the toddler just shy of two years as the man most likely held him by the legs and swung him like a baseball bat. He probably killed the kid out of boredom or frustration with the demands of a small child or because he'd been bopped around himself as a child or God knows why. The man had taken off then, been caught by the cops and now sat in jail as they figured out what level of murder he'd scored. The dancer they got later, when she came home from work and they'd flung some kind of neglect charges at her. The woman cleaning the room bubbled up in my ear again as I stared at the block wall and she said with that small, cooing voice American women sometimes favor when indicating feeling, "We kind of made a collection and customers chipped in and we bought him an outfit for the burial." She told me they got the clothes at Penney's.

I drove back to the paper, wrote an impressionistic piece pivoting on the frozen bottle and all the hopes and basic desires found in a beer chilling for a thirsty throat, and then phones starting ringing at the city desk and I was hurled at the funeral.

Now I am studying the back of the mother's head as she sits in a separate alcove off to the side. She has fine hair, a kind of faint red, and I knew a woman with hair like that, and as I stare I can smell this other woman, and feel my hands tracing a path through the slender strands. I can smell the soap, the scent of the other woman, the small smile and fine bones and clean even teeth. In my memory, the coffin is open, the boy's face very pale and blank and he is surrounded by donated teddy bears that have poured in from a town that told itself these things were not supposed to happen and, if such things did happen, were not supposed to happen in our town. That is part of the world of sex that is called crime, the insistence that it belongs to another country and does not touch our lives or feelings or lusts of the midnight hours. It hardly matters that the toddler died for reasons that probably did not connect to child molestation. For me, he became the entry point to rape and other categories of sexual abuse.

Just before the service ends, I have a hunch, a feeling that the cops are going to get the mother out of there through the back door so that the press cannot snap her image and I cannot scan her face. So I get up and leave the chapel of the cheap mortuary and go to the back, and sure enough, suddenly the metal door opens and two cops burst through with the lap dancer handcuffed and sagging between their grip. The light is brilliant at eleven a.m. and merciless as it glares off the woman. Her face is small, with tiny bones, and her age is no longer possible to peg—somewhere between nineteen and one thousand. She is wearing tight pants on slender girlish hips, and a black leather vest over her blouse. The waist is small, the hair falls to her shoulders, the lips very thin. A moan comes off her, a deep moan, and I sense she is unaware of the sound she is making, just as she is unaware of what has happened to her. The only thing she knows is what I know. There is a toddler in a box with teddy bears and the box sits in a room full of strangers from this town where she had bagged a job dancing for other strangers.

The cops look at me with anger, drag her slumping form away and toss her into the back of a squad car. I stand still, make no notes. Then I go back to the newsroom and write the funeral. That is when it begins. For the next three years I live in a world where the desire, almost always of men, to touch and have their way with other people makes them criminals. I am told I can't get off this kind of beat because most reporters won't do it. This may be true, I don't really know because those three years are the only ones I ever spent working for a newspaper, and practically the only ones I ever spent working for anyone besides myself. I would quit the paper twice, break down more often than I can now remember, and have to go away for days or a week or two and through violent exercise kill the things that roamed my mind.

It was during this period I came to taking one- or two-hundred-mile walks in the desert far from trails. I wrote up these flights from myself and people began to talk about me as a nature writer. The rest of the time was spent with another nature.

I can still see the woman coming through the metal door, slumping between the paws of the cops. I am standing northwest of her and about twenty feet away. It is eleven a.m., the glare of the sun makes her squint, her hips are bound in impossible pants, her face has never seen anything brighter than the dim lights of a strip joint, and her wrists in the chrome gleam of cuffs are tiny. I can remember this with photographic detail, only I can't remember what became of her or her lover—just the boy, the splotch on the wall, the blue water bed and the frozen Budweiser.

Until this moment, I've avoided remembering what became of me.

The tree, I must tell you of the tree. The backyard is barren because I have systematically killed everything—roses, the citrus trees, the lawn. I do this because I know in my bones such things do not belong in my desert. The grass I spade out for weeks, shaking each lump to save the soil. When the bermuda returns from snippets of roots, I dig again. The third time, I pour on poison. The fruits go down to the ax and the saw. I grub out the roots with a pick. The roses I slaughter without a thought.

I spend days with a heavy metal bar chipping a hole through the caliche—an eight-foot thick stratum of calcium carbonate and captive rocks that runs like cement under the yard. Sweat pours off me hour after hour, day after day. I curse the caliche and hack away. Finally, the hole drains when filled with water. I buy a five-gallon mesquite, fill the hole with bags of good dirt, and plant. My father taught me to put five-dollar trees in fifty-dollar holes.

I water the small tree constantly. That first season it grows more than ten feet. A woman takes to stopping by and has designs on the house. She scrubs the kitchen cabinets, tears into the bathroom. She brings a gay friend over and the two of them pick the proper tile for the floors. The tile never goes down and we make love during the blaze of summer on the cool concrete floor. She does not complain, she likes it rough. But she mocks the tree. When I tell her how vast and towering it will become, how the tree will shade the yard, she sneers. She says it will never reach such a size. I love the tree, I know it is keeping me alive. I do not tell her of the roots and the sucking sound.

She pours contempt on the sapling, I feed it love and lick the bark.

Night, the warm hugging night of early fall, and they form up in the park, the women and their supporters with candles and flashlights, banners and will. The green pocket of trees and grass hugs the road, and when World War II ended, the road was the last pavement before the yawning maw of the desert took over. The people are going to march to take back the night. Women are at risk, after sundown they lose their civil rights, human rights, they lose their right to prowl the city streets, the cabarets, sidewalks, and they live imprisoned within the sanctity of their homes. He came in through the bathroom window.

Take back the night.

They go a few blocks and swing down one of the city's main thoroughfares. Safety in numbers, group solidarity, sisterhood is powerful, protest, demands, anger, laughter, high spirits. They find her later in a narrow slot between two buildings, more a gap in the strip of commercial facades than a planned path or walkway, the kind of slot that sees hard sun a few minutes a day and then returns to shadow. She is seven and dead. While the march to take back the night was passing through here, she apparently left her yard nearby and came over to see the spectacle. The police and press keep back one detail: she has been eviscerated. That is the food of a newsroom, the secret facts that others do not know or cannot be told, the sense of being where the action is and where the knowing people gather. So we say to each other: Opened up from stem to stern that night.

I come in the next morning ignorant of all this and am called in to a meeting. The city editor, the managing editor and the publisher are agitated. They have children, they want to do something, but they don't know what. I'm told to figure it out, some angle, something. The city editor is new to the job and he tells me he always figured if he got hold of a newspaper, he'd do something about stories like this. Now he's the boss and this is what he wants done. I nod and I say, you'll have to give me time. He nods back. The exchange is very short, this paper has no long meetings. I go back to my desk and remember one night. And when I remember, I don't want to take this assignment but I do.

He speaks in a small voice as his hands cradle his face in the hospital waiting room and he says, "My baby girl, my baby girl." His wife looks on stoically. The call comes in the middle of the night and when I arrive, there is the cool of fluorescent lights, the sterile scent of linoleum floors and the memory of her going down the corridor on a gurney with a face pulverized into raw flesh. She had visited her boyfriend near the campus and then left and gone out on the quiet street to her car.

That is when he took her. They drove out of town into the open ground. He raped her, pistol-whipped her, pumped two rounds into her, and then left her for dead. She saw a light and crawled toward it. The people inside feared her pounding in the night and did not want to open up. Somehow an ambulance came and now she is in surgery as I sit with her weeping father and stoical mother. At the time I am related by marriage. But that does not help. I am a man but that does not help. Nothing really helps, not words, not anger, not reflection.

Eventually, a red-faced detective comes by to placate the family and express his sense of urgency. He explains all the things being done but he convinces no one. How do you find a rapist when half the population is suspect? That is when I first hear the police read on rape: "Fifteen minutes for the guy, five years for the woman." For days afterward, as the hospital reports come in, as the visits to the room present a bandaged head with all the hair shaved off, as the unthinkable becomes normal for all of us, nothing really helps. We have stepped over into a place we refuse to acknowledge, a place of violence and danger where the sexual impulses that course through all our veins have created carnage.

I am in my late twenties, and my male friends all come to me with visions of violence, scripts about what should be done to him, what they would do to him, how these instances should be handled. I nod and say very little. I go over to a house where friends live, the kind of male dormitory where there's a dirty skillet festering on the stove, clothes tossed here and there, empty beer bottles on the coffee table giving off stale breath. It is precisely ten a.m. and one guy is just getting up from the mattress on the floor of his room. He is a Nam vet with a cluster of medals and two interests after his war: hunting and women. A stack of skin magazines two feet high towers over the mattress, and a fine .270 with a polished walnut stock leans in the corner. He tells me they should take those guys out and cut their dicks off and then staggers down the hall with his hangover to take a piss. I feel like I am watching something happening on a screen but that I am not really here.

I have a vegetable garden then and that is the only place where things make sense and fall into some kind of order. So I sit on the dirt amid the rows of bell peppers, tomatoes, eggplant, marigolds and squash, sip red wine and let my mind flow. What I think is this: consent. Lack of violence. That's where I decide he crossed the line—with the kidnapping, the pistol-whipping and the shooting. This criterion saves me from the thicket where women say yes but mean no, where women submit to avoid a brutal beating, where women and men . . . Because when you enter the land of rape, you enter your own country, a corner of your own life and imagination, except that this time everything is wrong and tastes foul to your mouth.

And I never cease scanning faces when I prowl the city, and what I wonder is, are you the one? I look over at the other cars when I am at a stoplight. This becomes an unconscious habit. Sometimes when I sit on the dirt in my garden, I think I have adopted the consciousness of a woman. Now I think like prey.

Later, a year or two later, a guy goes to a party near the campus, drinks and whoops it up and leaves with a woman he meets there. He takes her out and rapes her and tries to kill her. Turns out he is the one and they send him to prison for some years. By then it hardly matters to me. I know he will be back and he will be older and that will be the only change. I come to believe I have no solution and have gained no wisdom. I just have an understanding of how things work, and the knowledge of the way they work seems to change my life and the world very little.

I also have memory, the memory of the father sitting in the hospital waiting room, cradling his face and saying, "My baby girl, my baby girl." But I bury the memories and go on pretty much as if nothing ever happened. As does the woman who was raped, pistol-whipped, shot and left for dead. She moves back into the world and resumes her life. You can know some things and the knowing seems to help you not at all.

I feel these memories as I leave the meeting with the editors with my instructions to write about the slaughter of a seven-year-old girl during a march to take back the night. I sit at my gray desk and look at the clock on the east wall. It is early in the morning, seven or eight a.m., and the few details of the crime the night before hardly matter. The girl was playing in a yard next to her yard and then went home. Presumably the march attracted her, but no one really knows. I have no desire to investigate the incident and pretend I am a cop who will magically crack the case. The memories floating through my body from the night of that earlier rape dominate me as I sit there staring at the clock on the wall. I decide to look into the world where such things come from, though I do not know what that means in practical terms. I have no plan, only this sensation of powerlessness and corruption and violation and grief. I can feel my eyes welling with tears and I know instantly that this feeling will do nothing for me or anyone else. After that I follow my instincts, which is what the predators do also.

I am ready for the journey and it comes in steps and leaps with no sense of progress. I'll tell you what happened but I can't draw you a map. It wasn't that kind of learning. Dante invented a topography of the inferno and there really is an inferno, but Dante knew in his bones his geography was simply a way to give form to a seething plasma. So we go to the inferno, we speak of cauldrons, imagine witches chanting, and yet we know these things do not exist, that they are efforts to make hard-edged shapes out of slippery matters. And we are left—in the dark hours of the night when we find it difficult to lie to ourselves—with the memory of the fire and fresh burns on our bodies.

There is another tree, also a mesquite. This hole also takes days. I plant the sapling maybe twenty feet from the first one. I think the two will storm out of the earth, eventually form a canopy, and smother the ground with sweet shadows. In time, the ashes will go there, those of the city editor who hurls me into the sexual jungle of our appetites. But that is much later, years later, after we become close friends, after he struggles with life and then gives it up. At the time of the planting, I simply think of green, of blue skies and the importance of giving life as I wander the country of pain and death.

The trees are supposed to accomplish one thing: steady me. In this task they fail, but this is not their fault, any more than I can blame the women or blame myself. My appetite for flesh begins to grow. I do not question this lust. I water the trees, then vanish into the night. I am hardly home for days at a time and even then, often as not, only for some blur of rutting. But I am aware of this other clock, of the trees living their own time, the roots finding fissures in the caliche, then thickening and ripping the stratum asunder. The ground breaks beneath my feet. I stand under the tree, and I am breaking also. The sucking sounds.

I also talk to the trees but tell no one.

There are five rules I know to be true. These things come to me out of my explorations.

1. No one can handle the children.
2. Get out after two years.
3. Always walk a woman to her car, regardless of what hour during the day or night.
4. Don't talk about it, no one wants to hear these things.
5. No one can handle the children.

The fourth rule is the iron law. We lie about sex crimes because we lie about sex. We lie about sex because we fear what we feel within ourselves and recoil when others act out our feelings. American society has always been more candid about murder ("I felt like killing him," we can say out loud) than about the designs we have on each other's bodies. What destroys people who have to deal with sex crimes is very simple: you lose the ability to lie to yourself about your feelings, and if you are not careful you fail to lie appropriately to others. When we are in bed with each other we find it difficult to say what we want, and when we brush up against sex crimes we find it difficult to stomach what we see and even more difficult to acknowledge the tug of our fantasies. In the core of our being live impulses, and these impulses are not all bright and not all as comfortable as an old shoe.

A few things stick in my memory about my work and its reception. I am at the home of a friend, a very elderly, learned man. When we sit in his yard under an ancient mesquite and drink, he is open to any topic—whether it be the machinations of the Federal Reserve Bank, the mutilation of young girls in Africa, male menopause or the guilt/innocence of Alger Hiss. I have just put a story in the newspaper on child molestation that runs four solid pages without one advertisement. I vaguely remember the lead. I must do this from memory because regardless of the passage of years, I cannot look at the clips, yet: "The polite term is child molestation. The father said he had done nothing but fondle his son. The five-year-old had gonorrhea of the mouth. The polite term is child molestation."

As I sit with my friend and we wander the intricacies of the world and swap lifetimes of reading, he suddenly turns to me and says, "I want you to know I didn't read your story. I don't read things like that."

I am not surprised. After the story hits the press, the women in the newspaper come up to me for soft conversations and want to have lunch or drinks. They murmur that they are part of the sisterhood or secret society of the maimed. The men avoid me and I can sense their displeasure with what I have written and the endless and relentless nature of the piece. I realize that if I had not written it, I would avoid reading it.

The second thing comes from having drinks with a retired cop. We are friends, kind of—cops and reporters are natural adversaries, and yet in some matters, they have no one else to talk with (see rule number four). I ask him how the local cops handled rape during his time.

He says, "Well, the first thing we'd do is take the suspect out of the house and into the carport and beat the shit out of him with our saps. Then we'd take him downtown and book him for assault." He does not read the piece either.

Then there is the woman who is passionately into nonviolence and vegetarianism and speaks as if she embodied a state of grace. She comes to my door one night and we make love on the cement floor. Afterward she tells me that when she was a girl, her rich and successful father would sit around with his male friends and they would take turns fucking her in the ass.

I walk her to the car.

Some things have the exactness of a photograph and I can hold them in my hands and look at all the people frozen for an instant. And then I can lean into that photograph and the world will move again. I am sitting on the north end of a back row and I am facing the west wall. The room is institutional and full of therapists, counselors and other merchants of grief. It is an all-day session of professionals and they are sharing experiences on treating the victims of sex crimes. I am here as the reporter, eager to learn how seven-year-old girls wind up eviscerated during marches to take back the night. I scan the crowd, mainly women without makeup and wearing sensible shoes. I listen for hours as they outline play therapy, describe predators (with children someone close and accepted by the family, with rape often as not the mysterious stranger), call for a heightened public consciousness about the size of this plague. Their statistics vary but basically suggest everyone is either a victim of a sexual crime or the perpetrator of a sexual crime or a therapist treating sexual crimes. They all agree that children do not lie and that more attention must be paid.

Late in the day, a woman walks to the podium. I have been noticing her for hours because she does not fit in with the group. Her lips are lacquered, her hair perfect, she wears a tasteful dress with gray tones, one I sense she bought just for this occasion, and high heels. She is the only woman wearing high heels. She speaks with an accent and tells them she is not a professional person, she is a mother, and a neighbor molested her daughter, her very young daughter. And she wants something to be done about it. In her case, she continues, nothing was done, the neighbor still lives a few doors down, her daughter still lives in terror—they have had to seal her window with aluminum foil so "he can't look in."

The woman at the podium is on fire, and very angry. Her words slap the professionals in the face. She has no theory, she says, no program. She simply wants attention paid to the problem by her government, her police and her city. And she will not rest. She reads her words off sheets of yellow legal paper and her articulation is harsh, like the beating of a drumstick on the head of a snare. When she finishes there is a silence, the silence of an audience that sits stunned and does not know what to say. I can tell that the audience realizes she could be dangerous because her words show appetite and her hunger could wind up ripping out their throats.

Afterward I cut through the crowd and find her. I say I am a reporter and would like to talk more. She is flustered, she is not used to talking to audiences and not used to talking to the press. She gives me her number and we agree to meet. I notice her eye makeup and the sensual nature of her lips.

When I turn, another woman comes up to me. I had vaguely noticed her enter when the woman whose child was molested was speaking. She is about thirty, wearing leather pants and a motorcycle jacket. Her eyes are very intelligent and she tells me she is a Jungian therapist. Her smile is generous. We walk out and go to a nearby café, one empty and half lit in the late afternoon, and sit at a round table with a dark top. We both sip longnecks.

She says, "You were the only person there who interested me."

I am baffled by this remark.

Her life has not been simple lately. She is distancing herself, she explains, from a bad relationship. She had been living with a man and he is very successful. He came home and they made love. He told her she was the sixth woman he had had that day but he liked her the best. He never comes, she says, anything else, but he never comes.

He withholds, don't you see? she asks.

When I get to her place, she is in shorts and a shirt, roller-skating in her driveway. She tells me she wanted me to see her that way, free and skating with delight. We lie on the floor. She says, "Squeeze my nipples hard, squeeze my titties as hard as you can." Later, we are in the bathroom because she wants to watch us in the mirror. We go back to the bedroom and she rolls over on her stomach.

She says very softly, "Yes."

Things begin to blur for me between the woman with the gray dress and the high heels and the hard flaming words and the woman who roller-skates and has bright eyes. Somewhere in those hours my second marriage ends. I know why. I too tend to say yes.

The therapist has a lot of patients who are fat women and they fascinate her. She herself has not an extra ounce of fat, she is all curves and muscle, her calves look like sculpture, her stomach is flat, her features cute. She is very limber. Once at a party, she casually picks up one of her legs while talking to a couple and touches her ear with her foot. She is not wearing panties when she does this feat. She runs daily, has been part of a female rock 'n' roll band, takes showers three or four times a day, and is proudly bisexual. She tells me one of her best tactics for keeping boyfriends is to seduce and fuck their girlfriends. She smiles relentlessly.

What fascinates her about the fat women is their behavior. Not the eating, she cannot even fathom the eating part since she never gains weight and eats whatever she wishes. Her place is always cluttered with bowls of macadamia nuts for guests. No, it's their sexual lives she is interested in. Their sexual lives are very simple: they will do anything. That, she tells me, is why men like fat women. They will do anything, name your fantasy, try out your imagined humiliation.

She tells me how she got into Jung. She went to visit her own therapist once and he questioned her openness, and she wound up doing golden showers in his office. After that she fled to a Jungian center on the West Coast and studied very hard. No, she says, she is not bitter about it. She learned he was right, she was not open enough.

I find her smile addictive. We sit in her kitchen and she makes a Greek salad. She always becomes a blur when she is cutting up the feta cheese and dicing olives. And then we go to the bedroom. She tells me I have green blood and smiles with the promise that she will make it red.

I am sitting on the tailgate of my truck with the woman who wore the gray dress, the woman who spoke to the audience of the molestation of her child and told of putting tin foil on the windows of the child's bedroom to keep her safe from dangerous eyes. We are to the east of the city, parked down a dirt track and hidden from view by a bosque of mesquite. On the hills above us, there are strange holes in the ground left by Mexicans in the nineteenth and early twentieth centuries, when they burned cords of mesquite and made charcoal. An old man took me up there once and showed me the ground where he toiled so hard as a boy.

Flies buzz in the midday heat and breezes lick at the woman and me. Her lips are full and painted, her scent startlingly fresh amidst the pall of desert dust, her eyes quick like a cat's. She is wearing a dress and unbuttons the front down to her waist. Then she reaches behind her back and effortlessly unsnaps her bra. Her round, full breasts spill out with large dark nipples.

She smiles at them and looks at me.

She keeps her panties on. We have been talking idly of child abuse and the need for me to write something that will educate the public. The breeze plays across her bare breasts and they glow with pale force in the shadows cast down by the mesquites.

She says, "Touch them."

Here is how play therapy goes. You look through one-way glass at very small children on the floor. The child holds anatomically correct dolls, ones with actual sexual organs. Through coaxing, the child acts out with the dolls what has happened to the child in the past. It is something to see. The dolls look like Raggedy Anns and do pretty much exactly what adults do with each other. My guide in this place is a gray-haired woman who is very well spoken and has the quiet calm of a Quaker. She used to work in the ward with terminally ill children. She tells me this work is harder.

Ah, now the child is moving the two dolls.

There is resentment on my part. Someone will ask me what I'm working on and I'll say, "Kiddiefuck." Or I'll recount to someone how I prowl through the police blotter savoring the rapes of the night, the woman who leaves the bar at one a.m. with the stranger, no, can't sell her, the woman who decides at three a.m. to take a walk in shortshorts and a halter to the all-night market for a pack of cigarettes and then gets bagged, she's out too. The girl who rides with her boyfriend and his gang pals and goes into the men's room with her boyfriend to give him head, then the others follow and gang-bang her. No sale. I course through the dull sheets of pain that reduce things to dead categories such as sexual assault, I flip through the pages hunting for the right one, and the right one is the one I can sell, the one where the reader cannot say, well, that could never happen to me, the one where they can't run away so easily.

A woman rides the freights into town and then hooks up with two guys at a café and they say, if you need a place to crash, come with us. She does. She decides she needs a shower and they say go ahead. When she comes out of what she calls "the rain closet," they're on her. She later goes to the cops, describes herself as a motorcycle mechanic, and tells them of the rape. The paper takes one look at my story and says, forget it. And of course, they're right. Rape, like many things, is kind of a class matter. You have to not deserve it for the world to care even a little bit. This I learn.

Sometimes for a break I drop in on a small bookstore where a heavy woman with a British accent sells used volumes. A gray cat is always nestled inside and the place has the feel of afternoon tea in someone's living room. One night she is raped in her home. The store closes, I don't know what happened to the cat. Eventually, she leaves town and settles in a city somewhat distant. Finally, I hear, she kills herself.

I keep hunting, talking with fewer and fewer people, except for those who live in my world or at least understand its dimensions.

I sense I am considered peculiar. But then I am. I'll be somewhere, maybe kicking back, feet up on the coffee table, glass of wine in hand and someone will play "Midnight Rambler" and my mood will sink and go black. To this day I loathe that song and think ill of people who like it.

We talk for twenty-two hours. Not all at once, no one can do that, but for very long stretches at a time. We become very close because I do not really ask questions, I am more of a prompter. Also, we are in the physical set, the home, and so what she says we can act out. Enter the rooms, stand where she stood, see the same walls. That is how the lady in the gray dress with the hard words, the lady who stunned the audience, begins. With talk.

We sit across from each other with the coffee table and a patch of rug between our chairs. She is cautious, this is her story, and like most people she wishes to tell her story, but only to the right person. The person who listens. I have no tape recorder, just a pen and a notebook and we begin spiraling into the tale. It is night, her daughter is in the tub, she mentions pain and points. The mother hides her alarm, asks gentle questions, does not judge and it slowly comes out as the minutes seem to crawl past. He is the older man, the pal of neighborhood kids. Always a smile, perfectly normal, you never would have guessed. Of course, the telling takes a long time and then we go over the telling and much comes out, and we repeat this for hours and then days and then keep going.

There is a point where the past has finally been peeled away, that dull varnish hindering our view, and the future has been set aside also, all those concerns about what I will say and write and how it will look in a newspaper, and this other moment occurs, always, the continuous present, where the person, in this case the woman with a soft voice and hard memories, is back to the past, back in that night and its aftermath but she is really in the present, she is there, not trying to remember, there, not trying to cast it into suitable language, but actually there and she can see everything and hear everything and she becomes like a seer and the words, no matter how slowly they emerge, seem to come in torrents, in a seamless monologue. And she cannot stop, cannot let go, not too quickly anyway. That is part of why it drags into days. Someone is listening for the first time in a lifetime.

The voice oddly goes flat at these moments, as if coming off an oracle. There is a sense in her of no inhibition as she recounts shouting an obscenity at her husband who was going to visit the neighbor with a twelve-gauge. She is a church lady who never says those words, she is a petite woman who abhors violence, a demure woman used to tacitly letting men lead. As she talks, her daughter plays in the yard, and from time to time I'll catch a glimpse of her as I look up from my notepad or glance away from the woman as the monologue flows from her full lips. The child is gamboling in sunlight. For a second, none of it ever happened. I see this apparition through the sliding glass doors and then the woman's words pull me back to the night, the aftermath, the weeks and now months of coaxing the child back first from terror and then from a sense of having betrayed her special friend by telling—and of course, she was warned not to tell.

All the while—and we pause for coffee or Cokes or glasses of iced tea—I am thinking of how I can take one small tale and make it speak to something larger and I am sensing a change in me as if I were being led through dark chambers where secret lore is being revealed and shattering my fixed notions.

During these sessions, the woman and I share a kind of trance. When I leave, the trance still holds and I talk with no one about what I am doing. In fact, I keep it a secret and make a point of filing other stories to disguise the hours I am spending with her. I live in worlds within worlds since the woman's identity must not be revealed because by law and custom the child's identity must not be revealed and so for me things become generic and universal, and yet at the same time I am looking into one woman's face, specific, exact, full of color, scent and feel.

I write the story in one long fury, and when I stretch out with the printout on the floor, it runs about twenty feet. Sometimes the Jungian roller-skater drops by and finds me crawling on the floor with my felt pen and she does not approve of this act. It is too involved, not suitable for things that should be done at a desk with a good lamp and a sound chair. I sense I am failing her by falling into myself and our sex grows more heated and yet more empty. This goes on for weeks. I don't know what to do with the story and then finally, I turn it in and they print it. Fifty subscribers cancel in less than an hour, I am told.

I have become furious but mainly with myself. Certain protocols in writing about such matters anger me. I decide never to write the phrase *child molestation* or *sexual assault* except in a context of deliberate mockery. I am angry at the pain as I make my appointed rounds and I am angry at the hypocrisy of it all. We cannot seem to talk about what we disapprove of without also denying what we actually are and what we actually do. I cannot put this into words but I find I am living it.

So I revolt. I fly to Washington, D.C., to pick up a press award, one of the many baubles that American reporters hand out to each other, and I am to speak in a big auditorium in the Hilton hotel to a crowd of five hundred executives of the chain, plus worthies such as Rosalynn Carter. I write no speech and sit on the dais waiting and drinking glasses of wine. I remember my first words to the audience: "I don't work for you." And then I inventory all the pain I find and write about and all the wounded people I deal with and I tell the audience that I work for them, for those people, for the injured, maimed, raped, murdered, violated folk. Afterward I go to a bar, meet two women and am taught for the first and last time in my life the proper way to consume cocaine—make a line, she smiles, roll this bill. I leave at dawn for the airport while someone is calling down to room service. And I return to what I understand, to where I know in my bones I belong.

A woman is at the door and she has three balls on a string she wishes to insert in my ass and then she will pull the string at the moment of orgasm.

A woman is at the door and she says she has cuffs.

A woman is at the door late at night and we make love on the concrete floor. As she leaves, she says she can't see me again because she is getting married in the morning.

Two women are at the door . . .

The images of how we ought to live have ripped out our tongues and made it difficult for us to talk about how we actually live. We are whores, studs, saints, moms, dads, lovers, various categories. The devil in blue jeans. My life in those days erased boundaries and paid no attention to whether I was a predator or a victim or a newspaper savior with a byline. I don't think I consciously sought out women or that they sought me out either. I think we lived in a state of hard knowing and we collided or we found each other or we got lucky because we felt this loneliness of knowing and this emptiness from living alone with it. There is a way to go so deep into the secrets and the hungers of your own culture that you break free by this very act of embodying it, and at that moment you live without concern for the mores and with a keen sense of your own needs. I have seen this state of being most often in the old, who finally realize that the rules of conduct are optional and read what they wish, say what they think and live in sin without a qualm. That is what I most remember about my time in the world of sexual hungers gone astray, in the world of rape and children taken and children killed and women beaten and terrified and humiliated—a sense of feeling everything, as if I had become some open wound, a sense of eating because I was hungry and drinking because I was thirsty and bedding because I felt alone and cold and sought warmth and tender arms. They say this feeling happens in wartime.

War always walls off the combatants from the folks at home. That is why I think I have fallen silent for so long about those years, kept my own counsel and largely buried what I saw and learned and felt. To speak is to invite the categories and have the Marlboro Man and the Woman in Red enter the conversation. Something like the plight of combat veterans who have to fend off talk of heroes and cowards and patriots and the enemy. I have hard memories of my life, but of the work, I have nightmares. I still drive by commonplace haunts and see weeping women, bodies, a terrified child, an eviscerated girl. This will never end.

There is a knock at the door.

The days of the week cease to have meaning, as do the weeks of the month and the months of the year. The only sure things lie in little facts, like holidays are bad because families will be together and thus have more opportunities to hurt each other. Orderly progress, like the neat list of classes found in one's college records, is a fantasy. I learn things on the run and without intention. I am not working on a degree or a career. Knowledge comes like stab wounds, and pleasure comes like the surprise of a downpour from a blue sky in the desert.

The woman in the gray dress sits up in bed and asks, "Aren't my breasts beautiful? Aren't they the best you've ever seen?"

I nuzzle her hair. Time has passed, the story is long gone, the woman in the gray dress with the hard words and the maimed child is now the woman.

She tells me her husband has been suspicious of me.

I ask her what she told him.

"Don't worry," she smiles, "I told him you were a queer." Then she slides over, gets up and rolls a joint.

Rule number four: *Don't talk about it, no one wants to hear these things.*

This mandatory silence becomes a measure for me of my plunge into sex crimes. One day I get up and realize that the things filling my head can be shared with very few other people. I'll tell you something that is not generally said to others outside the work. The rapes are bad but not that bad. The mind is protected from what adults do to adults. There is a squeamishness about the rapes, an embarrassment among the men who investigate them, and an anger among the women who investigate them and treat the casualties. But the rapes can be handled to a degree. Of course, it's not as easy as homicide. People stay in homicide forever and never lose pleasure in their work. Sex crimes generally cycle people out into some other kind of crime work in two years. It's because of the kids. No one can handle the kids. It goes against nature as we know it.

She enters my life at lunch. She works with maimed children and that is how we happen to come to the table. The lunch stretches on for hours. In the parking lot, she says, "Let's go to a motel."

I say no.

She presses, asks why.

I have no ready answer.

Much later, I pull into a gas station after working long hours. I hear her call from another island. We embrace and I pull her against me and feel her hips against my own. First, we fuck on a cushion I've spread on the cold concrete floor. She apologizes for her body, she feels she is fat. I tell her to never say that to me again or to anyone else. Then I kiss her.

We drink cheap champagne I find in the refrigerator. The bubbles feel good. She is dressed now, she feels more comfortable clothed. I peel off her jeans and place her bare ass on the concrete. She opens her arms.

Later I am in the yard under the mesquite. Both trees are growing fast and I can hear the leaves softly swishing in the night.

There is no more to it than that. No foreword, no afterword. Make of it what you may. You already know the facts.

Of course I am drawn into the American passion for fixing things, the deep faith that problems are really opportunities in disguise. Once I was helping a guy move—him, his wife, the two young daughters. A box I was carrying broke open and small paperbacks spilled out on the ground in the bright sunshine. I gathered them up and then idly flipped through one, and then another and another. They were all cheap things from no-name presses about men—daddies, uncles whoever—fucking kids. I was stunned and did not know what to do. I felt violated, as if it were wrong for me to have to know this. So I put them back in the box and the box in the truck and said nothing and did nothing.

That is part of what I feel as I enter the gray police station and go to the office where the sex crimes unit works. They've got a treasure trove of child pornography seized from perps, and in my memory the stack rises six or seven feet. The police want to outlaw the stuff, not simply manufacturing it, but possessing it. I am skeptical. They leave me at a table, and what they want is for me to look at it and come out with an article recommending that people who possess such materials go to prison.

The collection mainly features boys—seven, eight, nine from the looks of them—and they are sucking off men, taking it in the ass, being perfect pals about everything. I am struck by not what I feel but how little I feel. It is like handling the treasured and sacred icons of a dead religion. Careful constitutional qualms are filed in my mind—mainly that to think something is not a crime and anyone buying these materials or gazing at them is thinking about something. Fucking kids and taking pictures, that is already against the law. I look for hours and still feel nothing. I am in a place beyond the power of empathy.

A few months later I get a thick packet that contains fifty or sixty typed pages. The writer is facing a long prison sentence for having sex with Boy Scouts, as I recall. He writes with courtesy, clarity and an almost obsessive sense of detail. It reminds me of another long manuscript I received from a woman who was plagued by a radio playing in her head and various sinister probes, particularly of her anus and vagina in the night. She explained carefully how her many appeals to the authorities had brought no response and of her suspicion that her plight was caused by rays and lasers and various ominous waves of energy. The man awaiting sentencing for fucking boys uses language with the same exact tone. He says nothing ever happened except that he tried to comfort and love his charges. I doubt him on the details but come to sense he means his general thesis about love. He loves children, totally, and locks on them with the same feeling I seem to have for adult women. That is what I take away from the photos that the police want outlawed and the autobiography of the man they eventually send away to be raped and probably murdered in the state system, a criminal who saw himself as the perfect friend. Other crimes are being committed by people who see themselves as the perfect lover. And of course, a lot of things are being done by people full of hate, who are going to get even by causing pain, humiliation and sometimes death. There is no single, simple explanation of sex crimes. But in the case of men who use children for sex, there is often this fixation, this sense of love. Which always leads them to betray the very idea of love by using children for their own selfish ends.

I listen to music all the time. My tastes change slowly, without my awareness, and start sliding backward through the decades. One day I decide to look up a style of music in a big Merriam-Webster dictionary. *Torch song*: from the phrase to carry a torch for (to be in love); first appeared in 1930; a popular, sentimental song of unrequited love.

There is a crucible and in it music bubbles, *she's gonna drag me over the rainbow, I shot my baby*, and as I sit here now and think of then, I listen to the music screaming out of a guitar and know there are things I must address. What about the causes of sexual crimes, what about the endless wheel of pain where children are molested and then grow up to be molesters and rapists and what about all the studies detailing an inmate population fucked over (literally) since their most tender years? And what about the corrosive effect of pornography on the way men perceive women and children? And what about tougher laws and castration and community alerts to the release and residency of perverts? And what about the movies and what about sex icons and their sinister consumption by the masses? And what about the booze and the drugs driving people to these demonic acts? And what about date rape and sexual harassment at the office and magazines full of naked women and hostile thoughts? And what about what is in your eyes and in my eyes as we talk over a drink and listen to the music bubbling up from the crucible and then go into the night with eager loins?

So I will address these matters. *What about us, baby? And I love your perfume.*

I was basically an innocent about crime and cops and I slowly learned there are inner rings to this hell of human cruelty and violence. There's a place even lower and more destructive than the life of a narc, and that is the world of sex crimes. A narc becomes a stranger to his fellow cops, his wife and his children, disappears for much of the day into a place of needles, booze, snorts and busts. But with luck, he can keep some kind of inner self safe from the place he works and hunts. I know a narc who came home late at night, let himself into his sleeping household, heard someone moving in the hallway and swung. He found his wife unconscious on the floor and thanked God he hadn't gone for his gun. That was close but in this other country where men rape women and children, where two-year-olds turn up sodomized, no gun matters and no fist can guard the castle gate.

The walls are block, the fluorescent lights replace windows and we sit in rows forming a semicircle as the woman speaks. She is very nicely done in a sedate professional suit, tasteful hair, low-key makeup, and a serious, clear voice. The other prisoners mark time as I go through rape therapy in the joint. I am not here because of a story. I have come to find something beneath the stories or behind the stories or deep within myself. The fellatio, cunnilingus, anal sex, binding, teasing, caressing, the playing out of fantasies comes not from a criminal world but from the everyday world. Rape is an eerie parody of accepted life, an experience using the same wardrobe but scratching the word *consent* from the script. I have listened for hours to women tell of the horrors they experienced and what they recount as acts are usually within my life, and what they recount as true terror, the sense of powerlessness, strikes chords within me also. I can't even abide being here, I can't take the bars, guards, walls. But I am here anyway, listening to the hum of fluorescent tubes as the woman teaches the class.

The men, struggling to earn good time, feign attention. They answer questions appropriately and wear masks of serious thought. I don't believe them for an instant, and I think this class is a farce and that nothing will deter my colleagues from their appointed rounds when they leave this place. The woman herself, from a good family with sound religious values, has been attacked—"I am part of the sisterhood," she once told me shyly—and she has brought me here so I will see hope and share her hope. So I sit with the current crop of convicted rapists—"There are no first-time offenders," a cop once snarled at me, "just sons of bitches that finally get caught"—and feel no hope. Of course, prison is rape culture—"just need a bunk and a punk," one local heroin dealer offered in explaining his lack of concern about doing time.

The session finally ends and we bleed out the door into the prison corridor. I am ambling along in a throng of convicts, the woman walking just ahead in her prim suit with a skirt sitting snugly on her hips. The guy next to me is singing some kind of blues about what he's gonna do to that bad bitch. I've blotted out the actual song, I can remember the corridor (we are strolling east), see her up ahead, hear him singing next to me, his lips barely moving as he floats his protest against the class and her fucking control and all that shit, but not the lyrics themselves. They're gone, erased, I suspect, by my mind out of self-defense. Afterward she and I go to a truck stop and eat apple pie and I can still see the whiteness of her teeth as she smiles and speaks brightly about her work.

Later, I taste the therapy for men who have fucked their own children. They sit in a circle and talk while their wives run the show. It's either show up at such sessions or back to the joint—so attendance is rather good. When it's over, I go off with the boys and we have beers. Each and every one of them in recounting his lapse from accepted behavior describes the act itself as fondling. Apparently there are hordes of diligently caressed children out there. I sit nursing my beer and say little and listen. I am pretending to try and understand. But I understand nothing at all. I have seen the end result of fondling and it does not look like fondling to me. I cannot reach out and put myself in their place. I cannot see children as sexual objects, it does not seem to be in me. I fixate, I realize, on women. And my fixation is sanctioned. Such thoughts lead to a place without clear light. We all share a biology and deep drives and what we have created—civilization, courtesy, decency—is a mesh that comes from these drives and also contains and tames them. I learn that whatever is bad is not necessarily alien to me. Or you.

I sit here, right now. To my left are two clay tableaux made by Tarascan Indian women in the village of Ocumichu, Michoacán. Devils fuck women in the tableaux, which are always made by women. One devil fucks a woman on her back. Another from behind. I look at them as I work. There is a pre-Columbian poem about what life and death and everything is really about.

> We only come here to sleep,
> We only come here to dream.
> It is not true, it is not true.
> That we come to Earth to live.

I think of the poem also. Then there is the Peruvian carving of a man with a giant erection. A friend gave it to me after his trip there. He said, "Here, this belongs to you."
I didn't ask why.

She loves pornography. It's around midnight, and she is standing in the motel room clutching a bottle of champagne against her black garter belt and peering intently into the screen of the television as fornicating couples, powered by the handyman of American fantasy, the telephone man, frolic. This is one of the seedy motels that cultivate hourly rates, water beds and hard-core cinema, a place much like the room where my life in this world began with the splotch on the wall left by the toddler's head. She is a counselor, one of the many I now deal with, and she likes sex and is fascinated by pornography. This is not unusual, another woman I know has several hundred pornographic tapes. But the interests of the woman in the black garter belt are kept off the table at her work and left to the night hours and random bouts with me. Days are for the maimed, in her case children with cigarette burns and sore orifices. Some nights are like this.

I glance at her naked ass, see the serene concentration on her face as she tracks the movie, and I am empty. She and I share the same country and there is a big hole in us and so we come here. We live in a place past the moral strictures of sin and lust, we run on empty. For us, sex has been drained of its usual charge, delight is beyond our reach. This is a fact. As the months roll past, I have felt this slippage within me. I will have lunch or dinner or a drink or coffee with someone and wind up in a place like this. Romance is not a consideration. There is seldom anyone to talk with and when there is someone, a person stumbling across the same terrain like the woman in front of me, there is nothing to say since we both know. So we come here. A proper distance has been denied us, so we seek moments of obliteration. I have never regretted these moments nor fully understood them. They just come with the territory.

But the slippage bothers me. I seem to drift and the drift is downward—not into sin and the pit, but into that emptiness. I am losing all desire and have become a mechanic going through the motions of life. Food no longer tempts me. I flee into the wild country with my backpack, flee again and again for days and days, but increasingly this tactic does not work. Once I lie by a waterhole in July, and it is a hundred and four degrees at one a.m. (I get up with my flashlight and check my thermometer.) I am crawling with crabs. When I get back, I buy twelve bottles of the recommended cure and for a day have coffee or drinks with a succession of women, handing each a bottle. I take this in stride, as do they. One woman is briefly anxious because she fears I have called her only to deliver the medicine but I assure her this is not true. I think we go to bed. It turns out this mini-epidemic has come from the Jungian therapist who showers three or four times a day. She also is quite calm about it and prefers to talk about her new favorite movie, something entitled *Little Oral Annie*. She tells me she resents the smirks of the male clerks at the video store and I politely sympathize.

The moments of my impotence increase and I am not alarmed by this fact but clinically engaged. I sense that I am walling off everything, all appetites, and have room for nothing but this torrent of pain and squalor that pours through me from the daily and weekly harvest of rapes and killings and molestations. I once read a statement allegedly made by Sophocles in his eighties when sexual desire left his loins, and he said he was glad to be free of the madness. So I am becoming classic and care not at all. I repeatedly try to leave the work but I do not try hard enough. The city desk always wins because a part of me feels bound to the crimes. So I protest, and then return. I tell myself it is a duty but I know it is really a sentence I must serve for knowing these matters at all. And yet then, and now, I cannot really say what this knowing entails. I just feel it as I lie with caring women in countless cheap motels as the movies roll on the screen.

The end comes in the bright light of afternoon on a quiet street lined with safe houses. One moment a seven-year-old girl is riding her bicycle on the sidewalk in front of her home on a cul-de-sac, the next moment the bicycle is lying on the ground and the girl is gone, with no one the wiser. I am thrown into the case by the city desk—this crime is of a kind that seizes a city's imagination—and I go gladly into the fray. I am on fire. I have learned a great deal and now I will share it with others. Legions of dead children seem to live within me and they all come out as I work the story.

This one is my torch song. The rudiments are simple. The alleged perpetrator is a man in his twenties from a very good home in another city, a man whose life has been a torment of drugs, molestation of himself by others and of others by himself, a man who has slipped from his station in life into dissipation and wound up roaming the skid rows of our nation. None of this concerns me and I leave ruin in my wake. I fly to that distant city, talk my way through a stout door, and gut his mother like a fish. When I leave she is a wreck and later that night her husband goes to the hospital for perturbations of his heart. I get into files—legal, psychiatric—that I should not have and I print them fulsomely. The child favored a certain doll and I buy one and prowl the city with it on the cab seat beside me, a touchstone as I work. I am standing in the backyard as the mother of the missing girl makes a plea to whoever took her daughter to bring her home safe and sound. The woman's face is grief made flesh and I note its every tic and sag. It turns out the alleged perpetrator stayed for a time with a couple in a trailer court. I visit, and the man is facing child molestation charges himself, the woman is a hooker with a coke habit.

"Do I have to tell you that?" she whines.

Leave them, drive to a saloon, set my small computer on the bar top and beg a phone for the modem. I sip my drink and write in one quick take. The story flits through the wires and descends into the next edition. The following night a local PTA meeting takes a recess, walks over to the trailer, and it goes up in flames.

My temper is short, my blood cold. A woman who works in the newsroom comes over to my desk. She is a young mother and asks me what I think the chances are of the girl being alive. I snap, "Fucked, strangled and rotting out there." And keep typing. Her face looks as if she has been slapped. As the story flows from my nimble fingers, the sheriff leaps into the public wound and starts leading marches of citizens holding candles and decrying violence and the rape of children. It is much like the time not so long ago when people marched to take back the night. I pay no notice to these marches, they are for others. The reporters on the story all speculate about the girl—even when the arrest comes and the girl is still missing. I do not. I know. Bones, rot, out there. It is months and months before her remains turn up, but this hardly matters to me. I know, this is my country.

It ends several times but at last it finally ends for good. They cannot find the woman whose son, a famous local rapist, has just escaped from his incarceration. I ignore the efforts of the city desk to uncover the mother and interview her. Then they come to me and ask my help. I leave, chat up some neighbors, and within an hour I am in a state office, a bullpen of women toiling over desks and processing forms.

She has done everything she can—changed her name, told no one of her son, gone on and tried to fashion a life. I approach her desk and tell her my errand. She pleads with me, don't do this to me. She leans forward and whispers that no one typing away at the other desks, none of them know anything about this. Leave me in peace, she says. I look into her careworn eyes and I say yes. I tell her I will now leave and she will never read a word of my visit in the newspaper. Nor will I tell anyone of her identity.

When I enter the newsroom, the editor comes over and asks, "Did you find her?"

I say, "Yes."

"When can I have the story?"

"I'm never writing the story."

He looks at me and then says nothing, turns and walks away.

That is when one part of me is finished. I know I must quit. I cannot take the money and decide what goes into the newspaper. I do not believe in myself as censor and gatekeeper. And yet I know I will never write this story because I have hit some kind of pain limit. The phone rings, it is a woman's voice, she says, "Thanks to you she has had to go to the hospital. I hope you are happy."

I tell her I am not writing the story. I tell her I told the woman I would not write the story. She does not believe me. This does not matter to me. I have gone cold. My hands are cold and I know from past experience this means I can give no more. I am righteously empty.

The other ending is more important because it does not involve the work, the little credos and dos and don'ts of journalism. It involves myself. It happens the night the arrests come down for the missing seven-year-old girl who was snatched off her bicycle on that safe side street. Around three in the morning, I have wrapped the story and I reach into my desk drawer where I have stashed a fifth of Jack Daniel's bought earlier in the day. I do not drink hard liquor and I bought the bottle without questioning myself and without conscious intent. So I finish the story, open the drawer, take the bottle and go home. I sit in the backyard in the dark of the night, those absolutely lonely hours between midnight and dawn. I drink, the bite of whiskey snapping against my tongue, drink in the blackness. The trees are tall now, they have had three years' growth. I have become careless in my watering since they reached a certain size where I could sit under them in a chair. So I drink in silence as the trees caress me with small cool tongues lapping off the luscious leaves.

After a while I feel a wetness and realize I am weeping, weeping silently and unconsciously, weeping for reasons I do not understand but certainly weeping for what I feel. I know this is a sign that I am breaking down, this weeping without a moan or a sound. I feel the tears trickle and step outside myself and watch myself clinically in a whiskey-soaked, out-of-body experience. That is the other ending.

I quit the newspaper, never again set foot in the newsroom, go into the mountains off and on for months and write a book about them. That helps but not enough. I sit down and in twenty-one days write another book about the land, the people and the city. That helps but I barely touch on the world of sex and crimes, which broods beneath the sentences about Indians and antelope and bats and city streets. Nothing really helps.

This is what I am trying to say. Theories don't help, therapies don't help, knowing doesn't help. A few days ago I punched up the Internet and checked out articles on sex crimes. The experts say they have therapies that are cutting recidivism and maybe they do but I doubt it. I live with what I am and what I saw and what I felt. I have never been in an adult bookstore. Two years ago I was at a bachelor party in a lap-dancing place and lasted fifteen minutes before I hailed a cab and fled. This is a residue that will linger to the end of my days in the cells of my body. This is not a virtue or a position. I have no desire to outlaw pornography, strip joints, blue movies or much of anything my fellow citizens find entertaining. Nor have I led an orderly life since my time in sex crimes. I write for men's magazines and pass over without comment their leering tone and arch expressions about the flesh. I am not a reformer. So what am I? A man who has visited a country where impulses we all feel become horrible things. A man who can bury such knowledge but not disown it and a man who can no longer so glibly talk of perverts or fucking rapists or cretins or scum. A man who knows there is a line within ourselves that we cannot accurately define, that shifts with the hour and the mood but is still real. And if we cross that line, we betray ourselves and everyone else and become outcasts from our own souls. A man who can be an animal but can no longer be a voyeur. A man weeping silently in the backyard with a bottle of whiskey who knows he must leave and go to another country and yet never forget what he has seen and felt. Just keep under control. And try not to lie too much.

I am in a bar in a distant city with a district attorney. He shouts to the barkeep, "Hey, give this guy a drink. One of our perverts whacked a kid in his town."

The bartender pours and says, "Way to go."

I drink without a word.

I can't tell much from the back of her head. But there are five rules.

After the phone call from Barbara, after Paul blocked the view out my hotel window and swung oh so slowly, his body barely moving in the cool light of the studio surrounded by his art, his installation art, the bric-a-brac of objects carefully found out in the alleyways of our lives and then cunningly arranged to be just so, after that moment, I went downstairs to find the International Brotherhood of Teamsters, the bad boys of the American union movement. I looked for their sign, two severed horse heads on a badge.

My grandfather was a teamster back in a time when this badge meant not a damn thing. He had a wagon and a team of horses and when the train came, he picked up the freight and hauled around town to the small merchants dying slow deaths in the cornfields of Iowa. He would not know this brassy hotel in downtown Los Angeles. He was from a different world. He would know bootleg booze from his still, the cold morning feel of a shack in the Sand Hills of Nebraska, the savor of salt pork and beans, the warm feel of a goat's udder as he milked her each morning, the slight drag of a straight razor as he shaved each morning and the completeness of his life of strong drink, one wife, eleven children and relentless poverty. He died before I was born and might just as well have lived in some dusty century before Christ, or been one of the hungry ones huddled in the Anasazi camps chopping up the men, women and children as others lit the fire for the evening meal. He was disconnected from my being and yet the scientists tell me he spirals on, right this instant as I walk halls seeking the

Teamsters, spirals and pirouettes within me cradled in the burden and possibility of my DNA.

He was named Sam but he went by the name of Butt. No one remembers why. He worked as a jockey when he was younger and then did some stints as a barkeep before my grandmother complained of his terrible on-the-job thirst. I have some photographs and he never smiles.

When I was a boy, I swallowed whole all the family lore, thinking somehow it connected like dots and that this linkage added up to a bridge to a greater world, the one sounding ponderously in the history books or raucously in the movies. This was not to be. The dots did not connect except in a genealogy no one could keep straight and the greater world continued to live out there in cold, self-satisfied serenity and only came knocking in case of war, when the men would vanish for a while and come back even more thirsty. Or when the sheriff arrived with various charges.

I soon surrendered all notions of progress or any cavalcade of people and places on the march toward some destination. I remember my father scoffing at such things as a family tree and advising me not to look back lest I tumble into a nest of horse thieves.

On the ride in from the airport yesterday, we cut off some big road into the entrails of downtown Los Angeles and as we circled down to street level arcing along the round section of a cloverleaf studded with trees, the small round patch hosted an encampment of bums, bearded, well-tanned men in cast-off clothing huddled in some sacred circle and drinking as the sun faded and the city traffic flew by blind to their presence. They had cardboard signs tossed hither and yon, the message boards they hoist at stoplights to beckon the spare change of drivers. I have always wondered why bums half-crazed by booze seem to write their signs in felt tip with such a clear hand and almost perfect spelling. As they hove into view, the producer, my chauffeur from the airport, was explaining how he'd managed gypsy productions for years, sets and crews that dodged unions with fervor. He told me he couldn't make the movies if he paid scale. But even if he could pay scale, he'd never have a union set. He said it was a thing with him, a piece of ground that mattered to him, and that he would never surrender. His voice tightened on this point. He was never giving in to them. And of course, neither were the bums, those who had chosen or been chosen by booze or mental illness to live outside the bounds of a wage economy. They are the meek terrorists of our time, smiling beggars ready to spring at the first sign of weakness and light the fires under the cooking pots. I once had such a man tell me of holding down a woman in an alley while she was raped. And he told me it was his woman.

The men who were camped in the sacred circle of the cloverleaf cheek to jowl with downtown Los Angeles seemed as relaxed as a band of warriors who had just ridden into their traditional stronghold. I've fed them in soup lines, ladled out the grub as their blank faces staggered past. I've interviewed them wholesale for newspaper features and I've never found one who was homeless, who lost through mishap the family farm, the bungalow in the factory shadow. At best, they'd had moments as night clerks in dying motels. They simply didn't fit in and so they rode outside the light of our fires and lived off the bones we tossed into the dark. But they never howled. My town is infested with bums and they lodge along the arroyos as silent as cats on the hunt. I've had them invite me to stop by for a visit. One guy near my house has partnered in domesticity with his pal in the same stretch of wash for seven years. Every once in a while kids burn their camp out but they are tenacious and rebuild. They are the artists of our debris and their installations are beyond the mean hands of curators.

Now I am amongst the severed horse heads, they grow thicker and thicker as I wander the lobby of the huge hotel, and then I drop down a floor to a warren of meeting rooms, swing open a door and see the leadership of the International Brotherhood of Teamsters breaking bread as the day comes on. The tables have white cloths, the china is heavy, and uniformed waiters, all dark in skin, flutter here and there tending to the needs of labor chieftains. I am wearing jeans, a shirt with copious pockets fit for my supplies—pens, paper, cigarettes, a passport, matches, various tools to tear and tighten and hammer, weapons and what-not, a wrinkle-proof blazer highly recommended by seasoned travelers who come out of the bush and yet an hour later must be spruce for drinks, dinner and dancing. And I am wearing shoes made of leather with neatly tied laces.

I know not a soul in the room but still they have beckoned me to their midst. A few weeks ago a call came and I said yes. I tend always to say yes because otherwise you don't have a prayer of getting the girl. And so I said yes and a few days later walked across the bridge into Juárez, Mexico, and started talking to Mexican truckers who almost without exception had never heard of the International Brotherhood of Teamsters. I was to write a story for the union's magazine on what it was like to drive a big rig in Mexico and what it might mean if these brown truckers came north, highballing into the United States as a treaty said they would and must within a few short months. I agreed to do the story because I wanted to write for a union, to have on my little résumé this exotic task as a credit, even though Labor no longer existed, newspapers no longer mentioned the fact of such folk, unions were dying in some cancer ward sheltered from public view and carefully sedated lest they howl in the final throes.

As I crossed the bridge, past a streaming flow of people, all brown and poor and toting little plastic bags of items purchased on the distant shore in El Paso, Texas, I could feel the rhythms changing, sense the pace slowing into some internal trek of desire. The women had scent, the children scampered underfoot, the world seemed inhabited rather than simply crowded. I stopped in midspan and looked down at the concrete bank of the Rio Grande and on the Mexican side saw that the portrait of Che had been restored. Months earlier Guevara had looked pale and drawn. Someone had hurled a paint bomb of white at his fierce visage and blotted out his glower and defiance. Now he had been absolutely renewed and he stared with hatred toward the gringos of the United States.

I first met Che during the sixties when he was a wall poster everywhere in the college town when I camped and he looked exactly the same then as he does on the concrete bank of the Rio Grande in Juárez. The man simply does not age—I suspect Cuba itself is his portrait of Dorian Gray and that its sacrifice allows him to keep his hard young face. Back then he emerged from a corona of red, his eyes clear and yet focused on something beyond me when I looked at him, eyes staring off into the mists of the future when the revolution would have triumphed and there would be a chicken in every pot, done in the style of mole, of course. I was quite taken with him then, as I was with anyone who struck blows against the confinement I sensed on every hand. Marxism, Leninism, Trotskyism, all the unreadable isms, the leaflets put out by graphically brain-dead leftist presses that I glanced at and cast aside. But Che survived the literature that embraced him. He became a big star.

Big enough to be hunted by the Central Intelligence Agency in Bolivia and slaughtered and then have his hands cut off so that the authorities in Langley could make sure they had their man.

And then he seemed to go away, he couldn't keep up with the hundred-twenty beat of disco, he was useless as tits on a bull during the boom of the eighties, he had nothing to say that mattered to anyone when the wall tumbled down in Berlin. He was dead, but that was not the problem, he was worse than dead. No one played his music.

But cannibalism saved his reputation. I was walking across the Rialto bridge in Venice, it was November and the light was low and yet golden because it had to slice through so much sea vapor to reach the stone walls of the ancient city, and the air felt cold and crisp. I saw this kiosk peddling neckties, the kind where you flipped open the big tongue on the reverse side and discovered a naked woman and on every single tie she was smiling, and right next to these magic neckties I found Che. He'd become a billfold that said, "Ernesto Che Guevara, Hasta La Victoria Siempre." He still had those eyes, that strange stare into history, and one panel of the billfold had a photo reproduction of Fidel and the gang riding horseback into Havana with the Cuban flag fluttering in the dank tropical air, and by God, floating just above the bearded guerrillas on horseback, floating way up there in the sky, was Che about the size of the Empire State Building in New York City, looking proud and huge and still with that weird stare.

Naturally, I bought the billfold and have carried it with me ever since. Che Guevara, Capitalist Tool. Consumed, devoured, recycled, commodified—wow, have we got the words. Retro. A language of cannibalism.

I leaned on the railing of the bridge and looked at Che, ignoring the Indian woman squatting on the ground by my feet, her hand outstretched for coins, her dirty child underfoot. God, I loved the smells coming off the city, the stench from the river, the whiff of garbage, the perfume of the young girls, the diesel fumes from the trucks, and Che looking up into history and behind him on the big hill over Juárez a message in stone that shouted THE BIBLE IS THE TRUTH.

Paul, before he hung himself in that studio, was a fiend for recycling and commodification and cannibalism. I've got a photo of him as a kid, maybe eight, nine, ten, in a Chicago alley, his head half-buried in a garbage can looking for something. He was always finding stuff and devouring it and then spewing it out as something yet again in his art. He'd have loved my Che billfold.

But I'm not sure he'd have liked this deal with the Teamsters, although the breakfast they're devouring in the big hotel looks fine. I can hear the clatter of the stout knives and forks as I stand in the room in my wrinkle-free blazer and smell Juárez in my nose and feel Che's eyes on my back. Barbara's voice still rings in my head from the phone call and she is always such a friendly sound, even now when half the time it seems she is crying. She tells me she wakes up every single morning and discovers she is weeping. But the coffee helps, she says. As soon as she has that first cup, she stops weeping, presto! just like that.

Everyone around me has a big medal badge with those two severed horse heads. A guy takes me by the arm and says come on over, I'll introduce you to James Hoffa.

2

The ceiling light paints the windows milk and we sit in the ranch house sealed off from the summer night. On the walls are huge oil paintings of Indians and of mountain passes. She is talking and there is this simple strand of things I notice—her quick bright words, the light painting the windows milk, the big paintings. The house is not her house, it is not my house. It is a kind of no-man's-land. The torch songs always drive me to such a place. The occupant is a friend of mine and he is on the run. That is why he has come here to Chorizo, because it is where so many are on the run from something and yet have come to ground. My friend's story is simple: he got caught, he agreed to wear a wire, his testimony put ten or fifteen Mafia guys in prison. Now for him it is no known address, no phone, a nine-millimeter by the bed, an AK leaning against the wall in the corner, a sawed-off shotgun, and always a careful look over his shoulder.

Our history comes from running away. At first from all the failed continents starting with that whoop and a holler as we crossed the land bridge at the Bering Strait, and then with time, we streamed in from Europe, Latin America and yet again from Asia. There is the wound, always bleeding, from the Middle Passage, and on a windless night even, in Chorizo, we can hear the shackles clanging and the soft moans from the stale air of the hold. Later the fence comes down and we cross singing *corridos* from Mexico. There is no place we have not been and to a man, woman and child, we have fled some kind of failure, some lack of salt in the kitchen. That is our bloodline and we are the spawn of losers making a life from escape.

God, I love the vigor of our family trees, gnarly, twisted sons of bitches, tortured, lusty trees, bent, ungainly limbs, thorns, every foot prickly and on guard. The roots deep, hungry, probing, pushed by an awesome thirst. So we came, the people from nothing, guns cocked, a child squalling in the backseat of the jalopy on a bad road, bones cold in the night, brows sweaty by day, we came, we come, we keep coming, as if the moving were all we knew how to do or would ever know.

After a while, we hit our stride. Always come from the East, always head toward the West. I remember the guy showing me his little nine-millimeter. He had a spare barrel, a throwaway for that moment he might use the gun, kill someone and not want to leave evidence. Leave no trace. Let them find the body in the gray light of dawn, when he'd be far down the road with his faithful pistol fitted with a new barrel that would not match the markings on the bullet. Simple.

Now, stick out your thumb.

The light is clean, the air cool, the two males, sixteen, are hitching by the road hoping for a ride into Chorizo. They are ready, the afternoon is fine, a car slows, then stops.

It is time.

They get in—they know the guy, what the hell?—and talk to the man who has been hanging around the El Tonto for the last week or two.

The car moves, runs through the gears, and it is nice, it is good, moving down the road with nothing facing them but the lazy afternoon and the promise of night.

For her it is not the same but similar. She . . . is very quick with eyes that can only be called bright—blue, alert, intelligent, hungry. I'll tell you a simple story that will save time. The Border Patrol likes to descend on Chorizo like wolves and prowl about people's property looking for dope. These visitations violate various parts of the Bill of Rights and she cannot abide such behavior. So one night she hears the squad car prowling down her country lane, and she leaps out of bed around four in the morning and storms out. She is standing in the glare of the headlights giving the officers a piece of her mind, when she notices that she is buck naked.

She came to Chorizo in 1976, she tells me as the night rolls on and on. She hitchhiked from New York State with her four-year-old daughter in a car with some drug dealers, pausing in Missouri—*Well, I was almost gang raped.* Such people tend to land in Chorizo. The most recent wave began in the late sixties, when immigrants, whom the locals call hippies, drifted into an old mining claim called the Arroyo. A lot of people didn't like the newcomers, with their long hair and beards but they stuck and are still here, along with their children and grandchildren. No one wanted to admit it but they represented the legend of the Old West, the lawless freedom—except that they did not look like John Wayne or act anything like him. Everyone lived in teepees and scrounged for food and didn't do much of anything. The mountains were beautiful, the hills pulsating with the seasons from withered brown to lush green, and Mexico was just over the hill. She was on the line, on the border, on the edge and she says, "I knew I had come home." The first day or so she made it the ten or twelve miles into Chorizo, bought some canned goods for herself and her daughter and then carefully stacked them in the teepee. She took a walk through the hills and when she came back the cans were gone. She thought, "These people are hungry," and she did not get upset. After all, she had two hundred dollars, plenty to start a new life with, especially when you have finally found home. Jenny can remember the scorn in town when she first arrived, the sense of us versus them, but now she talks to people who once turned their backs at her approach and somehow time has healed things—or maybe no one in Chorizo really has the energy to keep things going over the long haul. After all, the newcomers enriched the local world. For example, after they came a new kind of work developed here, drug smuggling, or perhaps more accurately, an old line of work became rejuvenated. Stash houses began to dot the landscape and other odd matters occurred that were eventually absorbed into the mores of Chorizo, tucked away like a child in bed. Most complaints seem to be against the Border Patrol and the various police agencies that prowl the area in ingenious and transparent disguises.

I keep noticing the way she talks, that quick, well-enunciated speech, the words almost crackling with the snap in her voice. And from time to time there is laughter but it is always choked off, a kind of self-mocking laughter, and when she laughs she does not expand the way many people do—their chest heaving, their bellies going slack, contracting, their faces melting into new forms—no, she does not release something from within herself but tends to suddenly look downward, at the table where we are sitting, and pull back. And then after the laugh passes, her head comes up, the eyes flash, the black mane of hair shines, the skin is smooth and clear, and she moves on as if the moment of laughter were an interruption, a delay and now she must make up the time. Because she has something to say, a line running through her random talk like a hard wire. She wants to capture this place, Chorizo, to protect its past so that what has happened will be a conscious part of its future. She wants to be a historian yet escape the contamination and limits of that word and that way of acting.

(She shows me a photograph. A teepee stands on a hillside and the landscape is white from a snow. She is standing there in blue jeans and a sweater, hair long, safe by her lodge. She says she built the teepee when the Forest Service tore down her shack. The mesquites look white and alarmed as they bend in the background with the unexpected weight.)

Out there, past the window, that glass eye blinded now by the ceiling light, there waits the land, oak-dotted mountains with the lion, the javelina, the deer, the cow. Flats with mesquite, cactus, brown soil. And then the heartbeat, water, the stream flowing lazily through Chorizo, and the *cienaga*, the big bog where a slab of tilted slate drives the moisture to the surface and creates a broad green tongue that laps at the valley, a tongue rimmed with cottonwoods. The water is the blood of the place: for at least a thousand years human beings have lived here in small numbers because of water. Everyone stops by this spot for a drink but few stay, and fewer leave any record of their lives. Also there are many, many holes in the hills, deep holes where people have dug into the earth seeking minerals. For centuries this place has been mined and for centuries the mines have failed—at the moment they are all pretty much dead—but this does not stop men from looking in the hills for the big rock candy mountain.

(Virgil, an old man I know in Chorizo, says that when a horse is gentle-broke, the horse works with you but when you simply break a horse, you work the horse. The old man sits in front of his trailer at dusk shooting coyotes that have foolishly forgotten their fear. He sips his beer from time to time.)

Chorizo is a prospect, always a prospect, but never a success. It is still unincorporated and no one knows exactly how many souls live in the area—one thousand, two thousand, five thousand? No one seems to care. This is a great place for pretending, which is what I am doing now. The name *Chorizo* is not the real name. I will not use the real name out of caution. There are not enough places left where people can freely pretend. Somehow the United States has become a nation with a permanent air of unreality and yet, by law, custom, or magic, has managed to severely restrict the choice of fantastic roles available to players in this unreality. Halloween is the last night left.

Chorizo is a redoubt, struggling not to be a Masada. The fanatics here have a special twist. God did not seem to call them to this place.

I cannot really remember how I first came here but I can still taste that beginning. There is Jenny with her quick speech. And her husband, Chris, with his handmade words, rough blocks of adobe ripped from the earth, a language made from the dirt itself. Chris springs from ranch people and is the third generation on this ground. The ranch is all but gone—the cattle business is a casino with more losers than winners—and what remains is a hundred-and-ten-acre stub cradling a dry-wash and hosting an abandoned house. The feeble well gives up every June before the rains come. Chris's big silences are part of my taste for this place. He tells me about his ranch house that's been sitting empty for years, a place free of phones or electric lines, a secret place tucked away on a dirt road. Am I interested?

We sit in a bar and talk and I say yes. That's it. Very few words seem needed. Chris likes to talk silence. But the ravens are what really push me over the edge. I go out to this stub of a lost ranch and stand on the knoll by the empty house and I say yes again. I never enter the building. It does not matter. But the ravens do. There is a flock of them carousing in the cottonwoods by the wash, a mob of ravens. They are two-year-olds. In the nation of ravens, the young stay with the parents for a year or two, then they push on and form adolescent gangs that roam the countryside raising havoc for another year. At age three, they accept the world, mate for life, and settle into their responsibilities. I stand by the abandoned ranch house and watch this noisy interlude of raven freedom.

I say yes without a question or a doubt. That is when the taste of Chorizo begins.

> They have made it a desolation;
> desolate, it mourns me.
> The whole land is made desolate,
> but no man lays it to heart.
> Upon all the bare heights in the desert
> destroyers have come. . . .
> —Jeremiah 12:11–12

This place is nowhere. These people look to be trash. Dopers. Welfare bums, junkies, tax dodgers, traffic violators. Gun nuts. I have been coming here since I was a boy. Places like Chorizo have been dwindling for years, murdered in the lean hours of the night by golf courses, subdivisions, master plans and masters. But now they are coming back, sprouting up in the heart of our great cities, festering along the romanticized blue highways. Even a cornered rabbit fights. So too, apparently, do some Americans. As it happened, Chorizo was not dusted by the nuclear test binge of the fifties. But it was a close thing. For more than a decade, nuclear warheads were stored an hour away. A horse can cross the land in an easy day to the nearest abandoned Titan missile base. I have worried about Chorizo for years but I finally believe it will survive the current plague. That is why I come here. It is safe from salvation.

I will tell you why I fear salvation. It has the finality of the tomb. I have admitted my distrust of God—fuck His torch song. That is a given. I do not like God's ways. So His mercy, such as it is, I find weak drink, not near so satisfying as the bars of Chorizo, or as the purring coming from a bottle of red wine as I sit under a waxing moon on the brown hills amid the pagan mesquite and fall into my drunkenness. With salvation comes bliss and out of bliss comes grace and once grace takes hold, then the feeling goes and a warm numbness sets in and will not let go. When you arrive at this place, any horror can be accepted, not as a condition the way we accept the weather but as part of a grand design. And then you have moved lickety-split from enduring to endorsing, and at that point I leave the chapel and head into the hills with my bottle.

So Chorizo is the place of the independent, of those who endure but do not endorse, of the damned. Feeling clings here. Passion, stupor, rage, violence, song. Death. An unseemly crop of death. Men found in shallow graves with slugs in their heads. For a village, this place has industrial-strength death. Here you can still touch the land, feed hungrily in the dirt like a mesquite. Sometimes at night all I can hear are sucking sounds. The roots, you know. But then I am not saved and I keep a weather eye peeled.

The pretending is not the sole attraction of the place for me. I come for the failure. The West is full of schemers—every bare spot of ground a future city, every hill a mine, every desert a farm, every acre your-dream-home-here! every immigrant beginning life anew—but Chorizo never manages to pull anything off successfully. The mines fail, the ranchers fail, the developers fail and the tourists never seem to come in more than dribs and drabs and they leave very swiftly. There are three saloons, one general store, a café, a bakery, a feed store, and for a while the hot issue is to stop drunks from shitting on the two-block-long main street—a kind of antidefecation league. All this in the oldest town site in the state, though it never spawned a true town.

(The woman in the photograph looks arrogant, rich, and full of city scorn with her black hair combed tight to her smug skull, her dark sunglasses, red polka dot dress and that damn shopping bag hanging from one cocked arm.

A man with a tweed sport coat and fedora fills the frame beside her. I ask, "Who are these pricks?" She laughs and says, "That's me. It's Halloween and I'm a tourist visiting Chorizo.")

I am talking with Jenny—once she was in a play here and she had to play a buxom woman so she wore a bra stuffed with God knows what and looked as if her breasts were about 44C. There is a picture of her in that brassiere contraption, an image of her bending over that she says someone keeps threatening to circulate—*ah*, she gives off another choked laugh—evidence of pretending she cannot exterminate.

There are things the woman does not say and I do not say. She never says she loves this place. I am also silent on this point. But we both love it.

"Any killings?" I ask casually. She looks over at me quickly because the question here is burdened with possible problems. This small community, so close to the Mexican border, lives in part off drugs, the hills alive at night with strings of horses, men with packs, truckers running without headlights, the truck springs splayed out flat with the load.

Any killings?

Some men went to the lake, down there in the trees, and they were drinking and there was an argument, and one guy pulled out a gun and shot another man through the chest and the man died. A killing. Yes. When? God, years ago. Down by the lake, the bass noodling among the cattails, the catfish gorging on the bottom in the mud. She can't remember how many years, the names are vague too. It is one in the morning and I cannot see out the window because the light is blinding me to the night.

Yeah, we're livin' on the border with the border patrol
And everyone of them is a dumb asshole.
They've got guns and dogs and a bad attitude
And one thing's for certain, they're gonna be rude.
If you're drivin' down the road, then they'll wanna know why.
They say they just protect us, but that's a big lie.
You came downtown just lookin' for some fun,
But you're lookin' at a cop and he's holdin' a gun.

Chorus:
We got drums, guitars, mikes and amps,
We're white guys on food stamps.
We ate too much garlic, got stomach cramps.
We're white guys on stamps.
　　　　　—Mother Chorizo, "White Guys
　　　　　　　　on Food Stamps"

　　There's an old guy in Chorizo who has constructed a timeline going back into the deep pits of its past. His ranch has a yellow PRIVATE PROPERTY / NO TRESPASSING sign on the gate: NOTICE / ANYONE FOUND HERE AT NIGHT WILL BE FOUND HERE IN THE MORNING. The ranch where I stay is more civilized, with a polite sign advising, "Trespassers will be violated." I should mention that roads in Chorizo are not so good, nor are the roads into Chorizo. Local drunks regularly have head-on collisions with steers. People don't like the drive and this naturally keeps people out. For many residents, road improvements are an issue—they fight them. Some folks in town publish a map for a walking tour of historic this-and-that. But there is a feeling in the air that Chorizo does not seek company. The hunters come during the season, and fishermen drop by at the small lake a few miles out of town, but if you go in the bars at just about any hour, you see the same faces day after day.

　　There is plenty of time, centuries and centuries have left some tracks on this land. In the beginning was a dike, a large dike of stone reaching up toward the empty sky and trapping water and creating a lake (waves lapping over the town site of Chorizo), and the lake, well, maybe it festered and maybe it didn't because all this seems to have happened long before people walked to and fro on the earth. Later, my kind came along, dug in dry ground and found bones.

　　(Imagine their camps, pith helmets on their heads, typewriters resting on rickety tables inside sweltering tents. I'm sure in the old photographs we can see spectacles on their sunburned noses, and good stout boots laced up to the knees—the snakes! the snakes!—and off in the distance, perhaps almost fuzzy in these old photos, the flivvers are tied to the mesquites lest they drift

off after good grass in the dark hours. And in the frame, looking very serious and worthy of the ponderous burden and responsibility of science, we behold the incredible monster hunters, the tamers of ancient and forgotten graves. Did they have women? If they were women, did they have men? Did they enjoy the flesh, back in those days and months they spent inventing the lives of long dead souls they called beasts, creatures who had never passed an hour, I hope, without the sensation of some kind of lust.)

Some of these bones were very big and came from a long extinct elephantlike animal called a mammoth. And some of these bones were damn small and suggested a horse about three feet tall. Consider for a moment tiny *vaqueros* with lariats like shoelaces chasing Chihuahua-sized steers over the awesome Big Empty of the West.

Other grave robbers found hints of our own kind. About 300 B.C. a tribe appeared *(We do not know their own name for themselves, we do not know the sound of a single word in their language—we know next to nothing but we continue confidently to ransack their abandoned homes and claim we know all about them. Imagine a group of future historians explaining a vanished culture they have dubbed* MADE IN USA *and proving their theory by holding up beer cans and fragments of Tupperware that they have artfully arranged in chronologies based on soil stratigraphy.)*, which we call the Hohokam and they persisted in the area of Chorizo until about A.D. 1400.

After that . . . strangers came and they rode horses and the horses this time were more than three feet tall. These people carried lances, they fired guns and cannons, they spoke of a carpenter who had nails driven through his palms and his feet and asked his father for help and then watched an afternoon slide by while he writhed in agony. And three days after he died, a large stone was rolled back from his tomb and the crypt was empty and he appeared to people, then ascended into the sky and left almost a vapor trail behind him that some think spelled out the word *love* and others saw as letters with a different meaning.

This is the story they've come to tell, these people on horses, and eventually almost everyone in Chorizo forgets any other stories, although there are many arguments about the details.

Now dates appear. Father Eusebio Kino rides into Chorizo and marks the spot on his map of missions and it is the year of Our Lord sixteen hundred and ninety-five. Chorizo becomes a *visita*, an outpost, where priests fly through like circuit-riding Methodists to minister to the tender and innocent souls of folks they call Indians. Then in 1736 a man or a woman (or a child or a burro or an old hound dog) scrapes a place in the earth a little bit south of Chorizo and silver gleams into the eye. The silver lies like thick T-bone steaks on the surface and can be harvested by anyone willing to bend over. This fact attracts notice and people are sent north to look for more such bonanzas and naturally some come to the bog and mosquitoes of Chorizo. But the people who have long lived here disapprove of the people who have recently come and in 1751 they rise up and slay many of the newcomers. A large battle in this conflict is fought near Chorizo. But of course, the old settlers lose *(We can never imagine their winning, not for a second, because we are too committed to what we are now, to this computer that is flashing these words on a cathode tube as I pause briefly to bewail the slaughter of people denied the opportunity to be my ancestors. That is why we cherish this history, because we do not have to truly live with it.)*, their energies ebb, and they are overcome by the force of those whose hungers are greater. So great are these monstrous hungers that the newcomers continue to fling themselves outward into other places and other lives. We call them discoverers, explorers and the like. We also mold them into metal statues that inevitably, after a few short months or years, become invisible to everyone but the birds.

They're riding along, the three of them — here, pass me the bottle, I don't like this part — *when something happens* — Christ, I can't straighten this out, the stories vary, well, the two stories vary — *and the car pulls to the shoulder and after a while everybody is out of the car, and then the rock, and the swinging. The knife, ah, that seems later, five, ten, twenty shoves. And then there are two standing and one not standing.*

The sky is very blue. As expected.

*   *   *

In 1774 an experienced warrior of this ground named Juan Bautista de Anza mounts an expedition from a town nearby and the group camps in Chorizo on its trek across the skin of earth and eventually establishes a colony named after Saint Francis, a beggar man said to have loved animals. Many years later this city by a large bay will be called 'Frisco in between tokes on joints. But in 1776 the new people think of founding a fort in Chorizo (they call it a *presidio*) but the sickness that springs from the bogs drives them elsewhere. A vast silence descends (*no one is listening, no one at all*), and there are no records until the Gadsden Purchase, a real estate negotiation in 1853 (*There is an old hotel with a window of Tiffany glass that is named after this deal in a border town and the staff insists it is haunted—I have talked to people who work there and visited the rooms where the spirit walks . . . a woman is bending over an ironing board deep in the basement surrounded by bare concrete walls, and she raises her brown face and says, yes, yes, when I ask the question, then leads me onward into the gloom brooding past the glare of the bare bulb hanging over her workplace and she says, there, there is where the spirit comes and I carefully makes notes in a small paper tablet*) that plops Chorizo into an entity called the United States of America. Things begin to happen at the same old rate but with more attention to detail and this new sense of things, this keenness for cataloguing names, dates, and other facts is called history. Five years after Chorizo is bought from the Mexicans, who did not truly possess it (at the time of the purchase there are but five thousand Mexicans in what becomes an entire state, and this population is almost completely clustered in one fifty-mile-long valley), by the Americans, who are still trying to possess it, a strike of silver is made one fine day in the year 1858 in the brown hills around the bog.

Mines have always had a way of getting lost in Chorizo. In 1763 some forgotten Jesuit pens the *Rudo Ensayo*, a kind of inventory of the region, and this black robe clucks how "there used to be near this place [Chorizo] one gold mine and silver mines which are now abandoned." Part of the problem for the mines lies in interpersonal relations: the local Indians keep killing off the miners. Then in 1812 one

Augustine Ortiz buys up the whole area for about $750, puts in some cows and waits for the Indians to come and kill him and steal his herd. In a few years, naturally, he is gone. His heirs eventually peddle the land in 1856 to the Sonora Mining and Exploring Company, an outfit out of Cincinnati, Ohio. For a couple of years they play at being a business until they run into the same problems that have bedeviled everyone else in Chorizo and the outlying area: interpersonal relations.

(*"Our small party of five took turns in keeping watch and digging the graves. Burying the Papago in one grave, and the two Americans in the other, we wrote on a board—'Tarbox'; and under this: 'White man, unknown, killed by Apaches.'"*)

Samuel Colt of six-shooter fame bankrolls this venture and creates the first library in the territory so that boys swinging pickaxes can improve their minds. The ranch that feeds and fattens the miners lists sixty-one people (nine of them black, a fact that, like most facts in Chorizo, will soon be forgotten).

(*". . . hearing that a wagon-load of watermelons had arrived at [Chorizo], and having lived on jerked beef and beans for nearly a year, I determined to go on with Poston . . . About an hour and a half after these two men had left [Chorizo], they galloped back, showing in their faces that something awful had happened.*

"'What is the matter?' asked Poston.

"'There has been an accident at the mine, sir.'

"'Nothing serious, I hope?'

"'Well! yes, sir; it's very serious.'

"'Is anyone injured—is my brother hurt?'

"'Yes, sir, they're all hurt; and I'm afraid your brother won't recover.'

". . . Laying the bodies in a wagon just arrived from [Chorizo], we returned . . . That evening we had another burial . . . After this we . . . determined to leave the country by the nearest open route. The events of the past week, added to all that had gone before, began to tell on my nerves . . .")

After the Civil War ends, cattlemen flood the land, and steers become the true explorers of this ground and wander up every canyon, find a way onto every mesa, seek out like lovers each blade of lonely grass. In 1887

Apaches kill a rancher and the ground shakes because of an earthquake, followed by a smallpox epidemic. Then in the early and mid-nineties, the rains forget to come and the cattle die and when their vast dying is over, everyone notices that a lot of the earth is dead or dying also, and with time a word will come to spill from many lips, a long word, *overgrazing*. By 1895 Chorizo has two hundred and thirty-six souls and everyone takes a lot of quinine to keep the malaria at bay. Around 1912 a King 8, a Chalmers, a Ford and a Packard mosey into town. Four years later an army post is set up so that the troops can glare south at the revolution sweeping Mexico, and then in 1918 the influenza kills thirty locals. Another drought stops by in 1920 and 1921 and one guy organizes a bone yard, hauling away truckloads for processing into meal. Two years later, for lack of anything else to do, a six-mile stretch of the road connecting Chorizo with the rest of the planet is graded. In the late thirties the state health department finally notices the persistent malaria in the area and tosses some mosquito-eating gambusia fish into the bog. A real estate wheeler-dealer pops into Chorizo in 1948, announces the place would be perfect as an art colony, floats the idea of making a new Taos by the bog, peddles a hundred lots a week, and then leaves and the place goes back to sleep. Electric power straggles along in 1956 and the locals begin to study *I Love Lucy*. And then in 1972 eleven thousand acres of a big ranch that embraces Chorizo gets busted up into forty-acre parcels and new blood seeps into the old veins of the town.

And that's where the old rancher's timeline peters out because as he figures it, "The many new residents in the area as a result of available home sites together with the old residents of the town site will now be witness to a new chronology of events."

Oh, yes, and about that time a new group arrives.

Dope fiends.

Jenny holds the big white scrapbook in her lap, the large pages repeat like tongues eager to talk. Her fingers caress a set of sepia-toned images and she explains that this is Valentine Flat, a patch of low ground by a wild-looking river in western New York. The river looks cold, the rock cliff on the far side as ancient as God. Here, she points, is where the hippies gathered in the summer. The hills surrounding the river are where she was born and raised. Her eyes seem to sparkle as she speaks. Another photo looms up, and they are sitting on the ground, the men have beards—"my brother, there's his wife, that's their kid . . ."—and the women look kindly, the hair hanging long and it is a thousand or two thousand years ago and they are on Valentine Flat in the state of New York, and then—presto!—mesquite pokes up in the background of the next photo, mountains of rock grab at the horizon and there are teepees. Jenny's teeth are gleaming, her skin is glowing and it is the time before the dark time, that moment the people called the sixties.

The explanation is simple but garbled as we stare at the photo book: there is a mining claim—"How did you hear of it?" I ask. "Someone bought it," she says—and suddenly everyone in the photo at Valentine Flat is facing a camera at the Arroyo.

And so people magically appear.

They are all smiling, the men bare-chested, the sun pouring down like honey, in the foreground are tiny children and if you press your nose close enough, the smell of marijuana comes almost within reach. Jenny picks out another face, the man is bearded and smiling and on his head rests a cowboy hat with a flat crown and silver band.

"He was violent," she notes evenly. "Liked to beat up women, and somehow they never seemed to hear about the ones before. Once I ran into him at a party and he said something and I talked right back and he threw me over his shoulder and ran off into the desert. He stopped after a little while and threw me on the ground and said, 'Just so you know what I can do to you if I want?' Beat the hell out of two women. And then he was living with a woman up in the city and he beat her. She shot him dead."

Night is coming down, there is that kind of soft, dying light above Chorizo, as the boys throw a body down the mine shaft—thud, thud, thud. That was easy, why didn't they tell us about this in school? A faint breeze plays with the blue gramma grass, the sounds of people come from below. The night will surely be fine now. Beer, girls, fun. To be sure, there will not be a lot of money, the guy only had a couple of bucks. But what the hell. There is the car . . . and life is roaring ahead on the road.

Virgil stops by the ranch house every morning for one more early beer to help launch the day. In the past two or three weeks, he's knocked down twenty cases—of course, that tally does not include his brews at the El Tonto. Also, he comes by each morning to leave his dog, Baby, a small beast of two or three pounds. His truck, parked for hours in front of the El Tonto saloon, would be too hot for Baby and so he has a beer or two, then leaves the dog as he goes about his business in the liquid heat of Chorizo. He is a small man, I suspect in his early seventies. His manner is very deliberate, a slow, careful form of speech, an elaborate style of courtesy. He spent more than twenty years in the U.S. Army and is proud he left the service as he entered it, a private.

His past is frisky and like many of the inhabitants, it has led him finally to this place. Chorizo sometimes is the last place a person can go. For many years he trapped the hills—he has tales of taking a half dozen to a dozen bobcats out of a single canyon in a season—and one year when the price was good for pelts, he cleared $12,000. Now he is past such work and lives on his Social Security, the government food program that periodically dumps cheese on Chorizo (cheese that no one on earth seems willing to buy), and the profits of his penchant for the constant trading of horses and everything else. He is a collection of stories—riding the freights, working the oil fields, the army of course, and just wandering about the republic. Once, in making a point, he shed a shoe, pulled up a pant leg, skinned off his sock and showed me the scars on his ankle from some bad weeks spent on a chain gang in Alabama. Virgil is the kind of person whom modern governments are determined to exterminate through various programs called aid or rehabilitation or retraining.

(I was in a ghost town in the desert of the Great Basin and a man calling himself Silver Dollar Kirby had a saloon in one small room in the abandoned community—it was a proper ghost town, the table settings were still in place

in the long-closed hotel — and his establishment consisted of one board, two sawhorses, a quart of whiskey, and some shot glasses.

"How are you making out?"

"I'm doing okay," answered Silver Dollar Kirby.

And then he paused, as if considering whether his response was truly forthcoming, and slowly added, "I'm putting a little by.")

At one point Virgil had a saloon in Houston, a few blocks off skid row. He lived above the bar, slept on a cot, and augured a hole through the floor so he could constantly monitor his trade. He kept decorum by wielding a pool cue. He came to Chorizo courtesy of the legal notions of the American government. Some years back he was in the large city that festers about an hour or so to the north and entered a saloon for a cold one. As he walked in, he noticed all the patrons were stretched out flat on the floor and caught a glimpse of two men squared off in a pistol fight. The one he shot through the chest died almost instantly, the other took a slug from a .380 square in the head right under the eye and as Virgil says with a mixture of awe and contempt, "That was the son of a bitch that lived." They held him in jail for nine months trying to get a fix on the exact nature of his crime and finally released him on a ten-year probation. For a spell he hung around some small towns in the limbo of state supervision and then, with a wink and a nod, beat his way to Chorizo. He has never left. Of course, travel can be somewhat of a problem for him with no driver's license, a truck that has no registration, insurance, or plates.

He moves very deliberately and seems unruffled by the little that happens in Chorizo.

(It's years and years ago — in a place just west of Chorizo and things have been lean for a good long while when Jenny unexpectedly comes into fifty dollars. So she piles the kid into the old car and drives to the general store and stocks up on all the good-tasting things they have not been able to buy and then drives home again. She backs the car up to the door — she's nine months pregnant and looking for every break she can find — to unload the groceries from the trunk, and she's standing there with her three- or four-year-old daughter, when she suddenly catches a whiff of gasoline. Her house has no electricity so she goes in and gets the kerosene lantern, comes out on the porch, peers into the darkness and lights the lamp. The blast knocks her and her

daughter over. Seems on the rutted climb back to her place, a rock punctured the car's gas tank. Naturally, the machine's a total loss and all the groceries perish in the blaze. Her legs are seared, as is her face, and her eyebrows and some of the rest of her hair have vaporized. Her daughter is spooked—there will be nightmares—but unharmed.

She treats the burns with a salve she makes of aloe and so long as she lies down with her legs propped up, the pain is not so bad. Takes lots of vitamin E, also. But she cannot stand. The child is born three weeks later, at home, of course. Jenny has little use for doctors and their vile poisons and ideas. It's a boy. And that's the day of the big gasoline explosion. The car's still there, rusting away in the weeds.)

Now Jenny lives with her husband in the country, raises goats, keeps a big garden and bees, has trained up her children, and hews to a simple way of life.

> You've been working all day choppin' them logs
> You don't wanna have to deal with no police dogs.
> You came to party but they're lookin' up your cheeks.
> They must all be sick 'cause they all take peeks.
> The old folks say the cops are doin' their jobs,
> But the old folks polish each other's knobs.
> If you think I'm just rappin', well here's the point,
> I wanna be free to smoke a joint.
>
> *Chorus:*
> We got drums, guitars, mikes and amps,
> We're white guys on food stamps.
> We ate too much garlic, got stomach cramps.
> We're white guys on stamps.
> > —Mother Chorizo, "White Guys
> > on Food Stamps"

A young woman came to Chorizo around 1910 as the bride of a local rancher and she lived more than seventy years. *(Jenny's husband, Chris, hands me an ancient photograph of his grandmother. Her face is hungry and lovely.*) She'd been a schoolteacher in Houston, and she was anxious to break out and see some Real West. His grandfather rode out to meet the stage and get first crack at a new white woman in the area. They moved in together (*"Chris,"* Jenny says, *"you don't want to say that to him, you don't want people to know that."*), and then they married and the children started coming.

This is too brief, this telling. I can hear Chris's flat voice, the laconic roll broken now and then by the crack of a whip in his words. He is a man of silence but in this silence there is a deep peace that comes from knowing. And what he knows is the ground. Chris knows this thing I call the ground in a way that cannot be said but must be earned. This knowing is not a precious thing, it does not entail secret rites. It rides in the air and anyone can suck it into their lungs. You only must *be* rather than *want*. I never hear Chris want anything. The ranch is gone, the big money squandered. He works as a carpenter now and then, cuts his own firewood, slaughters his own beef, likes a beer come evening. We sit on the porch at times, him sipping a beer, me guzzling wine, and we hardly speak. I have the high-powered scope and the shelf of bird guides, but he always spots a new species before I do. He discovers that gray hawks—a rare species with only fifty to one hundred pairs in the United States—have begun nesting by the wash. I do not notice until he points them out.

Chris has the same curiosity about the manuscripts left by his womenfolk that he has about the gray hawks. In the thirties his grandmother wrote a novel, mailed it as a blind submission to a New York publisher in December and held in her hands a bound copy of her book in April. She composed it in a nearby city, where she was living for a time when her children got some schooling. All this creativity came about within the fellowship of a local group called the Scribbler's Club.

The local terrain appears with faint disguise—Chorizo becomes Los Alamos, a big peak pops up as Squaw Tit, the bog a cool oasis. She had lots of experience to pack into a book, days of riding the hills chasing steers, cooking over a woodstove, toting water from a spring, struggling to keep her mind alive as well as her love. In her time Mexican bandits still crossed the line on brief errands of robbery and homicide. The landscape is threatening, yet somehow physically faint, only the green trees and grasses around the bog come alive, full of smells and textures and life. The ground itself seems to exist only when it kills—the drought that downs and slowly chokes the herd, the violent storm that floods the arroyos and almost drowns the heroine. And the Mexican Americans who periodically grace the pages are simple, slow-witted fools feeding stock, saddling horses, sleeping out on the ground, going for the blind drunk in the cantina. If they are women, they are shimmering and predatory sexual threats singing love songs in the evening while they strum guitars, bold eyes that do not turn shyly away, clothing that fails to disguise their generous curves.

I am taken with the fact that to an Anglo woman at the time of the First World War, the ground was unattractive and hostile, although the nights are always beautiful in the book, with the stars and the moon and the scent of night-blooming cactus and the merciful blackness hiding the land from view. *(Chris hands me another photograph that has come down from his grandmother's days, one that someone has identified in white ink as "Spanish girl." The woman in the image is on horseback, dressed as a* charra, *and on her fine-looking hip rides a holstered pistol. Her face has that traditional countenance of invitation mixed with scorn, a face seen at any fiesta in any town in Mexico as the night plows toward the hot and sensual hours.)*

The girls are easy to find, and the drive down the back roads is dark, down by the river, a good long way from Chorizo—ditch the fucking car, the party is over.

A clean thing.

The nights are very cold and I roll up tight in an old army blanket. I am up before first light, grab my rifle and drift into the darkness toward the hills. The oaks brush my face, the rocks make me stumble, the air remains cold. I can smell gun oil on my hands, and cartridges ride cool with their brass in my pocket. I follow an arroyo as it knifes into the hills, marches upward and gouges a path into the mountains. Mexico stretches out a mile or two or three to the south, Chorizo snores by the bog a ways to the north. I am thirteen, fourteen, fifteen, and I want to kill a deer. Eventually, over time, I get my killing done, but that is not what I remember. I left the gun behind in an attic on the East Coast in a move made years ago, an ancient Enfield with a cheap scope and scarred military stock, along with a sewing machine and a bootjack—life moves on without a plan.

The smell is dry and dusty at midday, moist and cool in the evening. The deer are moving like shadows, the coatimundis, a raccoonlike animal of the area, rolling along in a troop, all females as is their custom, the mine shafts scattered everywhere and gaping open in the tall grass. I have never regretted the hunting and the killing and yet I know it was a shameful thing, the crack of the rifle, the bullet tearing through the flesh of creatures I had barely glimpsed for the first time in my life and the last time in theirs. In season I killed everything legal I could find, and out of season I killed anything that did not have a season. This went on from when I was eight or nine until the fall of my twenty-sixth year. I lived in a state of bloodlust and saw dead animals as my entry into the country. Others may hunt to put food on the table, to control the spread of wild populations. Not me. I never ate the meat, I always gave it away. I do not like the taste of wild game. I was in the game only for the killing. When I touched an animal, it was dead, the hair still warm, the guts slick and sticky as my knife spilled them onto the ground. A fever raged in me and then one day it stopped and I have never sighted down on a living thing again.

As I said, this was all shameful, a binge of killing anything that walked the earth or flew through the air. And yet I feel no regrets. Some things just are and I had my time of bloodlust. Now I can almost pass muster as a Quaker but I have no words on the matter of hunting. Except that hunting does not work. To kill, you move into the mind of the thing you kill, to slay the deer you become the deer and know in your bones the moves and habits of the deer. You can do all this. I did. But you cannot get into the country this way.

When I first started coming to Chorizo, the big slab of ranch around the town site had not yet been subdivided into little ranchettes, the dope fiends had not yet migrated and the road was still dirt. I remember coming down a hill in the rain, the clay soil sealed, and the truck sliding like a sled hither and yon down the greased path. As always, the El Tonto was open. So I have seen change, and for a spell I gave up on the town as a lost thing. But I suspect this view is wrong.

(Virgil is talking in his low, patient way over his morning beer. He speaks of an incident back when the new people came. A cowboy out riding in his truck got into some kind of wrangle with a group of hippies. So he strode to his pickup, sighted down the barrel of his .30/.30, levered in a cartridge, and blew the head off the ringleader. The guy went to prison for that one. And that's all Virgil has to say about it.)

Wolves were slaughtered around Chorizo in the late forties. One lobo was seen feeding on a kill in 1956. Now there is not one howl in the night, not the faintest sign of a paw print in the dust. Gone. Dead. Destroyed. Mean, hard, cruel change. And yet Chorizo still perks along, the coyotes flooding the night with sound.

Out at the Arroyo things can get a little lean at times. The leader of the outfit, the man with the beard in the old photograph taken at Valentine Flat, has survival skills worthy of a Green Beret. Everyone is living in teepees or shacks and there is no work nor much desire for work. The leader always keeps a woman with a young child near at hand because he knows that the food stamp people are helpless in the face of a lactating female. The supplies are always a case of hot dogs for him, oatmeal and beans for the woman and children. They also know a friendly merchant who, out the back door, will take food stamps for beer.

One day two women living at the Arroyo look down at the ground and discover a five-dollar bill. They have been out there for two years feeding on oatmeal and beans and they dream of raisins. They grab the five-dollar bill and start walking the twelve dirt miles into Chorizo. A bitch in heat hanging around the camp begins to follow them, and nothing they say or do will make the little dog turn back. After walking for hours, the two women make it to the general store, and as they shop inside for their dream of raisins, a cloud of local hounds gathers outside around the bitch in heat. When the two women come out and start up the road again, they are tailed by every male dog in Chorizo. The boys drinking at the El Tonto see this sight and think, hell, these hippie broads have cast a spell on our canines, they must be witches. By now it is getting late in the day, and dusk settles like a blanket over the valley. The women walk the dirt track, a Woodstock of lovestruck beasts following in their wake, and when they look back at the tiny hamlet, they notice a pair of headlights, then another, and soon it seems like a caravan is issuing from this speck of a community. The women think, my God, we may be raped out here and they take off cross-country through the hills and canyons. They make it back to the Arroyo at daybreak and they have their raisins.

Some hunters saw them—there is no accounting for bad luck or good luck, just ask anybody, it can happen either way. And when they saw these two kids pitching a guy down the mine shaft, they skedaddled, called the cops, and gave an i.d. on the machine's plates. Late that night the authorities fished the poor bastard out of the shaft.

The head was kind of messy from landing on the rocks below. But after a day or two, they figured out who he was from dental records.

The sign on the wall is a bit tricky, with its claim that the El Tonto is the oldest bar in the oldest town site in the state. It is only after a case or two of beer that I notice it does not claim to be a very old bar at all but simply the one with the longest record in this particular spot. But then time is not a keen issue in Chorizo. Virgil is here on his stool at the tip of the saloon's horseshoe bar, and across the way is Danny de Dios, a big man with big arms, barrel chest, bald head, beard, and glasses through which he peers at the world with an almost childlike curiosity. The first time I met him, he was peddling his homemade hoes with handles made of metal. I asked, "Don't these things kind of vibrate if you hit a stone in the ground?" He looked at me with pity and said, "I can tell by your question that you are not a gardener."

Danny's truck is a bashed-up thing, and his papers are not in order. They say that once upon a time he was a race car driver, and then on behalf of his sport, he did some deals that landed him in prison for a stretch. He has had, the locals say, hundreds of tickets for offenses of both man and machine. He sees the county jail as a place of peace and quiet and decent food and free dental care. Also, Danny is a man of the faith, and when he is in jail, he organizes prayer meetings and gets to preaching. In fact, sometimes this is so appealing to him that he has been known to call the sheriff's department from the pay phone in Chorizo and request that they come and haul him off. Increasingly, they decline. Recently, stunned by their feeble law enforcement, he hitched a ride to the jail, presented himself and his many offenses, and demanded incarceration. He was rejected.

Once Virgil got to explaining about a guy who used to live by him in a trailer on the edge of Chorizo. This neighbor had a liking for the bottle and eventually it got to him, and the doctors said he had to quit his boozing or he would surely die and very soon at that. So when he got back, he told Virgil he would have to dry out. Virgil looked at him, and the man was jaundiced and yellow, yet Virgil advised, "You might as well finish it." The man thought about that and took Virgil's words to heart. He went back to drinking, and in a not very long period of time, he was dead.

I'm driving a couple of miles down dirt roads with Virgil gently guiding—left here, right there—until we turn into a yard, the acres dotted with mesquite. There in that big metal shed is where Plug works. He fixes the local cars and trucks and has been at it a good while. He is somewhere around sixty. And just now he is sitting in a lawn chair on the cool concrete with three mangy dogs sprawled around him. After that ranch by Chorizo got busted into little pieces, he came here from southern Mississippi and bought his acres, his shed, his trailer. His brother-in-law works with him, and his wife of forty years tends to the home. He hands out beers—there are four or five cases piled high, and on his tool chest sit three fifths of tequila. The flies buzz, it is just after noon, and he has just finished a brake job.

Plug tells of the time he worked on the river at Natchez and they had these gambling barges tied up midstream between the laws of Mississippi and Louisiana. The oil crew he was part of went out there one day and lost everything. He says they shuttled you out in little boats and you couldn't leave until they'd cleaned you out. Well, after everyone had surrendered their paychecks, and they had walked down the gangplank to the shuttle boat, at the last minute a guy in the crew leaped up and raced back onto the barge, grabbed a fire ax hanging on the ship's wall, and raced fore and aft cutting through the mooring lines. The barge drifted downstream, smashed into the supports of a big bridge spanning the Mississippi at Natchez and then peeled off on its journey toward the Gulf of Mexico.

The flies buzz, Plug's brother-in-law is over there washing tools with gasoline, a lit cigarette in his mouth.

> If you think I'm out here flauntin' my rage
> Then you never should have paid to see me on the stage.
> The man hasn't stopped me from singin' my song,
> Though if he figures out a way, then it won't take long.
> They arrested Lenny Bruce and tried 2 Live Crew,
> And if you don't watch out, they'll be tryin' you.
> They're comin' down hard but we're not goin' to take it.
> The gov't sucks, they can't make it or take it.
>
> *Chorus:*
> We got drums, guitars, mikes and amps,
> We're white guys on food stamps.
> We ate too much garlic, got stomach cramps.
> We're white guys on stamps.
> —Mother Chorizo, "White Guys
> on Food Stamps"

∗　∗　∗

The sky is overcast for the party but everyone comes anyway. There's fifty, a hundred people, maybe more, it is hard to count the turnout because everyone is spread out and sitting in circles on the ground drinking beers, eating food, and the kids are running here and there, and no one seems to be paying much attention to their frolics. There's a bunch from the Arroyo—the men sport beards like biblical prophets, the tattooed women float past with clear eyes. A sign made from a piece torn off a cardboard box explains that two kids who were born and reared in the Arroyo have been arrested for hauling a load and need money for their defense fund.

(Highballing a load through the night, one machine with a couple of hundred pounds of marijuana, the other running up ahead as a blocker, roaring with lights off down the dirt road out of the oak hills toward the green mucky tongue lapping against Chorizo, the moon absent, stars out, cool feel in the air, and then suddenly a Border Patrol truck bars the road and the kid driving blocker rams it and is caught. He is eighteen or nineteen and suddenly he faces ten, twenty, thirty years.)

Jake's at the party. He's the unofficial mayor of the Arroyo, and one of his kids is now facing serious time for that night ride. I've seen Jake in old news photos from the sixties, the hippie with the headband, long hair and smile of chemical peace. Now he is gray-headed, gray-bearded and near toothless but still smiling. *(Jenny turns a page in the white scrapbook and two little towheaded kids maybe three or four years old stare up innocently from the page. They are the two villains captured on that night road running a load. One gets seven years, the other nine.)* A band is playing on a platform sited on the brow of the hill. One guy sits on a carpet wailing at a sitar and the droning sound floats out over the valley and against the green as a cloudburst walks across the slopes maybe five hundred yards behind him, and then lightning streaks down from time to time and I look at the big amps out in this weather and await an electrocution.

After the sitar band finishes, Mother Chorizo is slated to play and I talk to them about their music. They all sport T-shirts that announce the Mother Chorizo World Tour and list the itinerary: *Chorizo, Chorizo, Chorizo, Chorizo, Jones's Farm.* That last venue is a prison camp in the East where one of the band members has just spent a year or so after being caught with a load. This party is his homecoming. I ask the more-or-less head of the band just how big Mother Chorizo is and he patiently explains that it is really six guys, but every time they get up to full playing strength they seem to lose someone, and so on any given day Mother Chorizo is actually five strong. And then he smiles.

> I think you'll all agree that you want to be free,
> But can't you see that it's your liberty.
> The gov't tells you what to do
> And can't you feel that it's drainin' you.
> To deal with them you got to beat or join,
> But they're the ones makin' all the coin.
> Bush and Saddam are the same dude.
> This year it's oil, next year it's food.
>
> *Chorus:*
> We got drums, guitars, mikes and amps,
> We're white guys on food stamps.
> We ate too much garlic, got stomach cramps.
> We're white guys on stamps.
> —Mother Chorizo, "White Guys
> on Food Stamps"

As I sit looking at the window whited out by light, Jenny tells me that after she left the Arroyo, she moved to another mining claim and spent about two years and had two children. But mainly she read, just read and read and read. She is a fiend for reading. For a spell, she went to the city to get some kind of degree and this has helped her get work from time to time when the money is a little thin. Her biography is kind of scattered, like most of ours, and the telling is a series of quick glimpses, the same way the word of God gets compressed into the feel of beads as the rosary slides through the fingers.

(Virgil has a dream. He will have a truck that runs good, and a big horse trailer, the kind that has stalls fore and aft and in between squats a small cell with a bunk, and he will sally forth from Chorizo and wander from town to town buying horses here, selling horses there, drinking beers in various saloons, living the life of a native trader, much like the first European wanderer of the West, Cabeza de Vaca. Virgil will see the country a bit, make a few dollars, maybe even get a driver's license. It is all clear in his head and vague in his speech but somehow one image always comes to mind when he speaks of his dream—he is coming over a rise, the polished horse trailer in tow, a hand-rolled cigarette in his mouth, it is morning and the air is fresh.)

We drift back to the time of the killing when one man shot another man down by the lake and the bullet ripped through the tissue of a body and then death came. The murderer was sent up for a pretty good stretch and then to everyone's surprise he got out, and he showed up back in Chorizo. The guys, Jenny explains, were down on him, real down and gave him a hard time. I do not ask what this entailed. But the man did not leave, he hung on.

(There are so many variations on this matter of Chorizo homicide that it is a theme worthy of Bach and his student Goldberg. They talk of a man who lived west of town and had a claim that others disputed and one night—these things always happen at night, under the cover of darkness, the absence of the moon, the hand before the face and yet the eyes are blind— he exploded in a blast of dynamite. Not a clue. Or there is the handless man. He bought a piece of a mine or sold a piece of a mine—it all gets jumbled—and built a fine two-story house and then one day they found him in his new house with his hands cut off and his life gone. No one ever looked very hard for his killers, I'm told, because no one cared what happened to such a man.)

The man who got out of prison after the killing did hang on awhile. And then he killed himself.

(I'm drinking with a rancher in the bar. He speaks of the day he came down the canyon and saw this VW bus parked over by the bank. It was still

there a day or two later, so he decided to check it out. The windows were shut except for a crack where a hose slipped through and there was tape around this opening. The hose connected to the exhaust pipe. The man lay dead inside. I connect the two stories. Then disconnect.)

Turns out I knew one of the boys who murdered and pitched the guy down the mine shaft. Met him once in the saloon when he bent my ear telling me this joke. A black guy, a Jew and a Catholic approach Saint Peter at the pearly gates. He seemed like a decent kid, a bit slow, not retarded, mind you, just not real quick. A baseball cap was cocked on his head and a faint mustache struggled above his lips and drooped around the edges of his mouth. All the while he was telling me the joke, he clutched a yellow Sony Walkman, the music plunging through earphones clamped on his head.

The robbing/carjacking/killing turned out not to be such a good scheme. The guy who went down the mine shaft was so low on change that he'd just had to bum gas money off his old lady, a woman he was separated from. The car was handy for only a few hours before it was ditched in the mud by the river. About the girls, I cannot say.

Nobody in Chorizo talked much about it after the initial bust. By the next day, the incident had vanished from conversation at the El Tonto like a melting ring of smoke in the calm of the saloon.

I asked Virgil what it all meant, and he drained his beer and allowed that more needed killing thereabouts.

Once Jenny was driving down Main Street when she saw a friend standing in front of the El Tonto, pissing into the road. He looked up, saw her, and his face brightened. He waved with his free hand while continuing to void his bladder and said, "Hi, Jenny." Now when she thinks why Chorizo is special to her, she sees that guy waving.

I have seen people cut down mesquite, whack them right off at the trunk. Often as not, green sprouts shoot up from the stump. Mesquite can be harder to kill than a snake.

He wears a double-breasted suit and has a peeled lip from some sore. The tiny fragment of skin on his split lip wins me instantly. A man surely must know who he is to ignore this red blotch on his lip at a Teamster breakfast in the big hotel in downtown Los Angeles. The face is his own, intelligent, the face of the trained lawyer that he is. The body belongs to his father, short, squat and reeking of coiled power. They say he visited the old man constantly when the feds had him caged in the Lewisburg prison, did a regular commute where he relayed news of the outside world like some messenger to an exiled Mafia don. That was before the disappearance, of course, before the moment of rapture in the parking lot of that restaurant on the edge of Detroit.

The handshake is firm, the smile friendly enough, but the eyes, they are special. Very clear, blue, keenly aware, and yet there is a flicker of some kind of vulnerability, a wavering candlelight that comes and goes. I expected the handshake to be firm, what the hell, he is the old man's boy. Back in the fifties, way back before Bobby took a shortcut through that hotel kitchen, before the old man went to meet with some wiseguys at the restaurant, back when the Senate hearings were flogging the old man daily for being the corrupt union boss and he was glowering at the camera with a contempt that must have been the envy of every movie star that ever lived, back when James Riddle Hoffa had boomed his union into the tissue of every fucking thing that moved through the pathways of the American economy and had tripled the wages of all the no-neck guys heaving freight on the docks or driving the big rigs into the bowels of the night. One time he looked over at Bobby Kennedy, the pious punk whose old man was a pussy hound and bootlegger and stock market thief, looked at him and said, hey, let's arm wrestle, and of course, he'd crushed him, what in the hell is the surprise in that when he popped out of bed every goddamn morning of the year and pumped out a hundred, two hundred push-ups before he poured into his suit and went out and tore some flesh from the American economy to toss to the hungry wolves of his membership. Boom, pinned that punk's arm, just like that.

They had so much in common, two arrogant, angry guys who would be devoured and become things that floated free of family or love or anything, two symbols force-fed to the cannibals we have become, virtual men who would live on and on fucking Marilyn Monroe or sleeping with the fishes or hosting dark meets with dark forces. And in the end no one would own them, no one would have any property rights, they'd simply be forms and names out there, just as Che rides around in my britches as a billfold.

The son tells me he liked the piece, that thing on Juárez and those Mexican truckers. Says they'd like my help in the future, too. That's why I'm here, of course, going to do a press conference in a few hours and stare into the blank camera eyes of network television. Solidarity forever, the union makes me strong. And best of all, I work for the union 'cause she's so good to me. Printed 1.7 million copies of the article, by God.

I'm crossing the bridge again, hello Che, glad you got your face back, and then I scurry through the clot of Mexican customs guys who pay no mind to me, they're far too busy poking around in the shopping bags of the Mexican poor hoping for something to steal or maybe a few pesos as a bribe. Then I'm past them and into Juárez and suddenly the streets are alive, it is thirties America with a bunch of working stiffs, you know, guys wearing caps who do this and that and barely keep food on the table, smells are everywhere and for the first few blocks cabbies smile and ask if I would be interested in fucking some fine young girls, and then this curtain of flesh that hangs everywhere on the border is behind me and there is nothing but Mexico.

That is when the days start to tumble into one taco after another and the black exhaust of buses rumbling by on the street. The trucker is saying he works twelve hours a day, hauls by the load between Juárez and El Paso, and makes maybe a hundred or hundred and fifty a week. And he don't know about unions but he'd sure like to drive into the heart of the United States where those highways are paved with gold. His face is very serious and the price of a man who has given up drink and become the responsible father and husband. He is building a little house, he explains. His truck, well, it is not so safe and about one time out of ten the gringo inspectors flunk him at the bridge and will not let him continue. He shrugs.

His brother is another matter. He is older, at forty-five, and has been behind the wheel for twenty-seven years. In his younger days, he would prepare for a big trip, and here the trips are big, with two or three days of nonstop driving and no naps, *señor*, he'd get ready for such hauls by stocking up with a couple of six packs, some pills, some marijuana, and of course, cocaine for the hard night hours. It was not all hard, you understand, there are whores at the gas stations, lots of them, and of course, any woman who wants a ride is very friendly, you see? Now the years have caught up with him, and when he packs, he has cut back on the beer and treats his body in a more kindly fashion.

We stand in the dirt street at night drinking from cans of Tecate and the man is wide-awake drunk with the beating he takes from his work, with his contempt for government or the government's unions. With the electric joy of the road. Accidents? Of course. Every trucker I speak with has been in a fatal accident and has fled the scene. The police, you must understand, are very corrupt. My man guzzling Tecate fled a crash with a bus where eleven died. Robbery? Of course. Last year at least forty thousand loads were hijacked. All truckers are robbed, *señor*.

He is not wearing a shirt, his big gut hangs out and he caresses his fat lovingly. He is the appetite that has vanished from sight in my land.

There is a third brother who is quiet. He has lived in Los Angeles for fifteen years and works as a nonunion machinist. He has a little house, a woman and two children. Two years ago he finished all the paperwork and became legal. He is hungry to vote, he says. Two days ago he got up and decided to come home, home to Juárez. He has a dirt lot here and someday, *señor*, he is going to build a nice little house that will have cement walls and a cement floor and one good tree for shade. But his trip back takes me into dreams. He had finished work and left and then darkness came and his eyes grew heavy, and he was on the lip of the big dunes that wash across the desert and so he pulled over and put his fourteen-year-old behind the wheel. A while later he came to and looked over and the boy was pushing down the interstate at ninety-five miles an hour, doing pretty good, no? He glows with pride and I can almost see his eyes flickering over in the night and catching the glow off the speedometer as his son rushed into the future.

The boy looks at me and says in flawless, unaccented English, "I am a Mexican."

I cannot remember exact times from those days, just drinking and talking and more and more brown faces and the rumble of big rigs nearby, day after day, the accidents, the robberies, the cocaine, yes, *señor*, you can get it wherever you gas up. One man advised me, "Now you must be careful about eating meat on these long hauls. If you eat meat, you will get sleepy. And then you must use more cocaine."

He also said, "I just want a safe rig, a decent wage. And to be treated with respect."

He had never really heard about this treaty that might let him cross the bridge and drive forever. He had never heard of the Teamsters, either.

I did not ask about Che or James Riddle Hoffa.

The story comes out with scare headlines about them coming north and careening down our safe roads with dangerous trucks. The Congress pauses, the administration balks, that particular section of the treaty is postponed and I am in Los Angeles shaking the hand of James Hoffa, who has what I think is a split cold sore on his lip. The headlines are all a kind of fake. The trucks were never coming north then and everyone knew it.

I am among cannibals. The union movement has been eating itself for decades. The day the old man vanished from the parking lot, the

Teamsters had 2.3 million members. As I shake hands in the hotel conference room, they have 1.4 million. The old man himself has never reappeared. He has been devoured and made into a movie with Jack Nicholson. Things change, you know. Paul finally stopped cruising alleys looking for cast-off items for his work, and by the time he swung that rope over the pipe, he had a whole separate warehouse just to store his loot.

Installation art is by its very nature fragile, an arrangement of items that decay even as gallery visitors take them in. Decay is part of the message. Paul, clever to the end, hung himself inside his own installation. After he was cut down and carted away and buried, his installation was videotaped and boxed and hauled to yet another warehouse, where it sleeps with the rest of his works like a nest of vampires waiting for the relief of the night. His mother visits him there, just as James Hoffa visited James Riddle Hoffa in prison, just as the Hollywood producer visits his father in prison. Just as I visit the union movement in Los Angeles.

Because this is the AFL-CIO convention and I am here for my press conference, gonna sound the alarm on fourteen-year-olds slicing through the American night, gonna sing solidarity forever. I can hear the stone hammer smack against the fresh bones. The cookfires have been lit.

3

He knows all their faces. Washington from memory, the other presidents he gets from books. He's been nailing them with pastels, tempera, pencil sketches and oils since the late seventies. Sometimes he identifies them—Jackson, Washington, Lincoln, and the like—sometimes not. But mostly he just lays their faces out there for the world to see. His own name, that he always signs: Ike Edward Morgan.

Austin is his town—he was born in the area in 1958. He started painting here in the seventies, though at that time it was fire hydrants for the city. Since 1977 or so he's lived in the state mental hospital, and he works all the time. He rises, gets his morning meds around seven-thirty or eight, drops by staff member Dave Edington's office to say hello and then is off to work. When the fever of creativity is really on him, he might knock out fifty portraits in three days. They're not always presidents, but the presidents are the ones that first catch a person's eye. He's collected, hangs in New York and Europe. He belongs to a band of self-taught people who make what critics call Outsider Art.

He is a handsome man with fine dark skin, a soft smile. He moves with grace and concentration as he bends over a blank piece of paper, canvas or cardboard and begins to draw. The movement of his hand is light but not tentative. Nor does he wonder about color. He knows, he just knows. The face relaxes, his head ducks down slightly, and then the words come out of a well of shyness. He lives a life as dedicated as that of a Benedictine monk.

His images are on display at a gallery in Waxahachie, just a ways south of Dallas. I stand there in a huge room with dozens of presidents staring down at me, the whole A-team from Washington through Clinton, and I mean staring because if there is one thing Ike Morgan never misses, it's the eyes, the burning eyes of human beings looking out with wonder or caution at the world. He lives in a world of color. I'm seeing Ronald Reagan with a red face and green jacket and yellow shirt, a mop of hair, and some serious teeth. And Washington is across the room watching me with a black face. I'm standing here with Bruce and Julie Wheeler, the gallery owners, Ike's friends and passionate fans of Outsider Art. We look at Ike Morgan's one-dollar bill. It's about five feet by three feet, orange, and Washington's face is a rage of emotion, so dotted with daubs of paint that he looks a lot like those stop signs deer hunters shoot hell out of during the season. I kind of wish they'd use this design for a new model of the single, not because it would he hell on counterfeiters, but because it captures the rage and energy that makes me love my country, the high-stepping, hog-calling, hip-hopping style that never rests, the blues bleeding out of Mississippi and the Sousa marches wailing so soulful out of West Point and the constant flood of elevator music rising ominously above the levees, the lack of ease, the need for black coffee, hard liquor, support bras and automatic weapons, the pedal to the metal, freeway love at three a.m. and hold the mayo. It is all there in Washington's face raked with buckshots of paint, screaming off an orange background that is hot to the touch, I tell you this is blowtorch money, currency from hell, and it is hanging on a wall in a huge old gallery in Waxahachie about a half block from the courthouse square where a monument to the big war—the one that ripped this nation open and spilled its gut out, you know, Mr. Lincoln's war—stands tall and proud in the shape of a Confederate soldier at attention forever in the stone ranks of the lost cause. I need a wad of this orange money so it can sing to me in the morning and scream out riffs from Charlie "Bird" Parker at midnight.

I amble over to a big table and rifle through piles of Ike Morgan's paintings—the state of Texas has had to rent space to store Ike's work since he is a working fool and the state's in charge of him—and there is

Lyndon Baines Johnson. I'd already seen Ike's black Richard Nixon with red lips, intense blue eyes and a green background that looks electric. But Lyndon is special, he's part of what I've come for. I got up one day and had a notion: that in the state mental hospital in Austin, Texas, one Ike Edward Morgan, diagnosed psychotic, was capturing the color and fury and song—well, some of the song, since Ike is an eight-track man loyal to the musical technology loose in the republic at the time he was locked up—and love and history of my times. And that a mile or two or three from Ike, in a huge white building, a monstrous thing that looks, honest to God, like some white whale beached deep in the heart of Texas, a presidential library that opened in the early seventies to the howls of two thousand protesters (and the only one of the eleven libraries that has no admission charge), Lyndon is rising from his long black night, shaking his big-eared head, brushing those damned yellow rose petals off his britches and coming awake after all those years of JFK worship, after the ringing in his ears from punks like me shouting, *Hey Hey LBJ/How many kids did you kill today?*, getting up after the American presidency toddled through the Clinton years after crawling through the Bush years and spending what out of kindness we might call the dreamtime of the Reagan years, getting up as things go back to Bush II, and Lyndon's arising, clearing his throat and letting loose with a yowl that cuts right through the cloud of Prozac hanging over the republic and like the scream of a mountain lion coming off the peak in the night, his voice cuts to the bone and gets the blood up and we snap alert and realize that after this cavalcade, one captured in paint by Ike Morgan—this cavalcade of Nixon, Ford, Carter, Reagan, Bush, Clinton—Lyndon Baines Johnson, the man who took us to Nam in a handbasket, the man described by George Reedy, his own presidential press secretary, thusly—: "Were there nothing to look at save LBJ's personal relationships with other people, it would be merciful to forget him altogether. But there is much more to look at. He may have been a son of a bitch, but he was a colossal son of a bitch"—well, this Johnson may have been the last president who knew how to run the government and the last one to really have any practical handle on this vision stuff.

(I know, you think I'm into the paint thinner again, but listen up: Head Start, civil rights, education, fine arts, the humanities, Medicare, clean water bills, wilderness, urban housing—had enough?—we're talking real laws, hundreds of them, not spin. That terrible big government we denounce, and then we hitch up our pants and belly up to the troughs Johnson built. The man was compulsive. When we put the boots to him, and he went back to his ranch on the Pedernales, he told the hands, "I want each of you to make a solemn pledge that you will not go to bed tonight until you are sure that every steer has everything he needs. We've got a chance of producing some of the finest beef in this country if we work at it, if we dedicate ourselves to the job. And if we treat those hens with loving care, we should be able to produce the finest eggs in the country. Really fresh. But it will mean working every minute of every day." Yessssssssssir.)

You see, we've gone from the War on Poverty to this cigar thing. For years we've been gathered at the river in this sedated encounter group encounter and every once in a while the Big Therapist zips out to take in the results of the latest focus meeting and then returns to lead us in a new mantra. As my father would have put it in his delicate way, our heads have turned to mush. LBJ, gore smeared on his face and those yellow rose petals fluttering down as he rises from his crypt, successfully kicked the U.S. government in the ass and got it moving. John Kennedy went down in Dallas November 22, 1963 with a legislative program largely frozen since he took office and by June 1964 LBJ had rammed a herd of bills through the U.S. Congress and all those big notions rode on a five percent growth in the GNP.

So I snapped alert one day with this waking nightmare—that Lyndon Baines Johnson was back—and looked and listened hard to four cassettes called *Taking Charge: The Johnson White House Tapes, 1963–64*, tapes full of history. I realized I hadn't heard such talk since I and millions just like me chased LBJ from public life and put him in that big damned tomb of a presidential library a few miles from where Ike Morgan captures American history in the state mental hospital. So once this notion came to me, there was nothing really I could do.

Except go.

And visit the great artists of the End Time.

Vietnam Rap Artists / Wednesday, May 27, 1964

LBJ: Got lots of trouble.

SENATOR RICHARD RUSSELL: Well, we all have those.

LBJ: . . . What do you think of this Vietnam thing? I'd like to hear you talk a little bit.

Hardly got JFK underground and the family moved in and hellza-poppin' all over the place. Because it always is that way around Lyndon Johnson. And it never seems to stop now because of that monster library. Most presidents leave office and disappear into the boredom served up by American historians, a native class of the enfeebled. But not our boy Lyndon. I'm up in the stacks, thirty-six million documents all snoring in red boxes on black shelves, the air holding steady at seventy degrees, the humidity an even fifty percent so that the Vietnam War can endure and rage on here for centuries. All the voices still talk here because Johnson, that tricky son of a bitch, taped everybody who talked to him. He just forgot to tell them about it. On one tape he wants to get out front on this Negro issue—especially him being a southern man and all that—so he's going to appoint Carl Rowan, a newspaper guy, to be the head of the U.S. Information Agency. But Johnson knows he's got to slide this appointment through John McClellan's Senate committee and he knows McClellan of Arkansas is a stone cold segregationist. So he picks up the phone on January 16 and says, "John, I've got a little problem. I don't want to embarrass you in any way, and the best way to avoid it is to talk to you beforehand so you know what the problem is. Mr. Ed Murrow is dying with cancer of the lung . . . I've got a good solid man that's went around the world with me . . . But he's a Negro."

McClellan says evenly, "I doubt that I'm going against this. You do what you want to."

But Johnson is having none of this, he's seen the man operate. "I know what your problems are," he offers. ". . . I don't want you to cut his guts out because he's Negro. And I've seen you operate with a knife and I have seen a few people get de-nutted."

McClellan, well, hell, he's a United States senator and this sounds like a bit much to him, so he says, "I wouldn't say that."

Johnson fires back, "I didn't want you to send . . . him home one day without his peter."

"I'm not going to do that."

"I've seen you operate, John."

Harry Middleton worked for Johnson as a speechwriter from 1966 to 1968 when everything was falling apart. Now he runs the LBJ presidential library. But what he has really done is make one key decision: open up the tapes. There are ten thousand conversations, one third opened already, the rest to be made public lickety-split. When Middleton first decided to open them, he did not know what was in them—they were "a pig in a poke," he says.

But he wanted them opened on "my watch."

Because . . . he had to know that if anything was going to bring Lyndon Johnson back from the historical trash can, it had to be his voice operating, doing deals, and bullying a nation to his will.

Live oak, thin soil and blue sky cover the land. Just under the skin of the hill country is the rock, and when ground is abused, the soil flows away and rock slaps the world in the face. Fine limestone gates frame entryways to big ranches hidden in the trees and then the fist of the hill country takes over and lonely trailers or houses on piles pop up and goats chew the ground. The sign outside the smokehouse says YOUNG ROASTING PIGS. Down the road, a taxidermist touts white tail mounts with limited lifetime warranties. Just outside Johnson City, the dead raccoon lies by the road. And then LBJ's hometown is here, a hamlet of 932 souls selling pop and lunch to the straggling visitors to the dead god. The earth cries out for strong drink and gets Baptist churches. This is the place where white people learned to sink into the blues.

The sign in front of the LBJ National Park center gives a brief outline of the world he long ago found in these green soft hills of cactus, trees and thin soil: "No plumbing. No electricity. No place to buy a loaf of bread or a pound of meat." Just down the street is Johnson's boyhood home, a white clapboard thing with a swing on the porch and not much else—it's bigger inside than it looks, a park guard advises.

Fifteen miles or so west LBJ sleeps in his family's burying ground and the hills roll on and come spring and some rain the wildflowers bloom, and his ranch, the one he bought in the fifties with the loot that befalls a Senate majority leader, looks like the way life ought to be. You come from this kind of place, and you stay hungry. In the fifties, when LBJ was Senate majority leader, he prided himself on getting one of the early car phones. One day it rang while Johnson was out rolling around and it was Everett Dirksen, the Senate minority leader of the Republicans, calling up to tell Lyndon he'd just got a car phone. Johnson cut him off with an excuse me, he had to go since his other car phone was ringing. Johnson could never get enough love, enough applause, enough of anything and his hunger made millions dislike him. When his body lay in state in the white whale of a library in Austin he'd built to guard his reputation, Harry Middleton assigned a guy to count how many people went by the coffin. When asked why in the hell this mattered, he said, "Because I know that somewhere, sometime Johnson's going to ask me."

I stand there in the bright sun and let the clean air wash my soul and wonder when the war will end. Johnson City is the kind of crossroads where a lazy dog can cross the highway without a care. And Johnson lived and died a dumb shitkicker in the eyes of a lot of people. But then country boys for generations have been skinning out with glee people who say things that way. When Charles de Gaulle came to bury John Kennedy in November 1963, he said, now this man Kennedy is the country's mask. But this man Johnson, he's the country's real face.

Vietnam Rap Artists / Wednesday, May 27, 1964
RUSSELL: And I don't know how we're ever going to get out of it without fighting a major war with the Chinese and all of them

down there in those rice paddies and jungles . . . I just don't know what to do.

LBJ : That's the way I've been feeling for six months.

His handshake is soft and so, too, is his voice. He is not keen on eye contact but then he recognizes the power of eyes. It is about eighty today but Ike Morgan likes the feel of a lot of loose clothing, and so he wears two pairs of pants, a bulky sweater and a parka. It took the state of Texas hardly more than a month to decide he was not competent to stand trial back in the spring of 1977, and then after two years he got out of the state hospital for the criminally insane and wound up here at Austin State Hospital in the heart of the city with its generous smear of live oak trees. For a time he had spells when he still felt the anger but then the drawing took hold. One of the hospital workers, Jim Pirtle, noticed his work and showed it to a Houston art dealer and Ike Morgan was on his way from being state case number 086146 to being an artist. Ike still sometimes draws Jim Pirtle, even though Jim himself moved on years ago.

Since 1991 he's been on Clozaril, one of the newer drugs for psychotics. Dave Edington, for years his state-assigned social worker, thinks it has stilled Ike's anger and given him the feel for more speech. Now the state wants to put Ike out in a kind of halfway house, but he is not anxious to move. He likes the routine of the hospital, he tells me, and likes the room and the time for work. "I don't got nothing against being here," he rolls on with that soft voice. "I forget what the days are. I work and accomplish things. People wonder why I want to stay at a dump like this, but it evens out.

"I started doing artwork," Ike explains, "about the same time I learned to tell time—when I went to school."

So he stays in and draws turtles, birds, bears, rock stars, apes and presidents. Especially, presidents. He shows twenty-seven poster-sized George Washingtons he recently whipped out (four or five hours apiece, he figures). I particularly like the Washington with yellow hair, a purple-brown face, blue suit and yellow ruffled shirt. Ike goes with whatever colors he finds in his box and has no prejudice in these matters—"I like orange, red, blue, and green and lots of other colors."

I tell Ike Morgan I am very fond of the purple and brown Washington and he says, "That is a very nice thing to say."

Across the lawn, just past Guadalupe Street, the straight and woolly world of Austin begins. I point to it and ask Ike, who comes and goes and now rides the bus into town for classes three days a week, what he thinks of all that out there. He looks where I point and says, "I've been out there. I've got friends out there. And sometimes you've got to draw the line."

We talk about hot peppers, decent French cookware and why a career officer, a good Catholic boy from San Antonio, the father of six children, Major Ted Gittinger, 105th Battalion, First Cavalry, walked out on the United States Army. Now he is part of the staff of the LBJ presidential library; in fact a letter he wrote in 1956 to Senator Johnson seeking an appointment to West Point (didn't get it) is part of the collection. But by 1970, after a tour in Vietnam as an artillery officer, he was an ROTC teacher at Sam Houston State in east Texas and his graduates were coming home with tales of the collapse of military discipline in Vietnam. He'd already had a taste of that during his tour in Nam with an army starting to be devoured by cheap dope and a racial Grand Canyon where there was no color line when the bullets flew at the front and hell to pay between whites and blacks when on leave at the rear.

"I resigned," he says flatly. "I was sick at heart at what I had seen in the army and the country. I was afraid my country was coming apart at the seams."

So he left to become a college teacher and wound up at the library doing oral history. In a real sense, he's spent a quarter century or so still in Saigon.

Looking into this thing called Lyndon Johnson, Gittinger says, "I lost friends. He lost my war. But I'm not bitter. I just didn't have the heart to go on and do any job in the military. We weren't going to win and I didn't want to be the last guy killed in Vietnam."

So he goes over and over this war, especially that tape with those Vietnam Rap Artists, Ice LBJ and Senator Richard Snoop Doggy

Russell and he's left with, well, they meant well, and yet everything got fucked up.

Downstairs a guard tells me that one thing he learned on this job was to never ask Vietnam veterans about Johnson.

I asked why.

"Because a lot of them don't like him."

Gittinger doesn't feel that way, but still, he's not all that settled on the war yet. He thinks maybe forty years from now scholars will get a better bead on it, that things will kind of calm down once guys like him and me die. Because for a whole bunch of us, whether vets or goddamn antiwar protesters, it just doesn't seem to end. He eyes me and says, "You know how you can tell a bullet's close? You hear this shot and then this whump, that's from air filling the hole as it goes by you."

So we talk inside Johnson's tomb about this monster named LBJ. Part of what neither of us ever saw coming was that this paranoid, overbearing, egotistical braggart would overwhelm our defenses by abandoning his own.

LBJ is the dead man talking.

Later, Gittinger walks me away from this cacophony of voices into the outside pavilion and points to the blooming mountain laurels.

"Smell it," he encourages me.

I do.

"What's it like?"

I say it reminds me of a whiff off a fine cheap whore.

He smiles and offers, "Grape Kool-Aid."

I hear Jimi Hendrix's "Purple Haze" ringing in my head and yes we are trying to be one nation.

Sometimes, late at night, or at least I want it to be late at night, Ike Morgan dips into the money he earns from selling his artwork and orders up a pizza or some burgers. Or best of all, some chicken wings. And they deliver them to the Texas state mental hospital in Austin and it all tastes so good. Afterward he'll have a Camel, or if he's trying to save up for his art supplies, he'll roll a little Bugler and have a smoke and relax. Because it's damned hard to have more than two centuries of presidents of the United States pouring through your hands. Not to mention various singers and movie stars and other children of the Lord.

He is the official historian of the United States, the man who has left the busy streets since 1977, the eight-track man, the fellow who cannot hardly remember anything before 1977, or at least one day in April of 1977. And yet he does portraits of all those presidents of the United States and some of them are so damn obscure probably not even their wives can recollect them or bring to mind their scent or faces. That's the hell of it for the LBJs. You get to be king of the world and then you die and then it's 1999, the very damn lip of the millennium, and I'm in a fish joint in Austin just a bare mile or two or three from that huge LBJ presidential library and I ask the twenty-three-year-old bartender what she thinks of LBJ and she says, "I don't really know much about him, but I suspect he had some doing in the killing of Kennedy."

But Ike Morgan does. I've seen his portrait of LBJ and the lips are very red, red like lipstick, and the eyes very blue. And the face is black.

I tell the bartender I spent the afternoon out at LBJ's ranch and she asks, where is that?

I tell her about an hour west of my drink and she smiles real nice.

Vietnam Rap Artists / Wednesday, May 27, 1964

LBJ: How important is it to us?

RUSSELL: It isn't important a damn bit, with all these new missile systems.

LBJ: Well, I guess it's important to us—

RUSSELL: From a psychological standpoint.

I'm listening to these goddamn tapes, the ones that have convinced me he is rising and coming back and it is a Thursday, June 11, 1964, and LBJ is talking on the phone to Senator Richard Russell of Georgia, one of those guys that is always around and not talking a lot but actually running things, a man who loved the Constitution and fought the civil rights movement, and LBJ is whining about Vietnam, and this at a time when Kennedy is hardly cold in the ground and the rest of us can't find the place on the map, and LBJ wails, "I'm confronted. I don't believe the American people ever want me to run [end support of Vietnam]. If I lose it, I think they'll say *I've* lost it. I've pulled out. At the same time, I don't want to commit us to a war. And I'm in a hell of a shape."

Senator Russell offers, "We're just like a damn cow over a fence out there in Vietnam."

Ah, but Lyndon says, ". . . I've got a study being made by experts . . . whether Malaysia will necessarily go and India'll go and how much it'll hurt our prestige if we just got out . . ."

All this talk going on without me, going on before I knew where such countries were. And Ike not even ten and hadn't entered into his genius with color and his toils in history.

We love periods, order, sequence. I'm standing in Waxahachie with Bruce and Julie Wheeler going through piles of Ike Morgan's artwork that they have at their gallery. Waxahachie is an Assembly of God town—Jerry Lee Lewis once studied theology here before being seized by great balls of fire—and Bruce's grandparents settled here after missionary work in India. When they died, he and Julie came here to find space for their passions. They fit in fine—Bruce signed up with the Masons and Odd Fellows and created this sanctuary for Outsider Art. Ike, as it happens, began with a Dumpster Period. This covered the years when he'd scrounge behind the hospital in the trash for something to draw on—pieces of cardboard boxes, covers torn from tablets, sheets of paper. It's probably from this period that the four-part Lincoln came—the president on four sheets of eight-and-a-half-by-eleven paper taped together. A lot of the paintings have leaves stuck to them, a reality for the Outsider Artist. Sometimes Ike would tape things together, sometimes after working he'd fold them to save storage space—storage has always been a problem for a man with his work ethic. Also, there is a period when he drew noses in a particular way, and then these series would come, sometimes explained by a book that came his way, and sometimes not explained at all. Right now, for example, Ike is heavily into homage to Dr. Seuss. And Sarah Bernhardt. Unlike many artists, Ike draws without a concern for the market, and unlike just about any dealer, Bruce and Julie never suggest he make something the market wants.

Ike's life has apparent order in two places: inside their gallery with its carefully filed, loved and preserved art works, and inside that big blue book that Dave Edington sometimes consults, the one stuffed with twenty-odd years of reports and notes on the case of Ike Edward Morgan.

All of my life I've had trouble with this order, knowing it was a way to make sense out of things and yet sensing it was a way to squeeze the life out of things. Upstairs at the gallery, Bruce and Julie stash their collection of memory jugs, old gallon containers coated with papier-mâché embedded with human lives. Someone dies, you open that dresser drawer and scoop out the loose change, old buttons, favorite sea shells, little trinkets, a comb still entangled with their hair, pocket knife, all of it, and encrust that papier-mâché jug with the stuff and you have the memory of the person, one you can see and touch and know. If they could just get a memory jug that played music too, we'd have it, and I'd feel less anxious about the fact that the past is so walled off— not by time or death but by our terrifying fear of life itself.

For decades Ike and Lyndon have been trapped in their madness and we've said we couldn't make head nor tail of them. Ike stayed stashed in the state hospital, Lyndon buried in the tomb of the library he threw up in Austin. One huge inside glass wall of Johnson's archive opens up the stacks of documents like a window into a brain and I've stood there staring in at millions of pieces of paper, all those voices, and I leaned forward and could almost hear them shouting and screaming in their desperate effort to make themselves heard through the thick glass that keeps them in their place.

Douglass Cater, one of Johnson's presidential assistants, remembers how he had these newswire machines in his office—the kind with a roll of paper, keys flying like hell, and the whole thing inside a soundproof cabinet—and LBJ would get up during meetings and go over and stare through the glass and see what was going on in the world and then, if it really caught his eye, he'd open up the cabinet and "disappear down into the bowels of the thing to read it as it was actually being typed out of the spindle. He wanted to get even farther ahead of the news before it could surface." I tell you, you can hear voices in this library. Sometimes I've thought the place needs a Dumpster artist, an Outsider Artist. And then with the issue of the tapes from the first year of LBJ's reign, the voices came out of the Dumpster and began to twist and shout, and there he is, hair down to his shoulders, face painted with peace symbols and lipsticked across his forehead the word LOVE, and he's crooning in that cool cat way of his:

> When the truth is found to be lies
> And all the joy within you dies

None of those presidents Ike Morgan is making us face, not a one, ever got there by being shy and retiring. But still there is something about Johnson's ego that puts your basic power-junkie, self-centered-maniac president in the shade. On January 8, 1964, LBJ had given his first State of the Union message and that afternoon he called a big muckety-muck national columnist to get his reaction. His operators found the man traveling in North Dakota.

Johnson discovered the columnist had not even heard the speech, so he told him, "I got eighty-one applauses, in twenty-nine hundred words. It was a twenty-five-minute speech, and it took forty-one because of the applauses . . ."

And the horse you rode in on, too.

Vietnam Rap Artists / Wednesday, May 27, 1964
LBJ: I'm afraid that's right. I don't think the people of the country know much about Vietnam, and I think they care a hell of a lot less.

RUSSELL: Yeah, I know, but you got to send a whole lot of our boys out there—

LBJ: Yeah, that's exactly right. That's what I'm talking about. You get a few. We had thirty-five killed—and we got enough hell over thirty-five—this year.

RUSSELL: More than that . . . in Atlanta, Georgia, have been killed in traffic accidents.

LBJ: . . . That's right, and eighty-three went down in one crash of a 707 in one day, but that doesn't make any difference . . .

He knows things a lot of us don't. On Sunday, April 10, 1977, Ike Morgan, age eighteen, was told to do some cleaning by his grandmother, Margarite, sixty-one. It was Sunday night and she went into the bathroom wearing her nightgown to take a bath. The baby-sitter was over from next door to look after Ike's younger brothers and sisters. They heard some shouting. He slipped the nine-inch butcher knife into his grandmother's heart and stomach.

"I don't know," he almost whispers. "That's the hardest thing I could think of. I should have been in school instead of hanging out around the streets. I don't know how to explain that. I can't put all the blame on my grandmother. It was not a very right thing or good thing to do. I've tried to change what I can change. You can't be too hard on yourself. My grandmother loved me but she didn't like some things. When she was bringing me up, she was nice and sweet. Some of the nicest days I ever had."

And then he goes off and then he comes back. The murder of his grandmother is hard ground for Ike Morgan to visit and his memories over the years have been blurry, as if that day were hidden in the mists.

"I came up in those neighborhoods," he continues on. "I couldn't just back off, you know." And then he is back at the hospital, where he found safety. "These people," he explains, "gave me more reason to be strong, and that's all a guy needs sometimes."

He is drawing Dr. Seuss characters on the poster. Two big birds, a couple of trees, a bear, a rabbit, a worm, some turtles. In the left-hand corner is a bush with huge berries—"Birds love to eat berries," Ike explains. He holds the pen like a brush between his thumb and fore-finger and sketches out this peaceable kingdom. After decades he is the silent member of our community who now has the gift of speech, the one we ignored and then buried alive in our institutions and now he has color and form and gives us our presidents.

The neighbors later told the reporter that Ike had been walking up and down the block acting kind of strange for days. When they got to his grandmother in the bathroom, blood was running out from under the door.

The war is still raging damn near everywhere if you bother to look. Out of uniform, I'll grant you that, but still there guzzling in the whiskey bars, standing in line at the grocery check-out. Common as roadkill. I found him at a truck stop during a Teamsters strike and hopped in because he was heading west, and going east was against the grain. There had been shootings, so he rode with a .44 Magnum on his lap as he guided his Peterbilt toward L.A. It was the early 1980s and Ike was deep into his art by then, going out back of the hospital to scavenge paper and cardboard from the Dumpster. Lyndon was deep in his grave and pretty much forgotten except for biographers who periodically dug him up and flogged him with whips made in Saigon. Once in a while Republicans had at him and made the phrases *Great Society* and *War On Poverty* sound like something you did back of the barn with a chicken.

My truck driver was quiet at first and then we fell into those black hours after midnight—carefully studying each freeway overpass for snipers—and he returned to Saigon. He'd gone during the white heat of the war, 1967, and the next thing he knew he was an Ohio farmboy looking out the back door of a chopper as a gunner. A fellow in black pajamas was under him looking up, the pilot was barking into his ears through headphones, and he hesitated on the trigger and then cut the guy in black pajamas in half. After that, he told me, it got kind of auto-matic and then a year later the U.S. military dropped him back in Ohio as if it had never happened. He remembered walking around the yard at his folks' farm with his mother and he was wearing a suit and all of a sudden there was a loud sound, and he flung himself down in the mud.

He never forgot the look in his mother's eyes when he got back up all wet and covered with mud.

He decided to go to college and enrolled in the National Guard to help pay for it. A few weeks later he was at Kent State and heard gunshots again. He decided to hell with college if it was going to be like that and became a trucker. He showed me a photo album of favorite cargoes, and he told me he kept an apartment in Oklahoma City. He hardly ever got to visit the place but he made damn sure he had a home and damn sure it was in the heart of the country.

And then there was the carpenter who finished off my office and introduced himself as a baby killer. He'd come up from Chihuahua as a field hand, enlisted to get a footing in the US of A, and wound up with some weird secret team in Cambodia cutting throats in the midnight hour. When he got back to the world and walked off the plane in Oakland, some woman spat at him and he broke her arm. Told me it was a reflex. He said his wife would find him sometimes slumped in the corner of the bedroom weeping. He loved baseball.

And there were people talking guns and explosives over the beer and wine in the sixties. Finally the heroin hit and then the coke, and the whole thing vanished, slipped away except for the wounds. And I'm left standing in Austin with a presidential library and a presidential artist.

Vietnam Rap Artists / Wednesday, May 27, 1964

RUSSELL: It's a tragic situation. It's just one of those places where you can't win. Anything that you do is wrong . . . I have thought about it. I have worried about it. I have prayed about it.

LBJ: I don't believe we can do anything—

RUSSELL: It frightens me 'cause it's my country involved over there, and if we get into there on any considerable scale, there's no doubt in my mind but that the Chinese will be in there, and we'd be fighting a danged conventional war . . .

LBJ: You don't have any doubt but what if we go in there an get 'em up against a wall, the Chinese Communists are gonna come in?

RUSSELL: No sir, no doubt about it.

There is something about George Washington that touches Ike Morgan. "I like the first one more than the other ones—the vision of him. He's too nice looking, the scenery of him." And so he does him over and over and sees him with a red face, a purple-brown face, an orange face and a black face. We can't see Washington at all, he's not a man or a face or a form. He's a blur as we hand over the money, a cartoon on our currencies.

Ike has created his own iron constitution out of his own hard lessons from life. George Washington is scenery, a vision. Hard work and dedication matter. "If you don't try," Ike offers, "you'll never know what can happen anyway. Keep hanging in there. If there wasn't for people helping out, I don't know if I'd be here today. You just gotta be yourself. I can't do what everybody says to do—you gotta figure out what is right to do and make a decision and stick to it."

And then he turns back to his drawing and adds eyes to the rabbit.

"Go to a restaurant, get yourself a bite to eat. Get away. Do something special, you know. Early in the morning you can see wildlife pass through. Good to go bicycling. When the sunlight comes out, that is just enough. It keeps the body warm."

He sketches a crescent moon in the upper-left-hand corner.

"Sometimes people need moonlight."

Everything about the war is simpler now, and it seems like a detail that it devoured LBJ's presidency, his domestic program, his reputation, denied him a second term and chased his ass back to Texas where he built his library, grew out his hair and went to his grave looking like some deranged street person. Now the ground is shuddering as he comes back up into a world that thinks a virtual war like Operation Desert Storm is the real thing.

It is evening on April 30, 1964, and Johnson is on the horn with Robert McNamara, his brainy secretary of defense, and he's pissed about reports from this Vietnam.

"Let's get some more of something, my friend," he offers, "because I'm going to have a heart attack if you don't get me something . . . We need somebody over there that can get us some better plans than we've got, because what we've got is what we've had since '54. We're not getting it done. We're losing."

McNamara almost intones his brief reply: "I know it."

Great, the fucking secretary of defense knows he is losing a war in a place only he and a handful of bureaucrats know exists.

". . . Tell those damn generals over there," Johnson orders, "to find one for you, or you are going to go out there yourself."

And McNamara picks right up on the boss's mood and says, "That's one reason why I want to go back. A kick in the tail a little bit will help."

That's the spirit, that's the can-do shit that LBJ wants to hear. But he makes sure McNamara understands when he says, "What I want is somebody that can lay up some plans to trap those guys and whup hell out of them and kill some of them."

Nail that damn coonskin to the wall, you hear?

And while he's straightening out this Vietnam mess, the damn generals bogged down like some old truck in the mud, he's fiddling with the biggest civil rights act in the history of these United States and is deep into the longest goddamn filibuster in the history of the U.S. Senate, a southern chokehold on the bill that will rattle on eighty-three days before Lyndon Baines Johnson, that Southern Man, stops it dead in its tracks and signs the bill into law.

Besides that he's got this War On Poverty he wants to win and he's fired up to kick Barry Goldwater's ass in the fall election, and he's just gotten the country out of a winter of mourning for JFK and he's trying to figure out a way to ship Bobby Kennedy to some outer darkness, and if all that ain't enough, he needs some britches.

So on August 9, 1964, at about 1:16 p.m. he gets Joseph Hagger, Jr., of the Hagger Company on the phone and says, "You-all made me some real light slacks . . . Now, I need about six pairs for summer wear."

And by god, Mr. Hagger says, "Yes, sir."

But that's not enough, and LBJ rolls on, a man's got needs, and yes, even the president of the United States must sometimes stand naked, but also he must wear britches that don't irritate him and so listen up. "The crotch, down where your nuts hang, is always a little too tight . . . Give me an inch that I can let out there because they cut me. They're just like riding a wire fence."

And now you want to task me with this intern and a cigar story? Enough of that, I tell you he is rising, those yellow rose of Texas petals are a-fluttering off, and he's coming back, the president who said of JFK's womanizing, hell, that he had more by accident than Kennedy ever got on purpose, the man who laid them on his desk in the Oval Office and what's the chickenshit you're saying about a cigar? The man who took us to Saigon and Mississippi and Bed-Stuy and the humanities and the fine arts, the guy who got into all our business and finally ended this stuff about only white people voting, I tell you he's coming back, ready or not.

It's around 8:35 on Tuesday, August 4, 1964, and this monster calls up his wife Lady Bird and he says, "Darling?"

And she says, "Yes, beloved."

And he says, "Did you want me?"

And she says, "I just wanted to see you whenever you're all alone, merely to tell you I loved you. That's all."

And Lyndon Baines Johnson says, "I'll be over there."

Vietnam Rap Artists / Wednesday, May 27, 1964

LBJ: I've got a little old sergeant that works for me over at the house, and he's got six children, and I just put him up as the United States Army, Air Force, and Navy everytime I think about making this decision and think about sending that father of those six kids in there. And what in the hell are we going to get out of his doing it? And it just makes the chills run up my back.

RUSSELL: It does me. I just can't see it.

Ike is standing against a white wall wearing a suit he just got for his art show. The coat looks to be too small for the shirt, he's got his cuffs shot way out. The pants look to be too long and bunch up over his shoes.

His shirt is not tucked in but then Ike Morgan likes that loose feel. He wears a nice bold tie around his neck and a faint smile on his face. He is standing between two huge presidents, portraits that seem to be about six feet high. Both of these presidents are brown, a happenstance in Ike's world where color comes from a box and from his instinct and is never a burden on a man. The president on the left looks to be Grant, the man from the slaughter of the Civil War. Of course, the other brown-faced president is George Washington, the first, the man with the vision and good scenery.

I once was doing a walking beat with a skid row cop and as we entered a dive, a guy raced for the bathroom to dump his kit—syringe and what-all—and the cop, a huge guy, grabbed him by the throat and held him off the ground against a wall. The guy pleaded, "I'm clean, I'm clean." The cop said evenly and cold as ice, "You can't be clean here."

You can't be clean around Johnson. He got too much done.

He's talking, man's always talking, and it's June 23, 1964, second day into summer and it's about four in the afternoon and he's on the line to Senator James Eastland, the god of Sunflower County, Mississippi, and they're talking about a woman named Fannie Lou Hamer of Ruleville in Eastland's home county and my ears get big because I knew Fannie Lou Hamer. She was a piece of work, a woman I've thought about most of my life because when I choke I think, well, hell, she did not choke, and sometimes when I think that, I fire up enough nerve to push on. She and her husband lived in a shack. When I sat there I could look at a wall and see daylight coming through the cracks. She was the granddaughter of a slave and just about drove Lyndon Johnson and James Eastland crazy. For a while she worked for SNCC (the Student Non-Violent Coordinating Committee) organizing and helping black people to register to vote, a project Senator Eastland had never fit into his schedule. One day in June 1963, just about a year before Johnson and Eastland chatted on the phone, she walked into a whites-only restaurant in Columbus, Mississippi, and got jailed and the hell beat out of her. Folks would fire into her shack from time to time. But she never gave in and by June 1964 had welded together something called the Mississippi Freedom Democratic Party and was fixing to show up at Lyndon Johnson's convention in Atlantic City and demand the seats of the traditional lily-white delegation, the one Senator Eastland was so fond of. Also, three civil rights workers had vanished in Mississippi two days earlier on a sabbath.

So Johnson says, "Jim, we got three kids missing down there. What can I do about it?"

"I don't know," Eastland grumbled. "I don't believe there's three missing. I believe it's a publicity stunt."

And then he rolls on and my ears get big: "I happen to know that some of these bombings where nobody gets hurt are publicity stunts. This Negro woman in Ruleville [Fannie Lou Hamer] that's been to Washington and testified that she was shot at nineteen times is lying. Of course, anybody that gets shot at nineteen times is going to get hit."

But Johnson presses on, he's friendly but he senses he's got a problem with these missing civil rights workers, although he doesn't know they've already been buried in a dam. He's in fine form, asking Eastland about the weather and commiserating with him about the lack of rain, and then Eastland offers the insight, "It'll take a crowd to make three men disappear."

And LBJ says, "That depends on the kind of men, Jim . . . It might take a big crowd to take three like you! I imagine it wouldn't take many to capture me."

And they go on like that bantering back and forth, the boys you know, and I remember being there four years later, sitting in Fannie Lou Hamer's shack, being there after the dead boys were dug up and the civil rights bill was made law, after the big changes, and still it was lively, hell, Martin Luther King had just been murdered up the road in Memphis. But what I notice is that that call from Eastland ends and immediately Johnson is on the phone with J. Edgar Hoover, and Hoover says they found the car and it's burning so hot they can't peek in to see if there are bodies. And then bam, Eastland is back on the line and he says he talked with the governor of Mississippi, and the governor "expects them to turn up with bruises and claiming that some-body's whipped 'em. He doesn't believe a word of it."

Johnson drops the big one by saying, "Now here's the problem, Jim. Hoover just called me."

Eastland bleats, "Well, I don't know nothing about that."

I really hated Johnson back then and I'm not sure I've mellowed much as I listen in and hear Mrs. Hamer come up and remember those Mississippi days and nights. But I have to notice as I listen to the tapes that the filibuster is grinding out and the man is always on the god-damn phone and the government, that rude beast, is awakening.

And you can't be here and stay clean.

This ain't no disco, this is work and work is not necessarily what you have been told. It must be done, these things in the head must be born, be given color and form. Life has its drives. "Life is not building up too much stress," Ike advises. "Sometimes I wake up, and I decide I'm gonna do something nice for someone. They say you don't want to do work, well, then why eat. All you do is art, they say. And it is good to eat." He pauses—he's still working on his Dr. Seuss drawing—then he continues. "You know how some days are, all day out in the yard play-ing with water. Sometimes in life you just can't draw. And sometimes you can stay behind it."

When the weather is good, he likes to work outside, get away from the gray-feeling building with light green ceramic block walls, dull linoleum floors and the weight of government, the dim halls and the doors that open freely to get inside but are locked when you try to go outside, to go to the pastoral grounds with big trees and grass impris-oned by the whirr of traffic on each side.

So Ike Morgan takes his stuff out to the concrete picnic table, the one all splattered with paint from his work, and he'll be at it for hours. Sometimes Dave Edington will see him out there in the wind with four different paintings held down by garbage can lids, and Ike'll be bent over working on a fifth.

* * *

Like that other great American president, Elvis Presley, LBJ went to flesh in the end. After he left office and moseyed back to the ranch, he kind of seemed to give up on things. His hair grew out and the people around him didn't quite know what to make of him and his new do. A man with a bad ticker, he started smoking a couple of packs a day, boozing into the wee hours on that Cutty Sark and hitting the Night Hawk on South Congress in Austin and gobbling up burgers. One day in January 1973 he showed up at his presidential library to talk to an aide, Mildred Stegall. Johnson looked like hell, skin pink and gray, and he had the air of a dying man. He told her how to take care of the many tapes he made as president, of phone calls and meetings—they should be sealed for fifty years and some of them should never be opened. A week or so later he died at the ranch. A week after that Stegall sealed the material, as instructed, until 2023. This decision was later overruled for various reasons including fear of public lawsuits to open up the files. And because it was pretty clear Johnson really did want everyone to finally listen in on him. When Harry Middleton once tried to censor the release of some stuff in the papers, Johnson roared, "Good men have been trying to save my reputation for forty years and not a damn one succeeded."

But what strikes me is Johnson's attitude that January day as he gave his weary orders with his long white hair curling down to his shoulders. He had the air of a dead man walking, a man who didn't care. Where the Kennedy library, close by Harvard, gives us history as a veneer and never mind the garter belts, Johnson's joint is serving up history with the bark on. Just before his big library opened, he noticed that the museum section didn't have any hate mail and by God, he was a world beater in the hate mail department. So Lyndon Johnson, disappointed by examples dug up by his staff archivists, waded into the millions of pieces of correspondence himself looking for the meanest letter "I ever got." He finally settled on a postcard from Linden, California, that read: "I demand that you, as a gutless sonofabitch, resign as President of the United States." So it went on display.

Vietnam could do that to you. Dave Edington, Ike Morgan's social worker at the hospital, remembers finally finishing his tour and riding home with a plane of other guys who were coming back to the world after a tour. Just before they made it to Seattle, the pilot came on the intercom and told them to get all sharp objects out of their pockets and to tuck their heads down because the landing gear refused to come down. But no one gave a damn. They all figured they'd die in the attempted landing. The plane was perfectly quiet and serene as they glided toward oblivion.

Listen up now. This is simple. First, horror movies are okay, just so long as you remember they are not true. That's what Ike Morgan advised me, and he's seen true horror and come back from it. And second, we gotta stop dismissing people because the hour is getting late, they're about to blow out all the candles on the last thousand years and Saigon won't go away and neither will Lyndon. He's pulled the hat trick. No, not the War On Poverty, they said that didn't work even though it did. No, not the Civil Rights Act, that worked so damn good, everybody forgot what a bitch life was before it got passed. And forget the Great Society, everyone else has. What is bringing Johnson back is history with the bark on, with the past served up raw and bloody. John Kennedy, he's got his Harvard center tending to the holy remains and ducking every time an old squeeze shows up, but Johnson, he figured out something better than all the spin masters, all the pet house historians, all the loyal lying retainers a man could muster. He stockpiled the greatest show on earth, brutal and bawdy power lashing against our hides like a whip.

And he's coming back from his tomb, he's pulled that wooden stake from his heart just about the time we've wearied of focus groups, false piety and clambering about looking under the bed. We've lost our appetite for Rhodes scholars and are a little more open to Outsider Artists, to the self-taught, to the guys who have been there.

Ike and Lyndon are back with their reports. And it's not the way we think it should be and it is not polite and it is not always pretty. So come down the lane of pain and take a good look. Good morning, millennium. Time to chew some bones. The weather forecast today is purple haze.

Ready or not.

Vietnam Rap Artists / Wednesday, May 27, 1964

RUSSELL: It's one of those things where "heads I win, tails you lose."

LBJ: Well, think about it and I'll talk to you again. I hate to bother you, but I just—

RUSSELL: I wish I could help you. God knows I do 'cause it's a terrific quandary that we're in over there. We're just in the quicksands up to our very necks. And I just don't know what the hell is the best way to do about it.

LBJ: I love you, and I'll be calling you.

White, some splash of teal, but mainly an invisible gray feeling cloaks the Staples Center. The building is six years old and instantly begs the eye to tear it down and begin again. Community centers are the architectural oxymorons of my nation and walking into one has all the emotional charge of kissing your sister. Off to the side of the entryway of the arena, a couple of union maids run the credentials table with the air of being in charge of a ho-hum PTA meeting. I have entered the black hole of the word *Labor*.

But mainly I'm caught by the light, a thin gauzy light falling with fatigue over Los Angeles. Maybe a thousand or two thousand delegates and hangers-on wander the void of the Staples Center. I'd expected clinking glasses of double shots, big cigars, loud coarse talk, and here and there some women dressed to the nines. I peek inside the arena and the vast chamber swallows the union movement whole. The chairs are half empty and the speakers, one after another doing their five minutes of labor jive, are splashed on a giant screen. The actual people are hard to find, the podium is empty and after a while I find these little queues of folks in the big empty who talk into the cold eye of a video camera and thereby are translated into vast mouths and tongues and noses and eyes on the wall.

"Brothers! Sisters!" the voices say, and then they descend into the minutiae of labor, of using the elderly in stuffing envelopes, in properly running that local somewhere. No one listening will hear that the unions are dying, that new workers are being minted by the legion outside the grasp of organized labor, and that the AFL-CIO has the future of a Shaker community. I go up to the press room and find it hosting maybe a dozen scribblers. They are watching an in-house video feed of the emptiness down below on the convention floor. Most of them are writers from tiny labor publications. In the ocean of words that flutter across the republic, there is no space for a reporter who covers the world of work.

But the light is the thing, the sickly light of Los Angeles, the deadly light of the windowless arena, the starved light falling on my shoulders. I am a fiend for light, two gray days in a row and my spirit sinks and my temper frays. I once lived in the hills on a small New England farm and for an entire November the sun never broke through the clouds, not for a single instant. That time lives in my memory like some horror of captivity. I remember once getting out of bed in Wisconsin and looking at the gray sky, getting in the truck with a gallon of wine and some pills, and never stopping until my bumper crossed the line into Mexico.

I must have light or die. Now I am in the arena of something even more repellent than darkness. I am in the place that does not care if the sun ever shines. It is never morning here, not one time. The fires that burned so violently early in the twentieth century, the rage and hunger and lust of working people for their place in the sun, this blaze is banked. I am among the cannibals of that movement, the men and women who could create nothing but who can consume everything, the dukes of labor living off the dues of dwindling memberships and fattening on this island of high wages. The bones shatter as the rock strikes, the marrow is sucked out, and now, let's take a crap on the family hearth.

I ain't gonna work on Maggie's farm no more because they sold the damn place to agribusiness.

So I crawl into the nature of the light. Paul was a man of the light also, a person who lived as a giant cornea savoring light and manipulating light and caressing light and funneling light. And twisting slowly in a circle that kept closing in on itself until finally movement stopped and the sign said GET HOME, and the soft loving light poured through the windows of the studio onto his body and the installation was complete.

In the beginning was the light and light was with life and the light was life and the earth quickened, and we came out of the ground to yearn forever and never reach the light but to tumble through generations, our skins afire with this lust for the light and we go toward the light or we go toward nothing and we become nothing. That is all.

In the first light of day the colors return with the sun. I have watched the leaves go from black to gray to green, day after day I have watched, and nothing can control this, nothing can manage this, it is beyond the commissions and regulations and rules, it is the fire in our bellies and this fire must never be banked.

Paul fell into this place behind the art, this ground where art comes from and is hatched and slapped and shaped, this terrain where light sweeps across objects and exalts them and where the eye feeds in its peculiar optical way and we are no longer blind and minute shifts of light alter everything and make the commonplace suddenly divine and the divine suddenly garbage tossed in the alley just as Christ came off the cross a carcass for the hyenas of the Roman world to dispose of as they saw fit. But on the third day the rock moved, the vault emptied and the light returned and Paul is walking down the alley looking here and there, and suddenly he stops and picks up a hammer or is it a wrench? He stops and sees some object and the light pours down, and it is transfigured and on its way from the trash toward art. Somewhere in this very manner, and I am certain of this fact, somewhere when he was strolling through our garbage, he found the shrink-wrap machine and he took it back to his studio and that act was the beginning of the end for him and the beginning of the beginning. He must have loved that machine, it could devour anything and encase it in a new skin that denied feeling forever and forever.

I am holding a plastic cup of coffee as I stare out at the boneyard of the union convention in Los Angeles and on the cup is printed a cautionary tale that warns: CAREFUL, THE BEVERAGE YOU'RE ABOUT TO ENJOY IS EXTREMELY HOT. Yes indeed, forget the herbal capsules, stop chomping on garlic pills, they will not save you, it is extremely hot and still you will enjoy it. The light will punch through this dome and burn the community center with its fire. I must keep the faith.

Some like it hot.

Thirty years ago I went up the stairs. It was fall and it was Saint Paul, Minnesota, and I went up the stairs. They creaked, each step creaked as I went up them. The stairway had the odor of old things, dust long settled, air that had been trapped and begged for release back into the gas flows of the planet. The light was stolen from Edward Hopper's paintings, that light of terrible loneliness that isolates every thing it illuminates. I feel my foot on the next step, and then the one after that, I am going up there to meet the embers of the fire. I am lugging a tape recorder but I am incompetent with machines and this tape recorder will run for hours and capture nothing, not the light, not the creaking of the stairs, not the tormented, trapped air yowling and begging to be free, not a single fucking sound will this machine capture. You must know this now. There is no record of that day, except in my mind, and for thirty years it has been locked away in some cell in my brain and now it comes back, comes without warning, that afternoon, the light, the stairs, the voices, comes back demanding my attention as I stand on the convention floor and watch monstrous faces splash against the wall and gigantic lips move and say, "Brothers! Sisters!" and mean not a word of it.

But thirty years ago I met the men who had gone on a quest for the fire and they had been burned almost beyond recognition, and yet they still lived and spoke and I drank in their words and kept no record save in my soul. Paul was seven years old then and just beginning his alley prowls. Barbara was happy and saw dawn and called it the future. We were ignorant of the cannibals, all of us, well, almost all of us. The men at the top of the stairs were not ignorant. They had seen the bone crushing and heard the sound of marrow being sucked out. They were veterans of what would become my life among the man eaters.

Now we enter the dreamtime.

The dreamtime is at the top of the stairs and it is the place beyond cable television and op-ed pages and glib and clever words. It is almost beyond words at all, since it is the place of hunger and from hunger comes the only hope of love. The premise was very sound: I was to interview two or three old men who had been part and parcel of the early labor movement and I would record their words, and then a transcript would be made and these words would be put in a folder and stored in an archive as fodder for the men and women who, in due time, wrote the book of history. The folder, you must understand, would be in a gray archival box and none of the paper would have acid in its sinews and therefore it would last forever and forever. I fucked all this up. The tape never recorded the words. The transcript was never made.

We are now at the top of the stairs. I remember that we turn right and there is a naked lightbulb in the hall, and then there is an old door, half frosted glass, and I knock and it opens, and we go into the room where old men wait. They have casement windows open, curtains flap out the windows and lick against the brick wall of the building just as Edward Hopper would have painted it. The windows face south, absolutely they face south. I am very good at this kind of thing. It's the machines that show my flaws. I set the tape recorder down and this is thirty years ago and the tape recorder is huge and reel to reel and I adjust everything and start it, and of course nothing is recorded. Except in my head.

Dreamtime.

There are three men but they fuse into one. His face is gaunt, his body thin, his sweater old and smelling of mothballs. He is freshly shaven like a corpse and his skin is waxlike. The eyes are clear and hard. Not unfriendly, but hard. He still has his hair all gone gray. When he talks, he never raises his voice but leans toward me and speaks without hesitation. He knows and the words have the force and clarity of this knowing. Not confident words, or arrogant, just sure. He is beyond argument and beyond belief. His politics are like his manners, a matter of custom. The world that forged his ideas has vanished except in his memory, but still he clings to them.

They are coming home, he tells me, coming home from the wheatfields of the Far West, coming home from the hop fields, coming home from brute labor at the time the First World War is over. They are brothers, two brothers, or three, I can't remember, riding the rails, sun baking them in the fields, sleeping in the hobo camps.

I remember one phrase he said: "It was terrible."

They'd joined the Industrial Workers of the World, the fabled IWW, they were the working stiffs, the men in the old photographs with caps not hats, the guys cradling mugs of coffee, steam rising into the cold air of dawn, the ones who felt left out of wherever the country was heading. Joe Hill, I dreamed I saw him last night, Big Bill, the Cyclops of labor, the western miners, murders, lynchings, deportations, a list of wounds and massacre sites as if they were Plains Indians being slaughtered in a gulch at Wounded Knee. The Red Scare after the war, J. Edgar Hoover standing there at the dock as the death ship of the American left, the hulk holding Emma Goldman and a horde of other commies and anarchists, steamed out of the harbor into what the government prayed was oblivion in the new hell Lenin was building in Russia. The old man sitting before me in the south light that filtered through the flapping curtains ticked off these names and events like beads on the rosary of a dead religion. The mass strikes, the shutdown in Seattle, the days when all the wheels stopped moving in the Twin Cities, the swan songs of American socialism and anarchism and communism. But in the beginning the brothers were coming home, hopping freights, coming home tired and filthy and with damn little money, lean young men with anger in their eyes and defeat in their souls.

They are walking down a country road in Minnesota with their bundles on their shoulders, and there is the home place, some house and outbuildings huddled on the green earth. They walk into the yard and their mother waits. She makes them strip and boils their lice-ridden clothes in a kettle.

The old man looks at me and says: "It was terrible."

After that the pace quickens. It becomes trucks, big trucks, and the old man and his brothers start organizing the drivers and they train up a man. And this man trains up a guy named James Riddle Hoffa, a promising youngster who at seventeen had already led a loading dock strike in 1931 over a cargo of strawberries and won a thirty percent pay raise on the spot. And of course, eventually, this new kid goes bad. That is the way stories from the American left always ends: the sellout, or the corruption, or some other taste of failure.

For the brothers, it goes bad also. They drift through various isms, wind up siding with Trotsky in the faction frolics of the left. And eventually are nailed by a federal law and imprisoned. One brother kills himself. And when the cell door swings open, the world has changed and they are fossils from the history book of American labor and in this book their pages are blank as labor after the Second World War cleans its house, shakes radicalism from its skirts, and begins its descent into partnership with the American economy and the owners of that economy.

But he is not finished, the old man sitting by me as I watch the tape recorder fail to capture his words, that old man is not finished. He is irrelevant, consumed, digested and cast off, all of that, but somehow not finished. He believes in some kind of future. He believes, beneath the buzzwords of his Marxism and Trotskyism and communism and socialism, in a solid thing he tasted as he entered the yard and his mother made the boys strip and then boiled their clothes.

He believes the hard world he saw has not truly vanished but has simply been shunted offstage and that it will return, tooth and nail.

Cannibals. The eating and tearing. The rock glides down, the bone cracks, the marrow is sucked out.

It is back there. It is here. It is up ahead.

James Hoffa is standing in front of me, his body solid, his eyes soft and vulnerable, that split lip a dot of red on his face. Barbara's voice is in my ear, all the warmth of the midwestern mothers, a comforting voice, but now it is saying, "It's so hard . . ."

I crash down that stale stairway, flee this room of the ancients, the one with the curtain flapping in the breeze, break out into the hum of the Twin Cities.

There is a floor under modern life, and this floor is hard, and more and more people fall and hit it and this thud, thud, thud is denied or ignored. Or never happens. The floor has been removed, placed so distantly that no one can hear the thud.

Except when they cut the rope fashioning Paul to the pipe. And then no one knows what to make of the sound, including myself.

Also, the sound of the crack of the stone hammer hitting the bone as the cannibals gather and take everything and give nothing.

I remember the thirst and the drinking.

I can see the black kettle in the farmyard, smell the steam rising off the boiling clothes. Solidarity forever. I dreamed I saw Joe Hill last night.

I turn on a television. I am less grounded than Paul swinging from that pipe in his perfect installation.

GET HOME

4

The curtains are closed. There is nothing to see. Outside the temperature idles at about a hundred and ten degrees. The Arizona prison hunkers just across the road, an ancient colony of cages surrounded by fields all wrapped in a cyclone fence topped by concertina wire. Hard time arrived here in 1909. The town now hosts five prisons and on the census claims twelve thousand souls. But only thirty-eight hundred of them live free. Unemployment runs about two percent. In twenty-three hours the population will shrink by one. That's why I'm sitting in the fifty-year-old calm of the Blue Mist Motel. Michael Poland, who turned fifty-nine last Friday, father of four and ex-husband of Sally Ann, will be strapped to a gurney and administered a lethal injection tomorrow afternoon. He invited me. The certified letter read: "You have been selected by inmate Michael Kent Poland to be invited to witness his execution at Arizona State Prison Complex at Florence, Arizona, at approximately 3:00 p.m. on June 16, 1999. You are under no obligation to appear as witness to this execution. Under the law, this inmate has the right to choose his method of execution. Inmate Poland did not choose a method of execution, therefore, he will be executed by lethal injection."

The invitation was a long time coming in my life. So was the stay in the Blue Mist Motel. I've never met Poland nor had any communication with him. I'm here courtesy of his attorneys, who want me to witness how the state kills my fellow citizens. Poland is apparently not in any condition to send out a wish list of guests since he is at this moment embodied before the state supreme court in a petition asserting his incompetency to be executed. The grounds are simple: since Poland believes he can, by an act of will, prevent the state from killing him, he is not competent to be killed by the state. Few hold much hope for this petition.

Right now he is living his last hours isolated under a deathwatch, lest other convicts taunt him and lest he kill himself before the state has a crack at it. He is here because of two canvas bags, each holding a man, pulled out of a lake twenty-two years ago. When I mention the case to others who have been around Arizona awhile, they always remember it. And react strongly to this memory. When I say I am to be a guest at his slaughter, they fall silent and then ask, are you going? But of course I must, just as I must lodge myself in the Blue Mist Motel where everything is blue, dark blue and that light bright blue owned by swimming pools and "ALWAYS FRIENDLY, NICE, QUIET, CLEAN." I'd always thought that the motel's name—I've been driving by it since the late fifties—referred to its closest neighbor, the state's gas chamber. I was wrong—cyanide isn't blue anyway. Fifty years ago Gene Autry and some other folks built the place, Autry staying here during visits to Arizona. Later owners came up with the name Blue Mist, figuring it would suggest refrigerated air and an escape from the bake of the surrounding Sonoran Desert. Since January 13, 1984, a kind of renown has settled on the place. For eleven years, Roberta Moormann had booked a room here once a month so she could visit her adopted boy Robert, who was doing a long stretch for kidnapping and sodomy. That weekend he checked out of the state facility across the street for a three-day "compassionate furlough." The two stayed in room 22, just around the corner from my cell in 19. Robert tied up his mom on the bed, then gagged her and took to the knife. They found her feet in the trash at a local drive-in and the rest of her here and there around town. There is talk that the head wound up near the pool right down from my room. All these body parts were thoughtfully placed in trash containers. Robert Moormann is now on death row, also.

I choose the Blue Mist, just as I choose to accept Poland's invitation to death. Because like Poland, I have some unfinished business of my own. Oddly enough, after I check in, I think of a tree in my yard that has been ailing. I worry for its health, and then chastise myself for allowing such a trivial matter to intrude upon the business at hand.

When a tree probes the earth, the roots claw into the dark, the buried layers of soil and rock. I have arrived at the Blue Mist Motel in the same fashion, a blind mission that I feel and understand.

The sensation shares nothing with powerlessness. I am neither under control nor out of control, I do not take orders or give them. I taste and feel the sense of command and lack of authority of some fourth-century monk slowly going crazy in a desert cave of contemplation.

On May 24, 1977, a Purolator truck was robbed of about $300,000 in cash. The two guards disappeared. A year later Michael Poland and his brother Patrick were arrested. First the federal government gave them a hundred years apiece. The judge, an eighty-year-old on loan from New York, allowed, "If there is a God, each of you has much to answer for. And if there is no God, you have each lived a short and successful life." Then they were handed over to the state, which after two trials and some legal tussles sentenced them to death. For the first time in the history of the United States, the Department of Justice loaned out a federal attorney to the state to make sure the job got done. That's the short of it.

Capital punishment has a long trail around here. Arizona Territory voted in the death sentence in 1901, then voted it out in 1916, four years after statehood came on Valentine's Day. A killer in 1917, taking note of the abolition of capital punishment, boasted that he couldn't be hung. He was promptly lynched. In 1918 death was voted back in. Twenty-eight people swung until the matter of Eva Dugan came up on February 21, 1930. Miss Dugan had been a car thief and a serial house-keeper of men who tended to die. Her custom caught up with her. She entered prison in 1928 at age forty-nine, standing five feet two and half inches and weighing a solid one hundred forty-nine pounds. She took to heavy feeding and when she swung in 1930, her head came off and rolled about on the ground. When I was boy, people still talked about that hanging. No one remembered her name or the year, just that she was hefty and that the rope ripped her head off.

Arizona switched to poison gas and over the coming decades dispatched another thirty-five men. But with the execution of Manuel Silvas in 1963, legal motions began to pile up at the courthouses, and this fact, along with stuttering decisions from the U.S. Supreme Court, stalled death in Arizona for almost thirty years. Death row kept growing but death itself was kept at bay by petitions.

When I was a reporter in the early eighties, I was the designated hitter, the guy assigned to go in and make notes of the killing and then brief the rest of the press. But this never came to pass. State murder returned in 1992, and Arizona, a small state operating under the slogan "Ditat Deus," God Gives, is nevertheless a contender in the execution sweepstakes with Florida and Texas. So far we've killed eighteen. Michael Poland's twenty-two years on death row were a by-product of the legal battle across this nation over capital punishment. And his slaughter tomorrow will be the result of an American resolve to return to the killing ground.

Capital punishment is not a deterrent (except to the man or woman killed), paralyzes juries, gums up the legal system with endless delays, and occasionally kills innocent people. And in a nation such as ours, riven by class and race and gender differences, it will never be handed out in a fair or equitable manner. But executions will be used frequently for the rest of my life. We demand this killing and we will have our demand met.

I have covered crimes and seen bodies and wept tears. I have met people whom I believe have no right to live and, in some instances, usually involving children raped and butchered, would gladly have killed myself. But I am against capital punishment, with the cited exception of my own handiwork, because I do not trust the state to dole out the killing fairly, and I know the poor will die, and the people of color, and the affluent will usually live and so will the women, save an Eva Dugan now and then. I am sitting in the Blue Mist Motel drinking three doors down from Robert Moormann's butcher shop, and five hundred yards away, Michael Kent Poland is experiencing his last sunset—a storm is rolling in from the mountains, a wall of black in front of which is a wall of brown dust, and the wind is coming up.

Let me spell it out: I don't think Michael Poland is fit to live. I hold no brief for premeditated murder. All I have to imagine is that I am in a Purolator truck and two men are approaching it with guns. For a brief instant, I can feel the canvas bag against my face. But I'm not in a friendly barroom argument tossing a death sentence around for sport. I'm a couple of football fields from the slaughterhouse, and I can feel its cold breath on my neck. And in this moment I realize that I have no right to decide who lives or dies, any more than Michael Poland did on that day in 1977. No one has that right, not now, not ever. I'm the standard sinner with a typical appetite for revenge. But I dread tomorrow. Not fear it. Dread it. I have no taste for ritual slaughter, be it a lamb on an altar in some ancient Judean desert, or a man in Florence, Arizona.

They must have gotten up early, what with so much to do. Mike Poland is thirty-six, his brother Pat ten years younger. They've fetched up a police uniform they have bought and their wives have sewn on the insignia for a proper highway patrolman. An American flag on the sleeve, an Arizona state flag emblem plate on the front of the car. They've gotten a Sam Browne belt, the appropriate firearm. A light bar to slap on the roof. Taser guns. A badge. They have had three canvas sacks custom sewn, each six feet long and about three feet wide. They've rented two cars. Now they head north out of Phoenix on Interstate 17. This day, May 24, 1977, is rainy, unusual for the desert at this time of year.

Russell Dempsey, fifty-three, and Cecil Newkirk, fifty-one, have been a bit frantic too. The door on the Purolator truck is giving them fits, they can't seem to get it to close right. They're running an hour late and the banks in northern Arizona are going to open at ten a.m. and damn sure want the money. Dempsey and Newkirk have pulled almost twenty with the company and been partners all that while. They are company men and don't complain about their equipment, which runs a bit scant—no alarm system, no two-way radio. Just a van with around $300,000 in cash.

They may not have noticed the car parked on the roadside with the hood up, or the two women and all those kids—Sally Ann and Kathy Poland sitting on the shoulder with their broods, hoping to draw aside any highway patrol car that comes by, and talking ahead on a citizens band radio to announce the Purolator van has passed them and is on its way. Anyway, the armored truck is almost to Bumble Bee Junction and has rolled through beautiful stands of saguaro and the dark rock of Black Canyon and they know up ahead is the bench with grasslands and antelope and past that that the piñon and juniper and then the breath of cool high country with an enormous stand of ponderosa pine, the largest single block of the species in the United States.

They are sure as hell more worried about running late than anything else, when the lights of a highway patrol car start flashing in the rearview mirror. So they pull over. This better not take long. If the banks don't get their money, there will be hell to pay.

On June 9, 1999, Judge James E. Don walks into his courtroom like a gunslinger with a syringe in his holster. He is a Pinal County man, for years a prosecutor and then for the last twenty the judge. He works in a Wal-Mart temple of justice, with wood paneling reaching up the walls, plain acoustic tile on the ceiling and the hum of an air conditioner flooding his courtroom cell. Four lawyers in cheap dark suits plus a gaggle of legal aides represent Michael Poland in his competency hearing one week before his scheduled execution. A dozen or more prison employees wait outside. Florence snores in the heat, and outside the courtroom, dogs can almost sprawl in the middle of the baked and lonely streets.

At eighteen minutes to nine, Poland arrives in a brilliant orange jumpsuit, shackled with his hands pinned to his waist like a pope in a body language of prayer, his ankles bound also, his feet in delicate white prison slippers. He wears thick glasses, has gray hair, pale skin, enormous forearms and the air of a faceless clerk.

Court begins and Poland asks to speak. He says he has a high school education and explains, "I don't mean any disrespect to you or the court, but I don't see any real reason to be here." The judge leans forward and laboriously reviews his rights with him and then has him whisked back to death row.

The state had commissioned a psychiatrist of the University of Arizona Medical School to determine if Poland was really incompetent—meaning, did the inmate know he was going to be executed and why he was going to be executed?—but then declined to call the doctor when he decided that Poland was really nuts. In October 1998, two hours before his then-scheduled execution, Poland had been granted a stay by a judge because another psychiatrist believed he was incompetent. Since then Poland has gained twenty pounds and the state has gotten irked.

Last night the defense beckoned the current expert witness, the psychiatrist, to court for their side. Now he purses his hands before his skeletal body and says of Michael Kent Poland, "He believes he has a special power, a kind of supernatural, omniscient power to control things. He has the unshakable conviction that he has, can and will use this power in the future."

The judge leans back in his chair and stares at the ceiling's acoustic tile.

The doctor rolls on and explains that because of this power, one that Poland figures he may have always had but truly became aware of in the last half dozen years or so—and he can't be exact here on this dawning awareness, but whatever—because of this power, which prevents the state from strapping him to a gurney and injecting his veins with a lethal poison, he is on a mission to reform the prison system and abolish capital punishment.

Naturally, the doctor knows some folks may think Poland is malingering, faking this condition to cheat the death sentence. And that is possible. But most guys who do that, the doctor explains, go over the top in acting out their symptoms. Poland is the opposite, in fact is damn near shy and you have to "tease" this delusion out of him. Took the doctor an hour and a half to get him to fess up to his special power and his mission. At this point, the judge is damn near wearing a hole in the ceiling.

So Michael Poland is the real thing, something most folks might miss but a professional can spot, a delusional man who thinks he is on a mission and has special power. The doctor says he'll still be believing this nonsense when they plunge the needle into his vein. Of course, there is this problem for some: just before Poland's postponed execution in October 1998, he was plotting an escape, complete with an offered bribe to a guard, a getaway car, and safe houses, a half-witted escape plan, to be sure, but not the act some might see as that of a man with a special power to achieve a penalogical reform mission. Poland said he'd decided he could do his mission better on the outside. The next day the judge finds Poland competent to be executed. He cleverly notes that the only source of information on Poland's alleged condition is Michael Kent Poland himself.

A prison guard overheard Poland say something like, "I'm not going to let the state kill me." A psychiatrist testified, "I mean that [the delusional system] could continue all the way until he was executed. I mean he may die with that total belief." If Michael Poland truly believes in his mission and his special power, and dies with that belief intact, he is clinically insane. And he is also like a legion of martyrs keeping the faith as the fire licks their bodies tied to the stake or the hungry lions close in while an arena of Romans screamed in delight.

The legal skirmish comes not from the bench but from the pulpit. A prisoner not of sound mind is incapable of a key element required for an execution: penance. Only those who know their lives are ending can seek forgiveness and get right with God. This is an old point in the common law. Michael Poland must have a clear mind before we can blank out his consciousness forever.

The dust blew through, you could chew the dust. The heat held at least one hundred. Across the road, the prison sign that says stay back ten feet disappeared in the brown wind and then the sun fell and night came down. Across the road in the big house the lights came on, in the towers too.

Poland waits, visits restricted, the final twenty-four hours. Tall poles blaze with torches of light, the cement under my feet is hot. The lights look like sunflowers fighting against the blackness.

I have come here because I could not say no to the invitation. Like Michael Poland, I, too, am delusional and I, too, think I am on a mission. The hot wind brushes against my face. There is never a second that I do not think of bolting from the Blue Mist Motel.

He was born in 1940 in Indiana. Then his father went to war and the children came in two chunks, Mike and his older brothers before Pearl Harbor, and the three younger ones born after the fighting. His brother Pat is one of two fraternal twins in the postwar birthing. They moved after World War II to Prescott, Arizona, and the father became a sign painter. There is a vague taste of problems in this family home but nothing makes it into the court records. When Mike was fifteen, he moved in with an older brother in Phoenix for a year. He dropped out of high school after the eleventh grade. He married young, about twenty-two, with Sally Ann a few years younger. They had four children in short order. Mike worked trades—a draftsman in Phoenix, a surveyor in Kingman, Arizona, then a twirl in Colorado construction. He tended to exaggerate his experience and be let go when his real work skills became apparent. Sometimes he hit his wife. He was said to be a good father. He brushed his children's teeth.

In his thirty-fourth year, he took a different path. This part is always vague because whatever Mike Poland was up to, he left no arrest record. He is working in Glenwood, Colorado. A woman pulls into the construction job—this he tells a psychiatrist years later—and Mike talks to her, and by God, she is pleased by him and buys the whole $115 million mansion. She is Lucille Ball in this story. At least, this is what he tells the doctor years later. Like the high price of the house, these facts may exist only inside the head of Michael Poland. But some people don't notice his abilities. He goes to a bank—he does not at this time, he notes, have "overwhelming debts"—and the banker is snooty. So he has his brother Pat, who has also come up to Colorado, go to the banker's house, seize his wife and hold her hostage while Mike collects ransom from the banker. Mike is thirty-three. And he is smarter than they are.

After that, he and Pat are rear-ended by a Budweiser beer truck. They dream of a huge insurance payoff. Mike moves to Oregon and thinks of buying a ranch. But the payoff from the insurance is only five or ten thousand. This is not enough.

He moves back to Arizona. He and Pat and their wives and children are living in Phoenix. Mike loves to watch *The Rockford Files*. He dreams of being a private investigator. He studies the television show. He and Pat pull off the Dumpster heist—another banker's wife held under the gun, the ransom put in a Dumpster, where they have cleverly cut out a hole in the bottom to retrieve the cash. They also rip off drug dealers. All this is what the FBI later pieces together.

Mike is smart, Pat slower and easily dominated. They don't really work. They've got it all beat. Mike is a controlling kind of guy, he beats his wife now and again, makes sure that Pat stays under his thumb. But Michael Poland keeps the kids' teeth clean and brushes his own three times a day, twenty minutes a shot. Or at least that's his regimen in prison.

The schemes keep growing in scale. You gotta hustle when you don't have a straight job. Then it is the mid-seventies and they are all living in Phoenix, and Sally Ann is having an affair. She tells Mike. He goes crazy and beats her. Things are clearly out of control.

About that time, the notion of the Purolator job comes up.

The sun rises with an air of fatigue and seeps through the scud left by last night's dry storm. Out here the desert writhes in the fifth year of a drought. Across the road in the big house, there is no notion of weather, and in the mesh holding cell by the execution chamber there are hardly any notions at all. Today is Bloomsday and in Dublin devotees of Joyce are ambling through their ritual rounds of drink and literature as they reenact Leopold's schedule on June 16, 1904, the day author James Joyce met his beloved Nora.

Joyce, like Poland, was a control freak and *Ulysses,* his giant and generally unread novel, is so controlled that it is more like a statue than a story. Poland, in his decades of incarceration, has become a great reader and salts his letters with literary quotes. He dotes on his Shakespeare and likes to tell of sitting in on college classes once to cover for a friend. Michael Poland is always quite a guy in his own recounting. Joyce is not keen on quoting anyone but loves to invent and transform everything. Yet he is rigid. The section that takes up 3:00 p.m. on Bloomsday is "The Wandering Rocks." Here is how Joyce worked it out. The location: the streets. The organ: blood. The symbol: citizens. And the structure is that of a labyrinth.

Michael Poland is escaping his labyrinth at 3:00 p.m. today. Last week one of his lawyers worked ninety-three hours flinging various petitions into the maw of the state and federal system. By Monday, twelve separate motions have clotted various courts. And now the answers come hour by hour and they all say no. Yesterday the clemency board deliberated a few seconds. Soon the only thing standing between Michael Poland and the needle will be his special power to influence others and control events.

Frank Mowrey looks perplexed by the Indian casino where he heads security. He is not a gambling man. His manner is gentle and out of sorts with the bells and whistles of the slot machines and the video poker warrens. He retired after twenty-two years with the FBI, and for a bunch of those years, the Poland brothers were his obsession. He has quit the bottle now, and he is a devout member of the Assembly of God. But back then he was the shadow that trailed the Polands everywhere and became the door into the crime itself when Pat Poland confessed everything to him on death row in 1987.

He is a calm, bespectacled man as he returns to this knowledge of the killing ground. He remembers that after the brothers pulled the truck over on May 24, 1977, things went into a free fall. Dempsey and

Newkirk, running late with all that money due at the banks, opened the door to calm the highway patrolman and get their show on the road. Pat Poland is in uniform, his brother is crouching out of sight in the car. He tells the two guards they have been speeding and then pulls down on them with a .357 Magnum. They do nothing, so Pat signals his brother by saying, "Checkmate," their code word for having the guards under control. Mike then gets out of the car, comes up and they handcuff them.

Pat returns to the patrol car. Mike's assignment is to drive Newkirk and Dempsey and the van off the interstate. They are confident of the guards' reactions, they've been following them around for weeks and know their habits. Once Pat Poland even held the door open for them as they delivered money. But now Pat sees some kind of ruckus going on and gets out of the patrol car and returns to the van, where he finds his brother walloping both with a blackjack. There is blood everywhere and Newkirk seems dead and Dempsey unconscious. Pat Poland recalls his brother's eyes bulging and he seems in a psychotic rage.

Mike then gets the armored truck off the interstate and drives it down a dirt track, where it gets stuck. Pat follows in the car. It will take days for a police helicopter to finally find the van. Mike produces a nylon cord with a stick on each end, and he and Pat pull hard and strangle each guard just to make sure. They stash the money in the back of the car, from which they have removed the rear seat, put the bagged bodies in the trunk of the car and return to Phoenix. They'd earlier rented a storage locker and now they put the light bar from the car and Dempsey and Newkirk in it. Then they go home, change, and with their wives count the money. It goes like this: $66,000 in hundred-dollar bills, $36,000 in fifty-dollar bills, $61,000 in twenty-dollar bills, $39,000 in ten-dollar bills, $26,000 in five-dollar bills, $10,000 in two-dollar bills, $49,500 in one-dollar bills, $5,500 in quarters, 114 in English pounds, 85 Irish pounds and 86 Scottish pounds.

Then they go over to their dad's and borrow his pickup and the tarp, fetch the bodies in the canvas sacks from the storage locker and cover them with the tarp in the back of the pickup. They've called ahead to Lake Mohave on the California-Arizona border about a boat rental and take off across the desert. It is early afternoon.

Lake Mohave seems too busy for Mike and new construction has created too many houses with prying eyes, so the brothers roll on up to Lake Mead on the Arizona-Nevada border. They stop twice in their wanderings to buy gas and food. Pat is drinking heavily by now. It is night when they reach Lake Mead and they sleep in the truck with the bodies until dawn.

Mike rents a boat at the marina and uses his own driver's license as collateral. The lake is crowded with pleasure seekers zipping about. Pat drives the truck with the bodies. He makes it to the landing where they have agreed to meet, but his brother is late. He drives down to the shores and gets stuck again. The brothers unload the bodies and tie them with a tow rope behind the boat and take them out into the lake. Before cutting them loose, they stuff the bags with big rocks and also load a third bag with paraphernalia from the crime. They watch all three sink beneath the waves.

Then they walk out and find a tow truck operator, a guy who knows Mike from when he lived around Kingman, Arizona. He pulls them out and is tipped with a hundred-dollar bill. Years later Pat Poland explains his motives for the crime simply as a desire to have independence, provide a college education for his children, and ensure his family's future. He explains that "money is power."

The first two days of the perfect crime are over.

The sun bears down on the prison and will likely hit one hundred ten again today. The plowed fields sag under the heat. Each hour another petition is batted down by yet another legal tribunal. Michael Poland sticks to his routine. The twenty minutes of brushing his teeth. The lust for order and control. Last October he maintained his resolve until the stay came just hours before the scheduled execution. The Blue Mist Motel remains cool. The curtains, of course, are closed. In fact, someone has fastened them together with safety pins. One evening a woman staying here heard a lonely saxophone moan across the fields from the prison. She figured it was the essence of the Blue Mist experience.

For me, it is numbness. I have brought black slacks, a shirt, a sport coat and leather shoes. My preparations stop there. I am not planning the perfect murder, the State of Arizona has taken up that task. When they dispatched another inmate last June, the death certificate listed his cause of death as homicide.

At first there was a suspicion that Dempsey and Newkirk had ripped off the load of money and hit the road. Then a few weeks after the robbery, the bodies bobbed up to the surface half out of the bags. The perfect crime had a pilot error: the Poland brothers had tossed the dead men onto the lip of an underwater shelf. Just twenty-five feet further and they would have been in deep water that would have held the corpses forever. As it was, the wave action of the lake had rocked the bags and the big rocks in the bags had worn against the custom-sewn canvas and torn a hole. The rocks fell out in a neat pile (later discovered by divers), the bloated bodies rose to the light of day.

They were fished out on the Nevada side of Lake Mead and taken to Las Vegas. Here a curious statement occurred that would chase the Poland boys for the rest of their natural lives. In a short-lived effort to claim the killing as a Nevada case, the county coroner announced that the men had drowned, meaning they'd been pitched into the lake alive, presumably on the Nevada side. There was no water in the lungs, however, a fact given scant attention. It would be years before Pat's confession made it clear that the guards were dead before they hit the water, and by then it hardly registered, since both brothers were already on death row. But the horror of the pathologist's announcement would never go away.

The FBI found the receipt for the boat rental and latched onto the tow truck operator who had pulled the boys out of the sand. The Poland brothers became suspects and when the FBI checked up on them, they were spending money like drunken sailors—stereos, televisions, furniture, and so forth—and yet lacked jobs or any recent history of employment. Pat Poland had opened a business, a game room. They also noticed on that first visit to the residence that Pat came out of the house wearing a gun. Frank Mowrey and his colleagues rented a house across the street from where the Polands lived in Phoenix and just watched and watched and made no secret of their watching. Finally, in July they got a search warrant and found police gear and strange receipts for things like a taser gun.

Mowrey was determined to find the source of the canvas bags. Eighteen outfits made such things in Phoenix. When he walked into the last establishment, the clerk said, "What are you doing with our bags? Hell, I can even name the seamstress who sewed them." The circumstantial case that put the Polands on death row began to be built slowly, receipt by receipt. When questioned, the brothers told tales of being gamblers and gem dealers to explain their money. Or they floated the notion that fellows could make money by ripping off drug dealers (and the FBI did eventually find among their possessions a list of drug dealers and detailed maps of where they lived), but they could never provide proof of such activity.

Mowrey took to stopping by on his way home from work. Pat would be out front watering the lawn with a hose and they would talk. Mowrey would say, "Pat, you can't get out of this."

And Pat would get upset, the struggle going on inside him was as plain as day on his face.

Mowrey said, "You're letting your brother control you. You're going to be sitting in prison when I retire."

"Yeah, you're right Frank," Pat said. "There are a lot of things I'd like to tell you, but I can't."

Mowrey would see tears in his eyes, then Poland would clear his throat as though getting ready to speak. But the words would not come.

Once he offered, "Wouldn't want my children to think . . . ever did anything like that."

This went on week after week, month after month. Mike kept his silence, and Mowrey had decided early that he was beyond reach. But Pat kept trembling up to the edge, then balking.

The FBI hounded the brothers, while building the case out of scraps. In October 1977, Sally Ann, Mike's wife, tried to kill herself to escape the stress of it all. But nothing swayed Mike Poland. He had it all figured out.

Years later, long after it had all unraveled, he told an investigator, "I figured out A, B, C, but I forgot about D, E and F." And that was as close as he ever came to talking about it all.

Control comes from fear and fear has its price. When the Polands were finally arrested in May 1978, almost a year to the day from the Purolator heist, the feds offered a deal: confess and do fifteen years. And of course, give back the money. For the brothers this was a new experience since they'd never been arrested before and to this day their defense attorneys like to state they had no prior history of crime. So they turned it down and Mike Poland's need for control got the boys a hundred years—which under the conditions of that time could have meant as little as ten years. Then the state had a crack at them and hustled them off to death row.

About half the money has been accounted for and Mowrey, for one, is convinced that some stranger accidentally came upon the buried loot and took off with it. At one point, the Polands—during their last year in sunshine—showed up at a Safeway with a bunch of mildewed, squirrel-ravaged bills that they wanted to exchange for fresh ones. But the manager would have none of it. The FBI dug up half a county looking for the loot and came up empty on the missing $150,000. All this fed into Mike's dreams of control. In prison he hatched ways to leave— one scheme had his sons busting through the fence with a vehicle. Or he'd have a conversation with a guard and offer him a million or two to help out. All of these plans, like all of the Polands' crimes, were elaborate and overblown. And they always failed, especially with the prison staff reading the mail, listening in on their phone calls, and the guards wearing wires and dutifully reporting the bribes. But any cheap criticism misses the point. The point is control. Every bungled attempt had one saving grace: it put Michael Kent Poland in the starring role of an intricate plot that would bamboozle the demented authorities. He'd type out these scenarios, page after page without a single typo, manic efforts with exquisite details. (Look, he explained, you beat a polygraph by sticking a pin in your gum and the pain alters the flutter and you can lie like hell and the fools can't detect it—this, he rolls on knowingly, is a trick used by the KGB.)

Control requires constant attention. Getting rid of the bodies, for instance. Bury them and weather may eventually erode them to the surface or some kid wandering around will find the grave and tell. Put them in a mine shaft and vultures might swirl overhead, giving away the location. Obviously, you get some custom-made sacks and drive for hours across the desert to a big lake. When you start thinking this way, failure feeds your hunger for yet more control—what could be more stimulating to a control junkie than feeling the edge when things start to slip from your grip?

Mike Poland seldom lost control. While in prison, he discovered Sally Ann had taken a boyfriend. He told her he would bust out of prison, castrate her lover, plop his genitals into a bottle of formaldehyde and set it up right over the marital bed.

And then in 1984 he sat down and typed out a forty-one-page, single-spaced letter to his Sally Ann. She had just told him she was filing for divorce.

"PLEASE READ ALL OF THIS CLEAR THROUGH!!" the letter shouts at the top. It is dated June 17, 1984. This time there are typos. "Well, you really know how to hurt a guy," he notes, "but this guy just happens to have no pride left at this moment and is willing to crawl for you to give him a second chance. No one else will ever love you as I do nor make you feel as loved as I have and can. I have made mistakes, too many to still be alive, but since I am I know there must be a reason and I believe it is to make amends with you and go on loving as before, only better." Page after page after page, he reviews their marriage—great sex, apologizing for his hurtful words, insisting that she is breaking a vow with God by filing for divorce. And he is getting in shape so he will be handsome for her when he gets out, which he promises will be within a year because the courts, those fools, fucked up and he's going to beat this rap. Meanwhile, he wants her to know, "I began a regimented exercise program into which, although I still do a lot of weight work, I have now incorporated a greater amount of aerobic and mobility (stretching) and flexibility exercises and I have benefited tremendously . . . Patrick and these other fools are just in awe . . . My muscle tone is better than it ever has been and my purpose was and is to be in the best shape possible when I leave here so that we will have many good years together to catch up on all we have missed." The arguments, vows and claims twirl off the page. "No Lady," he lectures, "it is true LOVE and you cannot simply shut it off as you would a light switch and go on with your life." A hand keeps reaching off the page to grab the reader's throat, to command full attention and obedience. A moral hand clutching a Bible. "A somewhat funny joke," he offers, "that I want to pass on: 'Nothing lasts forever—except Herpes and AIDS.' People tend to joke about such things but not only is this true but I somehow think these were created on purpose to put a stop to the casual sex predominant in our society today as it is chiseling at the cornerstone of life itself, the family. Both these diseases are abominations on mankind, right? And where do we read of abomination and such? Right again!"

I devour the letter. For long moments, I become clinical. Then I snap alert and realize it is a real cry from a real human being. I wince when he promises his wife that he will get contacts and rid himself of the ugly glasses he knows she finds unattractive. I am invading what little privacy a man locked on death row can still possess and I do not approve of my prying eyes. Then I go back to my reading.

The letter failed and his wife became a nonperson to Michael Poland, just as his brother Patrick had been banished for disobedience. Control can be a deadly drug, but once addicted it is a hard habit to kick. Outside the pinned curtains, there across the road, Michael Poland has five hours to live. His attorneys are going through their swan songs. So far the authorities have doubted this claim. They suspect he is faking his condition. I don't think it's that simple. Michael Poland has proven he will pay almost any price to feel in control. Acting incompetent, denying the state's power to snuff out his life will leave him in the saddle as the poison flows through his veins. He has finally planned the perfect heist and this time he is stealing his sense of self and keeping it out of harm's way. This time no bodies will float to the surface, this time no brother will confess, this time no woman will leave him. This time he will wall all of us off and disappear into his own serenity.

I still think of my dead, of all those women and children left slaughtered at the hands of strangers. They have stayed with me since my time covering crime for a daily newspaper. I still live in the same town and for me, it is studded with kill sites—lonely desert trees where a child's bones were finally found, alleys where dawn found a woman naked and cold and cut to hell. I do not think of their killers, not a bit. There is no anger in me about these men, and as it usually happens, they are all men. I don't know exactly why I can still taste grief but can't reach the place of anger.

For years I told people about some of these men, how I believed they were evil and did not have the right to exist. And then I would add my arguments against capital punishment and leave the matter where it always ends up: inconsistent but actual. And as I sit here in the Blue Mist Motel watching the hours slowly pass, sit here close by the room where Bobby Moormann carved up his mom, sit here with the curtains closed and the purr of the air conditioner, I get no closer. Revelation does not come. Nor revulsion. Perhaps I am experiencing some kind of denial but I do not think so. I have read up on the choreography of prison executions and I know where to go and what awaits me. Two people who have witnessed earlier executions here have walked me through what will be my afternoon.

I would be more apprehensive if I faced a three o'clock dental appointment. My pulse is normal, my mind unclouded. There has been a slight toll to pay: for the last four nights I have been restless and I am told I have talked in my sleep. This inner turmoil does not surprise me. But I did not expect this numbness, this boredom. I leave the room and walk to the Coke machine and buy a bottle of Diet Coke. Then I look up at the palms and notice one seems to have set with dates and the others have not. For a moment I speculate that one is female and the others are male. But then I notice the big ones are a different species. For a brief instant, I feel alert. Then the pall returns. The air is hot and stale and feels of dust. The Coke is cool.

I go back to the room. I remember that it is Bloomsday in Ireland and for a moment I want a Guiness Stout. It is two hours and thirty-two minutes until the scheduled execution. For the first time, I notice that two huge identical prints hang on the room's walls, each containing zoological drawings of Indian sandpipers and some snipes.

We are separated: one room for the press, one for kin of the victims, one for the Poland family. I am with the family now. The entry was awkward, prisons always bristle with locked doors, searches, and guards who would rather no one ever came to visit. Everyone is very courteous. I hate prisons and would not last a week in a cell. I cannot do time. I can't even go to an office. And now I am here. For the first time in seventeen years, I am wearing a watch, a cheap one bought for ten bucks in a drugstore. I figure it is my duty to time things today because time is what this is all about—twenty-two years on death row is too long, Michael Kent Poland living out his natural life is too long, at three p.m. he must go, just as I was ordered by the State of Arizona to be here no later than two. Florence itself has a thing about time. When they built the courthouse in 1891, they put up a clock tower and then ran out of money. Ever resourceful, they painted four clock faces on it and for one hundred and eight years it has always been 11:44 in Florence.

Frank Mowrey, the FBI guy who put the Poland boys on death row, has a thing about time also. He is against capital punishment. "Our job," he believes, "is to punish them on earth, and if we send them to the hereafter, they may not be ready." And Mowrey wants them to be ready. He is a firm believer in Christ and thinks that executing people touches on eternity and that eternity is "God's domain." Over the years he has kind of kept in touch with Pat Poland, even sent him a modern-language Bible with commentary. Pat, in turn, has invited Mowrey to his own execution, which is scheduled for the end of 1999 or early in 2000. Mowrey doesn't know if he can bear to watch such a thing. But he does plan to visit Pat before he goes—"to make sure his soul is okay." He doesn't hold out a lot of hope for Mike's soul. Pat Poland in his confession emphasized that they never planned to kill the guards, that things just got out of hand. He also said that a year later his brother Mike, during an argument, let on that the third bag was for Pat. After Pat confessed, the brothers had a falling out and have been kept separate ever since. They have not spoken in years.

Confessions are always self-serving, we all know that. Personal salvation is the very floor under confession. Mowrey is not sure of the truth—whether they planned to kill the guards or whether Mike intended to kill Pat also.

Three members of the Poland family arrive—two sons and a daughter-in-law. One son wears dark trousers, a white shirt and black loafers, his wife a white blouse and long black skirt. The other son is dressed in gray from his cowboy boots on up. One son and his wife read the Bible and hum hymns. Four prison employees watch us wait. They are among a hundred and twenty-five corrections officers detailed to this execution, which is always referred to as "the event." There is a buffet—cookies, roast beef sandwiches, cheddar and jack cheese, oranges, pickles, lemons, grapes, black olives, carrots, celery sticks, breadsticks, Diet Coke, Slice, bottled water and coffee. No one eats but the prison staff. A deputy warden chomps on cookies and goes over his guests' master list and checklist of protocols for the lethal injection. I have not eaten but can feel my guts roiling. I close my eyes, let my mind drift and block out the murmured words of the Polands. We wait until two-thirty, then we are moved to another building. We pass by signs that declare: SECURITY/GOOD SECURITY DEMANDS GREAT ATTENTION TO DETAIL/GREAT SECURITY REQUIRES EVEN MORE!! They seem to have come straight from the mind of Michael Poland. Then we wait some more and at about ten after three are hauled off to the killing ground.

The room is small and fifty-two witnesses stand on risers. The air feels close. No one speaks. I am in the front row. A curtain is pulled back and Michael Kent Poland lies eight feet away on a gurney parallel to us but separated by a thick pane of glass. He lifts his head slightly, turns and smiles at his family. He seems to mouth the words "I love you." A black chest strap holds down his torso, his legs are covered by a sheet, leather straps pin his arms. Two tubes lead through the gray tile wall and a gray flap hangs over the opening. The needles are in his far arm, out of sight. A square of one-way glass sits above the tubes so that the operators can observe. Reflections of the witnesses dance on this glass over Poland's body. The warden comes out and asks Poland if he has any last words. A mike dangles from the ceiling just above his face. Poland says, "I'd like to know if you are going to give me lunch afterward. *I'm really hungry.* Can't think of anything else." He smiles again in his sons' direction. A deputy warden comes out and reads his death warrant. Then he leaves. Thirty seconds later the injection begins. The event is running twelve minutes late. Poland flinches ever so slightly, his lips part, his breathing becomes somewhat labored. In less than sixty seconds no signs of life are evident. In two minutes he is declared dead. It is 3:14 p.m. June 16, 1999. The curtain is pulled shut by a woman guard who has been crouching on the floor.

The curtain is a deep blue, so is much of the wall and the ceiling is a light bright blue like the bottom of a swimming pool, the color scheme of the Blue Mist Motel.

The sun slams my body into the ground in the prison parking lot. I am alive, Michael Poland, unrepentant, is dead, state-certified. The thing was very clean, the gray scrubbed tiles, the fluorescent lighting, the white sheets on the gurney, the props from the world of healing. I stand in the heat and feel cold. I watched and feel dirty for the watching. I have no suggestions, except skip the buffet or at least go light on the roast beef sandwiches.

I have returned to my room. Just before Poland's event, one of his lawyers visited him in the holding cell off the killing ground. All the petitions had been denied. Poland asked the lawyer when he'd be coming back. The attorney said he wouldn't be. Poland asked, "Why not?" So he died still confident in his own peculiar faith. I turn to one more letter. I've been saving this one for myself so that when Michael Poland is dead, I will have a message from Michael Poland alive.

On June 4, 1999, Poland wrote to one of his sons and daughter-in-law and little granddaughter. He was in good form. The family had sent him a photograph of his grandkid with some words penned on it. In the first paragraph he takes control: it "had black ink spots all over it as it looks like the ink was still wet when you sealed it. No big thing really, but I wanted you to know all the same so if you use that pen in the future just wait a bit till it dries, OK Lady?"

The letter is handwritten. He is isolated from other prisoners now and under a deathwatch. Only a son is allowed visits. Michael Poland touts a book on great scientists, recommends a Bible reading. "Society would be better served," he says, "if people would remember that there are no 'absolutes,' no black and white, but rather varying shades of gray and that no one's life should be judged by a single act or moment. As Mark Twain wrote, 'People are like the moon, they each have their dark side.' Just something to make you go, H M M M !"

He has twelve days to live unless his will kicks in but he seems not to believe it. He talks about the limited visiting now and how the warden won't budge on the matter. "We'll just have to wait," he advises, "until this thing is over and they move me back and you'll be able to visit again as before and I won't be on 'isolation' any longer. It's no big deal, so don't even bother yourself about it as it'll just be another week or so and then I'll be seeing your smiling face again."

They accidentally cut the roots on the big mesquite, the one that towers over the ashes of my friend in my backyard. It happened this way. A concrete pad had to be poured and they dug out for a footing, but then they hit caliche. They went at the rocky ground with hammer and tongs and the roots got severed. It was spring and the leaves were lime-green and fresh and newly opened to drink the sun. Suddenly they died, half the tree or more fell into a deathlike coma and panic raced through my body. Life seemed to be ending. I laid on the hose and gorged the tree on endless succor. Nothing seemed to happen for weeks. And then nubs appeared and the buds swelled and ever so slowly it came back from the edge of death and tasted the light once more. I would stand out there in the evening, my ears keening for a sound. Finally I could hear, ever so faintly, what I sought, and then it grew louder, the sucking, the violent sucking. We were made to water trees and not to sever roots. We are a species for spring, not fall. We hate the winter.

I'm going to pour a drink. I bought the bottle before the event. After all, it's Bloomsday, and while I'm not a fan of *Ulysses*, I still remember the power of reading its final pages, Molly Bloom's monologue that eddies into love and ends saying, yes, yes, yes. I'm still against capital punishment and I'm still against murder. And Michael Kent Poland died still in control, a drug injected into his body long before the State of Arizona got its hands on him. Cecil Newkirk and Russell Dempsey have been avenged. Seventeen of their relatives came to the killing, including one of the widows. I am not immune to this desire of blood for blood.

When I first got the invitation to the execution, I would joke with people that I was against capital punishment but in Michael Kent Poland's case, I might be willing to make an exception. I was wrong.

But what I think doesn't matter. We've got our blood up. And nothing is going to stop this business for a good long while. On the evening news the execution is the third story and rates eighteen seconds. Poland is the sixth to go this year—breaking a record set by Arizona in 1943. Back at the end of February and first week of March, two brothers were dispatched, one after the other like boxcars on some mystery train. And out here we've got a bunch more stacked up like cordwood. There is a nationwide backlog of human resources available for this work, and day by day more seem to arrive, faster than they can be killed.

There is no succor in using words with clinical coldness. A man is dead, a man who did not deserve to live and yet lived a life, and the state, my representative, has killed him, and nothing has been accomplished except the preparation of a buffet, the overtime for a horde of prison guards, the coldness of the death chamber.

It is possible to learn nothing and yet finally know something. And this thing I finally know is something drummed into me from my earliest years. This thing is something my mother told me as a child. It is too simple and plain to address the many issues. But it is all I have now, the one thing in my mind. My body aches, I do not know why, but my body aches and the pain is both dull and throbbing as I cling to this one thing my mother told me.

So I sit here with a glass of red wine and a four-letter word rides in my mind.

Love.

The word rises in my mind like a thunderhead. I spit the blood from my mouth. The curtains close.

Patrick Poland dies by lethal injection on Wednesday, March 15, 2000. The first taste of chemicals hits him at 3:03 in the afternoon and he is pronounced dead at 3:07. I sit in the yard, the calla lilies are in bloom, the mesquite coming into leaf, the air rocking with birdsong. The sun falls in gentle waves and I don't drink.

The day before at the clemency hearing—an appeal to the State of Arizona's executive branch since all judicial avenues had been pretty much exhausted—an unusual outpouring occurred. The two federal attorneys who had put the Poland brothers on death row, and Frank Mowrey, the FBI agent who had hounded them onto death row, jointly filed a single-spaced eight-page letter beseeching the Arizona Board of Executive Clemency for mercy. The letter had unusual force because the key prosecutor, A. Melvin McDonald, a Reagan appointee, had earlier made time in his busy schedule to attend Michael Poland's execution, seventeen years after he'd tried the case.

They based their plea on the fact that Patrick was dominated by Michael and that Patrick had expressed remorse and been a model prisoner. And because Patrick had been savagely beaten as a boy and this fact was never entered into consideration during the sentencing phase of the trial. The two prosecutors and Frank Mowrey confessed such matters were unknown to them at the time and did not come into the light of day until years later, when Patrick and Sally Ann, Michael's wife, finally broke free of the older brother's domination. The letter gingerly touched on this secret past, on how the father would take Patrick when he was five and choke him until the child blacked out. How he also, from time to time, smashed the boy's ribs, nose, collar-bone and other bones. How he wouldn't take his boy to the doctor for such minor matters. Once he broke Patrick's leg and ankle and even then fought getting his son to care. There is almost a wistfulness in the letter as the two prosecutors and the retired FBI man admit that the father had seemed perfectly normal to them at the time of the arrest and the trials.

As a teenager Patrick ran away. He ran to Michael's house. Michael took up the beatings where the father had left off. The letter does not detail the emotional abuse but it mentions that Patrick has a fraternal twin brother who also ran away as a teenager, but he ran to a brother living in California who was an architect, a brother who treated him as, well, a brother. And today this twin brother is also an architect. The image hangs there as a suggestion of what might have been.

But what the letter doesn't talk much about is Michael and his experiences with his father. In fact, Michael is constantly described in the letter as the essence of evil. But Michael as a teenager also ran away to live with a brother, and no one seems to know or talk about what he ran away from.

No matter. The clemency board was unswayed. And the execution went smoothly, like clockwork. On the gurney before the injections began, Patrick said, "I'm sincere. I'm sorry for the pain and suffering I have caused. I do thank you for your forgiveness."

He said to his girlfriend who was watching, "And I ask the woman I love to remember I will always love her."

When the poison hit, Patrick Poland jerked his head four times. In the desert where he died, the number four is held to be sacred by some of the Native American cultures. But perhaps this head jerking, this four-beat banging of his skull, was simply a happenstance and of no significance. Just as the beatings mattered not at all to the clemency board. Just as the life of his fraternal twin turned out so very differently.

In the instant before his final spasm into death, he turned to his girlfriend and mouthed, "I love you."

Then he blew her a kiss.

Love.

Her blue eyes blaze from her eighty-five-year-old face surrounded by tinted auburn hair. The gnarled hands belie her quick tongue. Evie Dubrow came into the movement in 1937, and now she sits in the arena in Los Angeles taking in the tired words from the podium like nectar. I am squatting in the aisle by her chair and listen hungrily for some rumble from the days of sit-down strikes, lockouts and clubs on the picket line. But they do not come from her. She is the happy warrior, the veteran of early service in the Americans for Democratic Action, the garment workers' union, and as a lobbyist scurrying around Capitol Hill. She likes Al Gore because she liked Al Gore's dad. She liked Barry Goldwater though he'd sometimes stop her in the hall and say, hey, I can't be with you on this vote.

She is the tonic in the hall of a dead movement, a large part of a century sitting primly and gaily amidst the fruits of her labor. When I listen to her, I cannot hear the rock hit the bone, or the sucking sound as the marrow is consumed.

That is the value of the arena full of labor ghosts, to block the eyes and ears. They are the guardians of some kind of fallen system of income distribution, the hagglers over pay envelopes and dues. And they sit in this cavern without a window on the outside world, and if they win, people called workers get a bigger slice of some pie, and if they lose, these same workers get less. No one talks about the bakery where the pies come from, the ovens of the economy. It is sacred now and there is not a single questioning voice left in this arena. They fatten within state capitalism and are content. I crouch by Evie and the huge faces boom from giant screens and the words fall like raindrops. I feel the thing buried beneath the building, the soil, the muck, the bones, the glowing magma crushed and burning in the heart of the globe. Deep beneath my feet there is something permanent and volatile, the forces of life, but here on the surface there is simply a bookkeeping exercise with a division of the spoils and nothing fundamental exists.

I cling to some primitive feeling that gases swirl about on the skin of the earth and feed living tissue and there is only so much of this tissue that can be sustained. That minerals lurk in the hide of the earth, and there are only so many of these peculiar molecules that can be found and gouged from the hide. That fish swim in the sea and only so many can be murdered and devoured before the seas go still and dead. That even a mesquite can reach only so far into the ground before its energy is spent and it can go no farther. That there are limits and that simply discussing a division of the spoils ignores the limits of the treasure house.

I want to grab a pickax and start hacking through the floor of the arena. I am among the cannibals and the black kettle is glowing.

So I am out of sorts.

Love, I don't know what it means, but I roll the word around in my mouth. Love is the answer. Love is eternal. Love is lust—no, can't say that anymore. Lust is not even lust. Hack through the floor, shoot a bazooka through the walls, break on through to the other side, find the union maid, feel the roots coursing through the earth, walk into the farmyard and have the old lady strip me and boil my clothes. Cut the rope swinging off the pipe.

I leave Evie to her labor pleasures and I go out onto a patio where a fat cook from the snack bar sits all in white and gobbles his cigarette as union heavyweights in very good suits consult their cell phones and make plans for good dinners.

I sink into a chair and soak up the sun and accept the wonder of it all. A weary woman sits across from me. Her dad was union, she is union. Her kids are a blank. She is UAW out of Detroit, she is black, she is an organizer and she is worn down by the success of it all.

She tells me not to sit in the sun. I ignore her.

She tells me that she visited Tijuana once, just a hop, skip and a jump south of where we sit, and it damn near broke her heart. She left the tour of the American-owned factories in the Mexican border city and went into a home and found a family living in one room.

She tells me, "It brought back memories, lots of memories, of my childhood in the early forties." And then she falters at the memories of being a black person in a city where no one wanted black people around and the filth and hunger of the lean times.

She tells me now, "These kids walking around with hip-hop clothes, chains drooping from their pants, cell phones clipped on their pockets—union wages paid for those things."

She stops talking at this point and looks wistful.

I understand. That is why I want to hack through the floor of the arena and find the earth and then in the earth find the root and then follow the root until I hear a sucking sound and feel the flow yet again. Two things I believe: the past is not over. The future is not over.

The present is the real question. It may be over.

5

He is barely a fable as the nicotiana waves its tassels of yellow flowers in the afternoon breeze. The sap is rising with the spring and the small patio flares with the orange of the *hierba azul*, the maroon red of the salvia, the flaming nectar cups of the chuparosa. A humming-bird hangs over the blooms and nearby the Queen's Wreath, what the people call San Miguelito, struggles up the rough wood fence and lashes its tendrils to whatever it can reach. A few days ago in an arroyo in Sonora, I saw a forty-foot paloverde completely topped and smothered by this vine. The force of life is strong now, and the air rich with sex and hope.

I am barely listening as I sit in the three o'clock heat with a drink in hand and the old cop talks of his days prowling the town's *calles*. That is why I almost miss the first mention of the man who is so distant now, he can hardly cling to our memory. I am more intent upon watching the buds form on the stalks of the harrisia, a ropy cactus that erupts throughout the good heat with huge white night-blooming flowers like any respectable cereus. He says, "Did I ever tell you about the night I was on patrol and was creeping around the Yaqui village, Old Pascua, looking for drunks and heroin addicts. I'd just started with the sheriff's department then. It was about three a.m. when I'll be damned I see this tree on fire."

I come half alert but it is hard because I can hear the sap rising in the fifteen-foot stalks of the nicotiana, and this gurgle and surge of life pounds against my ears with its lust. It is marginal here, like all of us.

We are this problem area of two nations, a void of hard mountains and harder deserts. No one has ever really known what to do with us or our ground except make it a border between two imaginary entities called nations. And into this nowhere have poured the rejects of life, the birds, the plants—nicotiana has crawled up from South America and gone feral in the arroyos and woebegone places—the animals, and of course the people.

The cop talking is a good example. He is half Anglo, half Mexican and his name is Arturo Carrillo Strong. We have been friends for years. His great-great-grandfather came over here about 1800. He was the wild boy of his family back in Spain, always chasing the women according to stories handed down. So they got him a place in the king's army, and he was shipped to the frontier of New Spain, a place we now call Sonora, in the hope he would straighten out. When he died, he was said to have had thirty or forty wives. This must be true since his descendants are everywhere on this ground. The family that issued from his loins has stuck and now runs deep in countless pueblos of this sheet of heat riding between the pretensions of Mexico and the United States. So the cop with his Spanish and his English, with his Mexican garden and old adobe house in a modern American city, with his remembered badge and obsession with old family recipes, is latent in the blood of this place.

This is happening in a dreamtime of mine. Art is in his late sixties in this dreamtime, and the tale's spinning goes back somewhere to the early or mid-fifties. He pauses, then confirms the range of dates, because he remembers that he joined the force in 1953 and went plain-clothes as a narc in 1956. So it has to be in that trough of national energy at the end of the killing in Korea. He's smiling as he talks, enjoying the memory. He's got a can of Budweiser in his hand, a full shock of gray hair, and he's deep in the riches of memory.

"So I rolled down the dirt road in Old Pascua," he says, "and came to the dance ground just before the church. This whole damn mesquite was on fire, and I could see a burning man hanging from a limb."

Naturally, he called this in on the radio. The burning tree.

What they found was pretty straightforward. About three a.m. a Yaqui man had gone to the mesquite before the church, really a *capilla* or chapel. He climbed the tree, fashioned a noose from rope, and sat on a limb. He doused himself with gasoline. He drank a can of lye. He struck a match. He put a .22-caliber pistol to his head. My friend saw him in the night burning out against the darkness. He did not live.

I slosh down some wine from my glass and out of the corner of my eye catch that hummingbird hovering again at the *hierba azul*.

"Shit," I say with a smile, "he did a hell of a thorough job."

Arturo laughs and agrees. He'd tangled with Yaquis before, once having to call a couple of cars of backup as he wrestled down a huge and determined drunk. Tucson was simpler then and much more Mexican and Indian in those days, before the huge post–World War II wave of Anglo refugees really kicked in. The Yaquis were refugees also, having come up beginning around 1900 and 1910 from their homeland in Sonora when the Mexican government stole a march on the Nazi future and launched a full-blown policy of genocide to get the twentieth century off to an appropriate start. They had been constantly at war with their official government since the 1820s and the fires never really banked until the 1930s and still give off heat to this day. The Americans took to the Yaquis since they were dirt-cheap working fools and gave them some land just north of downtown for a squatters' community, Old Pascua. They tried sending in missionaries to shape them up and make them pale churchgoing Americans, but it was a bust. The Yaquis listened and took the food or blankets or literature and went on about their lives as they had always done. By 1928 the town figured they'd turn them to some kind of account and started issuing pamphlets on their huge Easter celebrations since to the Anglos, the Yaquis were crazed with their primitive faith and rituals. In time a cottage industry grew up at the nearby university studying the Yaqui ways and then studying why they seemed to cling to their ways so tenaciously. Shelves began to fill with books about them. The Yaquis tantalized the Anglos because they seemed never to change in a world where the Anglos were seared by the velocity of the changes unleashed by their mutating technologies. And yet the Yaquis were extremely flexible, changing nations, jobs, damn near everything except a sense of who and what they were. And they never paid taxes. Never paid a *centavo* to Spain, never paid a *centavo* to Mexico, and now never paid a cent to the United States of America. They just went on about their business and the scholars scratched their heads for a couple of generations trying to fathom exactly what this business was.

I suck in the scent off the flowers, the hundreds of flowers in the small patio squatting between two mud buildings in the old barrio, and still the stench of burning flesh floods the air. This river of blood. Not gore, but the blood of kinship, the tug of common feelings rising from common ground. This sensation has been growing in me for years, probably decades. I look at maps and can no longer make out the lines signifying boundaries. I look in faces and less easily file the skins into races and cultures. I touch a leaf and think it is skin, stare into the eye of the beast and see a mirror. Río de la Sangre surrounds me with its flow and I ride the bloody currents.

The authorities throw up a metal wall south of me and say this will stop the march of the peoples across the line the governments have drawn in the baking dirt. Soon Mexicans erect ladders on their side of the wall and charge folks on the prowl for the use of the ladders as they hop over the barrier. A Central American arrives at the fabled line, climbs a ladder, and either tries to cheat or more probably does not know he must pay. The Mexicans rip his guts up with knives and he lands in an American hospital, where he can face a high-tech dying. In three months, the border town south of me tallies fifteen hundred knife and gunshot wounds at the public clinic. My head is full of these little items, these tiny bits and pieces. I read two or three newspapers a day and wear out my eyes on dull columns of economic statistics.

I snap alert—he is talking again. The next day, he is saying, he went back to the village. He had to take a tape measure and get the inches and feet of where this was and that was for his final report. He pulls his squad car onto the dance ground before the *capilla* and gets out with his instruments and his clipboard. There must be a report, it is the procedure. He ambles over to the charred tree and then he notices a white line in the dirt, a big white circle encasing the scene of the lye drinking, the gas dousing, the hanging, the bullet in the brain. Well, no matter, the measurements must be made. Suddenly, he feels a hand on his arm and looks, and there is a Yaqui shaking his head. He instantly understands he is not to cross the white line. He tries to explain about the measurements, the importance of the report, but the head shakes no at him again.

"Exorcism?" I ask.

"Yeah," he says, "something like that. An old woman, one of those *brujas*, had made the line with some kind of powder, and nobody was supposed to cross it or fuck with it. There was something evil around that tree, and the line would keep it in there, that's what I figured."

He laughs again at the memory. I do not ask him if he persisted and finally got his measurements. For some reason, that fact does not matter to me. If he persisted, I know what happened. The people would figure it's his ass and fair warning had been given. If he gave up and went away, the boys back at the sheriff's department would figure the hell with it and the hell with these fucking Yaquis. The village was a pain to the authorities anyway, a cesspool of booze and heroin. Besides, the cop had been raised on Yaqui tales. His people had suffered from the endless wars, from the raids and the killings. Cajeme, known also by his Mexican name of José María Leyva, was the great nineteenth-century war leader of the Yaqui people. When the cop was a child, the kinswoman who raised him would mark any misbehavior on his part with the epithet *"¡Indio Cajeme!"*

Crazy bastard, that is what the smile on his face says now, crazy fucking Indian. Jesus, he rolls on, the lye, the gas, the rope, the bullet. He sure as hell meant to do a bang-up job, don't you think?

Yes, I agree, he made sure he'd succeed. But succeed at what? I start peppering him with questions, the body flaming off the tree limb has pushed aside for the moment the flowers, the sap rising, the hummingbirds at the nectar, the Inca doves walking the ground nearby in their dull-witted search for seeds. He looks at me curiously as if to ask, what does it matter?

I haven't got a good reply. I'm leery of mentioning the river of blood. I can feel the river but as yet I cannot map it or spell out all its tributaries or describe the sea toward which it courses. I no longer think I am living in a world that is dying. Now I fervently believe it is being born. The birth is hard, the labor pains sharp, the medical assistance minimal. But still the birth is real and I feel big with it. What is being born is a new place fashioned from discarded, abused and tortured ground. What is being born is a new people recruited from trash, from rejects, from fugitives, from refugees, from the nameless and faceless and frightened and angry. And this people is desperate and bold and surging around me. I find them everywhere. They lack the passports, they have nowhere to go. They are fuel for the fire of this creation.

Arturo asks, "Why are you so interested in this case?"

I consider talking about Navojoa, a town on the Río Mayo. They are killing two or three a day there. The women march at night to protest the violence, the candles in their hands giving a glow to their faces. The store owners, after surviving a schedule of two or three robberies a day, are now all armed. Awhile back a state cop strolled into a store. The women running the place had been robbed twice that day. The cop said, give me your money. She threw up her hands in disgust. He shot her. The government throws a hundred *federales* into the town. They announce things have calmed down. Bank robberies have soared in Hermosillo, Sonora. Car theft is off the charts in Tucson. Juárez is a bloodbath. El Paso is a fort. Still the people stream into this blazing place, they come from the south and the west and the north and the east. They seem to have no place else to go. They are on fire, their faces are scarred. The river flows on. And the rivers are dead or dying in Chihuahua, the water is going bad everywhere, poisoned with bad chemicals, human feces, strange bugs. Cholera has returned, so has tuberculosis. The birth is very hard.

I tell him I don't know why I am interested, it's just something about the story of the man sitting on the mesquite limb with his gear all ready for the start of his voyage.

"Who was he?" I ask.

"Oh, Christ, it's been forty years," Arturo tells me. "How can I remember the name? Some of the details have stuck. He was a young guy, maybe twenty-five or so. He'd been in World War II, gone in real young, probably lied about his age like a lot of them did then. He'd gotten the shit shot out of him, that's for sure, and come back with a helluva lot of medals. A genuine hero. Christ, when he died, the Yaquis collected a couple of thousand dollars and planned a huge funeral.

"See," Arturo continues, "the thing was, the guy was a junkie. He'd gotten hooked in the military hospitals from all those wounds, you know, and then he'd returned to Old Pascua and couldn't kick. So he'd become a junkie and was ashamed of himself, and that's why he killed himself."

The name? Ah, God, it's been too long, he can't remember the name. But he'll never forget that night, the damn tree firing up into the sky and him dangling there.

The fire is not that unusual, I discover. Rosalio Moisés was a Yaqui who died in 1969. He lived on the Río Yaqui, he lived in Tucson, he lived in Texas, many places. This is not unusual. At one point during the wars, Yaqui communities stretched from Yucatán to southern California. Moisés filled his later years with writing down his life in spiral-bound notebooks. He had a belief that when a person is born, a candle is lit, and the person lives until the candle gutters out. Eventually, his book was published under the title *The Tall Candle*. But this, I suppose, confused some readers and now it is in print as *A Yaqui Life*. When Moisés was a small boy in Hermosillo, a man named Joaquín Perez walked to a hill outside of the city. He gathered together a pile of wood and then, Moisés writes, "climbed on it and burned himself up." Nobody saw this act coming. The next day the man's mother came to Moisés's home and the woman and his grandmother talked for a very long time. The mother said her son lately had been quiet and thoughtful but he did tell her he had done many bad things. Perhaps he had murdered without cause, Moisés speculates, or had hurt poor people or been guilty of "stealing eggs." The maestros in the Yaqui ceremonies, he explains, tell people that if they are bad, they will have to burn to earn salvation. "I have heard," he continues, "of other Yaquis who burned themselves up for salvation."

Ah, but spring is here. Life is good, I can taste pollen on my tongue. The birds are doing courtship on the limbs, the male hummingbird is inscribing a huge arc in the air as he tries to woo a female. I touch my face and feel the burning. Now we are the burned ones, *quemados*.

I live in a world that I imagine, and this imaginary world is the real world. Two nations claim my world but neither can control it. The boundaries are not set, both the land and the people here are in flux but already it consumes Arizona, New Mexico, Sonora, Chihuahua, and a chunk of west Texas. The American government calls my world the Southwest, the Mexican government speaks of the North or Northwest. But then these voices and names come from the imaginary world, not the real one that envelops me. These imaginary worlds are dying, the wages sinking for decades, the policies of trade a shambles, the jobs withering like vines in a drought. I can sense their panic. They hire more and more police. They solemnly assert sovereignty. They outlaw plants that give my head pleasure. They present plans while the land recoils, rivers going bad and dry, forests shrinking on scalped mountains, roads becoming dilapidated, air going foul and dark. The heat also continues to rise, everyone here knows this, but it is a matter seldom discussed by the authorities. This new world I live in is the result not of design but of fate. Here the lies of the governments clatter to the ground, and here the suffering ground devours the illusions of the nation-states. They have brought us agriculture in the desert and called it a miracle. They have brought us slave wages in factories and called it the new future. They have brought us squads of killers in uniform and called it law and order. The people here have come of their own accord, feeling some horror that is etched on their faces. They have come from bad places to this very hard place. And here a future is rising from random parts and this future is the river of blood, commingling, warring, embracing and seeking. No one planned on this, in fact all the plans were designed to make it impossible. But it is happening nonetheless.

The light is failing as she leaves the house to walk the dogs along the edge of the bog. This is in Chorizo, that village that is a home for my mind. The two border collies romp ahead as they cut into the federal wildlife refuge. The line on the map that officially separates nations is five or six miles south and studded with motion sensors. For a week or so now, the area has been infested with cops and agents. At night she hears the chopper overhead and sees the craft's spotlight splashing around on the hills of mesquite, oak and rock. There have been regular arrests and no one is sure why. The traffic in drugs here runs pretty much out in the open and provides the basic cash flow in the hamlet. People do coke on the bar top of the saloon and smoke joints without a thought. For a century, the nearby hills have been gouged with smuggler routes. Once it was rustled horses and cattle. Then with Prohibition, booze came north. Always there is the traffic in guns going south to eager hands. No one really thinks about this trade, it is part of the natural flow of the land.

As she moves through the tall grass of the bog, she sees a pickup truck ahead, the doors open as if people leaped out in a panic and fled. A man is standing by it who works for the wildlife refuge. He is every excited and agitated. She ambles over and sees sixty kilos of cocaine in the bed of the truck. The man explains that he saw this truck going into the bog and wondered what they were up to at that time and in that place. He says, stay here, I'm going to a phone to tell the authorities. And then in a brief while he returns with weapons to guard the truck. The light is going now and bats flap overhead snapping up insects. It is the heart of spring and everything is surging with life. The bog is a hotbed of endangered species and each day grows more electric as the land heals after centuries of human error and brutality. The woman looks at the load and thinks what two or three kilos would net her if she happened to stash them a hundred yards away in the growth.

The wait goes on and on. This seems odd. For weeks the ground has been seething with the authorities. After an hour and a half, the cops arrive. The sector, it seems, was totally empty tonight, not one cop assigned to it. That's about it. Except that the sixty-kilo load found in the federal wildlife refuge never appears in any newspaper. In fact, nothing that happened seems to surface outside that tight circle of people in the bog. On the street, the load would go for maybe

$300,000 wholesale. The authorities simply take it away and it is as if the load never existed and the night never happened.

The world they did not examine gains on them, a world stronger and harder than the dreams of their economies. I read their papers and hear their words. I understand their plans. Have more and more people make more and more things to grow this scheme they call the economy. They have left how to divide the economy to the magic ways of the marketplace. And they forgot that the earth is finite. So the numbers on their charts grow, the units they measure for wealth grow, but the number of poor grow yet faster. The fields erode, the irrigation districts go to salt, the forests become stumps and the air sags with chemicals, the wells sink, the ditches reek of sewage, the rivers kill, the fish die, the weather shifts and no one trusts the skies any longer. I am told it is all more complicated than this but I do not think it really is.

In my dreamtime, they are rolling down that highway into Mexicali, Baja Norte, and they are well prepared. They have automatic rifles, fragmentation grenades, a load of marijuana and other trifles. There are six or seven of them when the *federales* hit. This they did not anticipate. The men with the load and the grenades and other weapons are all official state policemen from Sonora. In fact, they carry written authorization from their commander. The bust makes headlines in the Mexican newspaper—it never appears in the American press. They are said to have come from Culiacán, Sinaloa—a legendary drug and murder center in Mexico— where they have done some work for one "Guero" Palma Salazar, the head of a cartel there. Such names of course change from time to time as people are demoted by bomb and pistol, but the structure is fairly durable.

The next day something predictable happens: the state police chief of Sonora announces that the arrested men are not really members of his force. Well, some of them are, he says, but not all of them. He does not explain the official letter of authorization they carry. Then a few days later photographs of two of the men appear on the front page of the Mexican newspaper. Their faces look very battered. The men are complaining of torture at the hands of the federal police. It is difficult to decide what to make of this charge. There are varying estimates of the level of police torture commonly available in Mexico. One human rights group feels eighty percent of all arrested people are tortured, another group asserts that ninety percent are tortured. Perhaps the alleged policemen are in the favored ten or twenty percent who are not tortured and their claim is a blatant lie to besmirch the reputation of the federal force. Still, their faces in the photographs look very battered.

As for the cops busted with the grenades, marijuana and automatic weapons, they simply disappear from view.

What I imagine is a real world where the policies of governments relentlessly produce poor people and these poor people flee and flood my ground. This is a thought that must almost be driven into the brain like a nail, lest it slip away. It goes against the rhetoric of states and against the unconscious dreams of all of us. We know words such as *recession* and *depression* for different degrees of economic stalls. But we have yet to mouth a word like *reversal* or *collapse*. Even in Mexico, with five hundred years of bitter experience, the thought is difficult to keep in mind. Given the projected increase of human numbers and the absolute inability to increase meaningfully the land surface of the earth, the future seems obvious, and this future is, if one goes by units of wealth as now measured, a future of decline. By decline I mean less wealth per capita, more malnutrition per capita, more infant mortality and more violence. There is no cybernetic highway that leads us away from this place, this future. In fact, the application of computers will most likely accelerate our movement toward this burning future because it reduces the number of people needed for work and redefines work in a way that eliminates its possibility for growing numbers of unskilled and uneducated human beings.

It is dawn now in the garden, the gray-light time when the birds come to the seed and suet and nectar, the moment before the bright light sears over the mountain and vaporizes the shadows. The world is soft now, the doves hungry but cooing. A candle flickers before a stone slab sculpted into an image of the Virgin of Guadalupe, and by her sits a bust of the outlaw *santo* Jesus Malverde. Scattered about are various Mexican and Indian wooden figures of deer, birds, rabbits, bulls and other creatures. There is a harmony at this time of the dawn that succors doubt and feeds hope. The river of blood pouring all around me seems benign, inevitable, and something to be accepted.

I live in a war machine looking for a war. The economy of the nation is locked into a military budget, a huge debt incurred in feeding the military structure of the state, and vast entitlements proffered to the populace lest they question this grotesque and distorted economy created by a half century of a wartime footing. For years income distribution has been skewed toward the rich and now, since government functions on this footing, it never considers this fantasy land as anything but absolute reality. Every proposed solution turns out to be a way to shore up this structure (various trade treaties, numerous claims of new kinds of work, periodic slashing of budgets that do not impinge on the war machine). Mexico has achieved the same kind of central obsession without bothering with a huge military. It is a nation that starves everyone to feed a few cities and particularly the rich families in those cities. Mexico City's metropolitan area, for example, hosts about a quarter of Mexico's population but has 42 percent of the nation's jobs, 53 percent of the wages, 38 percent of the industrial plant value, 55 percent of all public investment, and 66 percent of its energy consumption. The rest of the nation gets the leavings, and part of their booty is that the average Mexican has one of the highest levels of toxic substances in his or her bloodstream recorded on the planet. For decades now, we have flogged ourselves with statistics that point out the world's treasures are not divided too fairly. The numbers change but always seem to stay the same: 22 percent of the world's population lives in the industrialized nations and they wolf down 60 percent of the food, 70 percent of the energy, 75 percent of the minerals and 85 percent of the lumber. None of us really knows where these numbers come from or how accurate they are but all of us sense they are basically true.

The river is rising and I can feel it. Among the Yaqui Indians there is a natural way to tell when the river is going to break its banks, flood and destroy and rearrange the world. A man will be moving through the dense forest that lines the Río Yaqui and it will be morning. He will be carrying his ax since he intends to cut wood. Then he will notice that the frogs are not in the water but high up in the mesquite trees. Then he will notice that rattlesnakes are not in the tall grass but hanging off limbs high up in the trees. He will head for high ground.

I see snakes in the trees, I notice the frogs climbing. I am sure that the river is rising, rising despite the drought, the plunging water table in the wells, rising. The banks are breaking up, the sides calving into the hungry stream. Sometimes I cannot hear, my ears are deafened by the blaring announcements that come from the national centers. Still even with this irritating noise I can hear the river rise, the river of blood roaring out there, this thing with no clear face or language or color. It is brown, it is white, it is black, it is yellow, it is a mix of all these things. It is English, it is Spanish, it is Right, it is Left, it is the gun, it is the candlelit march against violence. It is rising. The river is very old, no one really knows its age, and for a long time it has gone out of sight—perhaps underground. For a very long time it is said to have gone dry and become extinct. But now it is rising.

It is 1924 in Pascua village, that settlement of Yaqui refugees in my town. There are three sisters. The first to go is fourteen years old. She boils some coins in water and then drinks off the brew, the "money water." Soon she stops eating, her color gets dark and she becomes quite thin. Within two months she is dead. Her two sisters do the same and soon they are also dead. No one is sure why. The guess is that they are sad.

Men do not drink money water. Sometimes in the night, they'll get up and hang themselves from a tree before their homes. Or they walk to the railroad track, lie down and get crushed and sliced into pieces. If the river is up, they'll jump in and drown. There is always the bullet to the head. And the fire.

Of course, that was a long time ago. Money water may appeal to more people now.

I was raised in a world that was indivisible and one nation under God to boot. I can remember giving the pledge of allegiance in the public schools of Chicago as the dust still settled from World War II and then was suddenly kicked back up by that thing in Korea. The morning light was feeble through the coal soot of the city as we recited the pledge and the desks were very dark wood and carved deep with the initials of legions of first graders who had been interned here before us. It was truly a simpler world. We had our divine mission and squared off against godless Communism. We lived in a growing economy that magically was dispelling decades of strife by creating new loot. A map rode on the wall with rock-steady borders—except for the pesky matter of the captive nations in Europe that would soon be resolved and live happily forever in the shade of big mushroom clouds. No one worried about money water and no one quailed before mutating maps.

This solid time of pledges of allegiance and apparent order was obviously a freakish and small interlude in the thunder and change that were fundamental to this century. But no one knew that then, and few realize it now. With the collapse of colonialism in the sixties, the maps went berserk with new names and borders, but even this change was acceptable since we were confident that with aid and lessons the new nations would evolve to become like us. Africa, after the killing settled, would become a series of Norman Rockwell paintings with black faces. Asia, based on the changes in Japan, would become the same with a yellow tone. China had disappeared—been "lost" was the official explanation—and took up a lot of the map and very little of anyone's time. India was going to be England except that everyone would wrap a towel around his head. And so forth.

All this is gone now but it still dominates our minds. Separatist movements occur everywhere except South America. The future of the nation-state seems less certain as trade treaties and new entities of administering trade and currency not only seize some of their functions but sap key elements of their power. As we become one world, a global village, new forms of nationalism and localism erupt and no one seems to have seen this coming. In fact, we are almost incapable of admitting that it is happening. We have been trained to man the parapets to watch for the enemy without. We have been schooled to scout the horizon for aggression and this training has ill prepared us for revolt from within. We have no background in fragmentation of ground after our long history of the consolidation and absorption of ground. That is one reason why what is happening on my ground is either missed or denied. It simply does not fit the lessons drilled into us during our long slumber.

And yet the very nature of states now makes disintegration inevitable. To tick off the forces is easy. One, as the economies go global, capital ceases to respond to local control or desires. Two, as the populations continue to grow, economic growth becomes essential for the state because only jobs and food and shelter can in the end preserve them from their nominal subjects. And three, the global economy creates structural unemployment—meaning permanent elimination of jobs as opposed to cyclical ups and downs—because global corporations seek automation, low wages and fewer workers creating more profits. We now live in an economy that is quickly becoming global, and that economy produces wealth as it annihilates work and workers. For a state this is a problem; for a corporation it is not even an issue. There is no reason to believe these tendencies will change because of new plans or international meetings or matters of state. The changes will come from below and they will be violent changes wrought by displaced people. People who realize they have no future can be convinced to endure their suffering. But people who realize they have no present will kill. I live on the killing ground. The people with no present swarm around me. They are currently lost to view and are misfiled in the giant information systems. Some are buried alive under the title of illegal aliens, others are criminals, others are simply put on hold in a limbo called job retraining. Others disappear from view when their unemployment benefits run out and the statistical tables assume they have been hired somewhere. This goes on day and night and yet their numbers grow, their bodies are real, their footsteps can be heard in the night.

That is why the river of blood rises and flows and is unacknowledged. We have a mindset that refutes or ignores or absorbs any evidence that conflicts with our worldview that growing human numbers and the free movement of capital and work cannot help but benefit us all. We increasingly do not have even a vocabulary to discuss such matters. We can hardly even determine what is an import or an export anymore.

The priests arrived in 1617. The first revolt came in 1740, but it was brief and settled on Yaqui terms. The next revolt came in the 1820s and it may have never ended. All Yaqui wars are over land, and no Yaqui war is to expand their lands but to hold their lands. They have memories like elephants and the children are drilled in the ancient boundaries. How we draw our maps hardly matters. For them the boundaries are eternal and any occupation of their ground by others is temporary. All this comes from a tree that once talked to them. Deer also.

At one point the Mexicans made them an offer. The land of the Río Yaqui would be surveyed, plots laid out, irrigated waters divided so that every Yaqui got enough ground. The old men heard this offer, went off into the mesquites and talked, came back and said, "God gave us the river, and God did not give each Yaqui a piece of river."

It is 1936 or 1937, the old Yaqui man writing his life in the spiral notebooks cannot be sure anymore. All he remembers is that a woman is sad. Her father had been shot and killed at Vicam for murder. Somehow her mother was shot and killed also. The woman went and lived with a man, but it did not work out. Around midnight—no one remembers the year exactly, much less the day—the woman walked out into the brush and poured gasoline on herself. Then she struck a match. The old Yaqui man scribbling away in his spiral notebook thinks he knows why she burned herself up. She was *triste*, sad.

Ramón Corral is surprised, and he is a measured and powerful man who seldom feels or expresses surprise. He came to General Martínez's home in Guaymas, Sonora, with solid expectations. José María Leyva, Cajeme, had been captured April 12, 1887 and now is incarcerated in the Martínez house. Corral admits he thought he was going to meet "a corpulent Indian, silent and with a ferocious expression on his face." What he finds is a slender man of medium height "with an astute smile on his wide mouth, friendly and good-natured and communicative." Cajeme is fluent in Spanish and Yaqui and English, a man cultured by any standard for nineteenth-century Sonora. He is also the man who has kept the Mexican government at bay for more than a decade and kept the Mexican army in fear for the same length of time. He is not what Corral is prepared for and his life has shown he is not what this ground was, or is, prepared for. His Yaqui name means "He Who Does Not Drink." Cajeme is a contained man, of measured speech. For Corral he is in a sense the ultimate nightmare, the man who knows the world of Europeans perfectly and yet also is a master in the world beyond the grasp or imagination of the Europeans, the world of native people who move lightly and dangerously at the edge where the lamp light gives out and some other reality locks in.

Corral is intrigued and for days makes notes. He is prepared to record this life, he is a man with a historical bent. Corral is thirty-eight years old. He comes from Álamos, Sonora, the town whose silver strike in 1683 essentially bankrolled the settlement of Sonora and southern Arizona and provided the money and energy for the Spanish to reach north and found San Francisco. He is an intellectual, a journalist and one of three men who effectively run Sonora. He owns ranches, flour mills, lumber mills, the electric company and many other things. And he loves his state and toils in his spare time writing its history. Naturally, in this work he must consider the Yaquis, a people twenty or thirty thousand strong who form an iron wedge through the heart of the state. For generations they have been the indispensable laborers in the mines, ranches and farms, and for generations they have been the barrier to the development of the water-rich and land-rich Río Yaqui valley. He writes, "They [live] outside the law and are a perpetual threat for Sonora; moreover there exists [among them] a focus of corruption, a center of banditry that naturally enlarges its proportions . . . [Their lands] are a great unexploited source of wealth . . . that only needs the pacification of the tribes and the labor and intelligence of the civilized man to yield abundant fruits and change the face of the State."

There it is, the charge: the Yaquis block this Mexican state from its deserved future. "Neither the Yaquis," he continues, "or the Mayos [their neighbors and language cousins] can be considered entirely savage. Their religious customs are those of Catholicism." Also they work hard at many necessary trades in the state. In fact, as he writes in the 1880s, he knows that Sonora would economically collapse without Yaqui labor. So he writes on, "In a word, they are true working people." But that is not all. He goes on to explain: "Their independence of legitimate government, their semi-savage customs, the scarcity of civilizing elements [among them] which could infuse ideas of moral betterment and make apparent to them the benefits that subjection to laws and civil society promise; all this conspires to develop in them the evil passions, and each year that passes their inclination to rob, kill and destroy, to wandering, drunkenness, and the array of vices . . . is more vigorous." And of course, they refuse to give up their land and have fought the government to a standstill.

This is some of the baggage Ramón Corral brings to General Martínez's house for his interview with the Indian called Cajeme. It is all about government, civilization, order—the state. It is about the matters that two and a half decades earlier dragged the United States into a civil war that left six hundred thousand dead on the field. It is about the irresistible surge of progress, that religion of the nineteenth century, the dynamism that swallows ground and people and makes them interchangeable parts of vast nation-states, makes them into citizens. When Ramón Corral comes to the door, there is hardly a soul in Sonora who doubts any of this except the man he is about to meet and many of his twenty or thirty thousand fellow Yaquis.

Corral is very intelligent—three times he will serve as governor of Sonora and in 1902 he will become the vice president of Mexico—and he swiftly realizes he is dealing with a different kind of man than he planned upon meeting. He asks questions, he makes notes, he walks Cajeme through the byways of his life. And Cajeme is happy to oblige him.

We are in the heart of the spring now. One day a ring appears around the sun and instantly the Mexican newspaper reassures its readers. It interviews scientists who explain it is caused by particles of freezing water in the atmosphere and is perfectly natural and portends nothing, nothing at all. It does not mean the end of the world, nor does it herald a series of calamities.

His father came from Guiviris, his mother from Potam, villages along the Río Yaqui. Cajeme was born in Hermosillo in 1835. His first eight years passed in Bácum, one of the eight basic villages of the Yaqui people. The Yaquis had first brushed against the Spaniards in 1533, when a slaving raid cruised north into Sonora. The Spanish scouts found warriors arrayed before them and the two forces met on a large field. The Yaquis marched right toward the Spaniards and threw fistfuls of dirt into the air. They made surly expressions and flexed their bows. An old man stood out because he wore a black robe studded with pearls to form the images of dogs, birds, deer and other creatures. The two groups collided in the morning, and the old man's dress blazed like silver. He had a bow in one hand, a staff in the other, and he controlled the warriors. The Spaniards left. When the priests arrived in 1617, they found the Yaquis spread out along the river in tiny hamlets, and for the purposes of God and agriculture, they consolidated them into eight major villages that proved so durable that eventually the Yaquis confounded the eight villages with the very beginning of themselves as a people. An early priest concluded that the word *Yaqui* means "*el que habla a gritos*," the one who speaks in shouts.

Cajeme was born into a world still being born. Mexico had become independent of Spain in 1821 and since then the nation as a whole and Sonora in particular had hardly functioned as a state. Various coups occupied the elites of central Mexico, and the people in the north were left to poverty and Indian wars. In the 1820s a Yaqui insurrection had been led by Juan Banderas, who fought under the banner of the Virgin of Guadalupe and demanded all Mexicans and Spaniards leave the Yaqui lands. He formed alliances with other tribes and sought to cleanse Sonora of any and all nonnative people. Three years before Cajeme's birth, the Yaqui forces engaged the Mexican troops in battle, but on the third day, according to reports, the Virgin hid her face. Banderas was shot on January 7, 1832. The war continued like an underground fire in a coal seam, and Cajeme's parents, like many Yaquis, fled the river. So he was born in the leading city of Sonora because of Yaqui efforts to destroy such cities.

Soon they returned to the river and Bácum. Cajeme grew up in a Yaqui world learning the three hundred fifty miles of border to the Yaqui country—a geography memorized on the basis of major trees, big rocks and the like. He witnessed the elaborate ceremonies. He was told of the talking stick, given a dose of the native brand of Catholicism—insights such as the fact that when Christ was crucified, his mother turned herself into a tree so she could embrace her son during his agony. He would be taught songs like this one of the talking stick:

> Sometime in the past the tree talked.
> All the elders do not know of it,
> But, yes, some wise ones spoke of it.
> When the world was becoming new here,
> There was one who could hear the sounds of the tree.
> The one who could hear it,
> That one told about it.
> They were old things from long ago,
> But only one could hear it.
> That talking stick was a long time ago,
> When the earth was becoming new here.

The discovery of gold in California set off a migration of Sonorans to the fields and Cajeme's family joined this stampede. An American tried to rob them and there was a shooting. The gold fields were very hard and they made little or nothing. During this time Cajeme learned to speak, read and write English. By 1850 or 1851 they were back in

Guaymas, the port just north of the point where the Río Yaqui meets the sea, and for three years Cajeme went to school and perfected his Spanish. Such an education was unusual for any Sonoran, much less a Yaqui, and Cajeme's command of languages surely made him stand out. These little scraps are about all we know of his youth and they were gathered during his interviews with Ramón Corral in 1887. Cajeme comes to us uncontaminated by many facts.

In 1854 the world briefly burst into the backwater of Guaymas. A Frenchman, Count Gastón de Raousett-Bolbón, attempted to break Sonora off from Mexico in the favored nineteenth-century style of a military filibuster. Cajeme at seventeen joined the local troops, the Urbanos, raised to resist him. The count was executed on August 12, 1854, and Cajeme was a seventeen-year-old former schoolboy who had tasted blood.

He drifted south to Tepic in Nayarit, a town on the edge of the Huichol country, near the old port of San Blas. Cajeme became the apprentice of a blacksmith and found he liked the work. Then he was drafted into a military group and his life went on a different path.

Since childhood, I have believed history was about the present. The past was but still is, just as I have never been able to separate myself from other organisms, not a dog or a cat, not a bird or the lice that have at times crawled on my skin. And yet I have had no theory and lived this belief with the faith of a priest or a dog. Science now tells me I share the bulk of my DNA with a fruit fly and when I read these announcements, I am relieved. And oddly confirmed. All the Cajemes are dead and yet I feel them present as I walk the public paths of my life.

Back in 1873, Ramón Corral started a newspaper in Álamos, Sonora. He called it *Le Fantasma y La Voz de Álamos*, The Phantom and the voice of Álamos. This is an interesting choice for a newspaper name since Corral spent his life being a force for reason and for the values of the enlightenment in Sonora. He was ultimately attached to the group called the *científicos*, the technocrats surrounding the nation's seemingly permanent president Porfirio Díaz. By the time Corral and his cronies were through, over twenty percent of the land surface of Mexico was owned by rich Americans, and foreigners also devoured a lion's share of the railroads, ranches, lumber industry, oil deposits, mines, and electric companies. The *científicos* believed the country had to be modernized and that to modernize the country it was necessary to host hordes of foreign investors. And that to modernize Mexico the native people—Indians and backward campesinos—had to go. He founded the university, he created more than a hundred public schools, he got the church out of education and he announced that it made no difference whether a Sonoran was Catholic, Protestant, Buddhist or a follower of Muhammad. And yet when he had to reach for a name for his upstart paper, *phantom* came to his mind.

And yet this thing we call history, the facts and scraps we have not lost but can barely pay heed to or comprehend, seems to breathe through the dust and bones. I can remember as a child suddenly thinking, this all really happened, these names once wore flesh. And this fascinated me for a while. And then as the years pummeled me, I began to sense that they not only had lived but also continued to touch the quick of my life.

It is like that moment when one realizes that the point is not to trace lineage to kings or queens but to understand that if one exists, one must, of necessity, be related to the first person who ever existed.

And then, in the night with drink, all the walls come down, and beasts enter one's blood. The fruit flies also.

Cajeme attaches himself to the service of General Ramón Corona and soon becomes the general's aide-de-camp. Corona is a liberal and hostile to the church. In March 1854 he joins in a revolt against President (and General) Santa Ana—the man generally given credit for losing Mexico's claim to Texas and much of the American West. By August, Santa Ana has fled to his estates in Colombia. Three years later Corona comes out in favor of the Constitution of 1857, which incorporates the reforms of an Indian named Benito Juárez. Cajeme becomes Corona's agent in Mazatlán, Sinaloa, and hooks up with the Sonoran general Ignacio Pesquiera. And then in late December 1857 Cajeme is suddenly discharged in Guaymas. He becomes the secretary and interpreter for a garrison stationed at the mouth of the Río Yaqui. When a new conservative revolt brings the Yaquis into play as their allies because the tribe views the liberals as atheists, Cajeme stays with the liberals surrounding General Pesquiera and becomes a corporal in the artillery.

When the French intervene under the pretense of collecting on some bad debts and put an obscure Austrian prince, Maximilian, on the newly invented throne of Mexico, Cajeme rises to be a sergeant in the Army of the North to fight the foreigners. He is at the key battles that eventually destroy the imperial forces and end in Maximilian's execution. When he returns to Sonora in 1867, he drops out of the army and, according to some reports, takes to drink. When some of the Yaquis and Mayos refuse to put down their arms, Cajeme enlists with some other Yaquis to fight his own people. And this leads him back to Bácum, where he was raised.

On February 8, 1868, the Mexican forces reenter the Yaqui country with 300 infantrymen, 100 cavalrymen, 250 Yaqui allies and two pieces of artillery. At the village of Vicam, they are told the Yaqui rebels wish to surrender but when the peace is made at the village of Cócorit a week later, the 600 Yaquis who appear turn in only two guns and 120 bows. The Mexican commander is not amused. He imprisons most of the Yaquis and tells the rest to rustle up the missing weapons. Two days later they hand over only forty-eight guns. The commander then marches 450 Yaqui prisoners to Bácum and locks them up in the church. He announces that for every gun turned in one prisoner will be released. He segregates the ten leaders with the warning that if there is any trouble, he will kill them. At about nine-thirty that night, 270 of the prisoners bust down a wall in the church, pitch bricks and sandals at the guards and make a break for it. The guards shoot and somehow the church is set on fire. By two a.m. only fifty-nine Yaquis are alive and there are a lot of charred bodies. Cajeme is said to have been at Bácum that night.

Then at the end of 1868, the Rió Yaqui rises after seventy-six hours of heavy rain and drowns many, destroys the crops, floods the villages and wipes out much of the livestock. The Yaquis are temporarily broken. General Pesquiera is now the governor, and he too is at low ebb. The wars of the 1860s that provide Cajeme with work have gutted Sonora itself, and the state's population has slumped to about 100,000. The governor reveals plans to develop and colonize the Río Yaqui with Mexicans and other non-Indians. Cajeme remains loyal to Pesquiera. One of the governor's opponents leads a rising in Guaymas in 1873, and by the time he is crushed, Cajeme has risen to the rank of captain. Throughout the various civil wars and Yaqui wars and the war against the French, there is one constant in the career of Cajeme: he rises. For many Yaquis he becomes a hated figure, the traitor, and a feared figure, the soldier and commander who delivers crushing blows to them. For the Mexicans, he assumes a different role. Suddenly, Pesquiera realizes that he has a trilingual officer under his command who is a full-blooded Yaqui to boot. So he made him *alcalde* of the eight sacred towns and of the lower Río Yaqui. Cajeme comes home to his people as the Mexican official who is supposed to rule them and, if they cause trouble, kill them.

The Yaqui problem seems finally solved and the governor returns to his development plans with new energy.

I hate the dates, the sequences, the pages reading like a roll call. But I hate the alphabet, and grammar also. When I was a child, I stumbled over the *begats* in my mysterious hours trying to fathom why the Bible was something important. And yet I sensed the writers of the old pages clung to the *begats* as a lifeline in the froth and fangs of life without end.

I go to the Yaqui casino on the edge of my town and Cajeme seems erased by elderly gamblers fixated on playing machines. History becomes rubbish to be tossed out and hauled away to the dump.

But still, I cannot do this. I cannot believe Cajeme never existed. Or existed and never mattered. I listen to the din of the slot machines and still believe, as I did when a child.

I am defenseless at these moments. Just as when I bend down and inhale the scent off a dog's face.

Rosalio Moisés, the old Yaqui busy scribbling his autobiography into the spiral-bound notebooks of a schoolboy, remembered a story told him as a child by one of the women of the family. She said what really tuckered Cajeme out was that he had a woman in each of the eight sacred towns and spent his time walking from one to another.

In 1875 Cajeme leads a revolt from his new base in the Río Yaqui country. He does it this way. The technical head of the Yaqui people, at least in military matters, is the captain general, El Jaguali (the Harelip). Cajeme murders him. Cajeme's supporters are the wild Yaquis in the sierra who have never surrendered, plus most of the councils of the eight towns. Next he takes on his old comrades in the Mexican army. The Sonoran leaders are dumbfounded. The man who knows three languages is now speaking with yet one more tongue. Yaquis who have dispersed all over Sonora and Arizona during the endless wars begin coming back to the river. General Pesquiera pauses over his plans for massive irrigation works, huge farms, and foreign colonies to make the Río Yaqui bloom and boom. His American investors hesitate in their schemes to develop the river valley's carbon beds and oyster beds and gold and silver mines. The past is not yet over, it seems; the Yaquis are once more a thumb in the eye of Sonora. State officials speculate that Cajeme has become addled, "conquered by the Yaquis' imperishable tendency to maintain themselves independent."

Cajeme himself makes a simple announcement: he will not recognize the government of Mexico unless the Yaquis are granted total self-government and sole rights to the Yaqui Valley. The officials at first discount these noises and tell themselves, "The Yaquis are not as terrible as they used to be." Under Cajeme's command, the Yaquis begin raiding ranches and farms. Cócorit is the one Yaqui pueblo that has already been colonized by outsiders. They burn it to the ground. The

Mayos to the south take note and they also rise up and burn a pueblo that outsiders had colonized. Pesquiera marches into the Yaqui country at the head of five hundred armed men to put down the pocket revolt. His colonel sends Cajeme a message suggesting a peace settlement. Cajeme replies simply that he will be waiting for the Mexicans.

The first battle lasts forty-five minutes and, according to the Mexican reports, leaves fifty-six Yaquis dead on the field. But the field becomes the problem. As the army blunders through the dense groves of Yaqui country they find deserted camps, some steers, but almost no Yaquis. Cajeme becomes a phantom and the only proof they have of his existence is the constant skirmishes that pick off soldiers. And then Pesquiera becomes involved in one of the endless power struggles that form the major activity among the nineteenth-century Sonoran elite. For three years, he maneuvers to save his regime, finally losing. The Yaquis are for the moment left alone, a problem that the Mexicans feel they will attend to in due time. No one seriously thinks that the inevitable development of Sonora can be blocked by a group of savages who like to dance wearing deer heads.

They do not look right. Many of the Yaquis today are overweight. In the old photographs, they are sleek, and all but naked peering over a rock with a rifle during the Mexican Revolution. They wear normal clothing also and shop in the same markets as I do. They live in normal houses on normal streets. They cannot have a past that matters. Any more than I can.

This thought comes and goes with me. But it is a thought. I never really believe it. I stay where I began: it really happened, Cajeme really lived. And it continues, silently like the shifts in the earth's crust along a fault line, the little tingles in the rock and soil of the earth that go unnoticed until the big quake shakes the surface.

Cajeme takes over the small port at the mouth of the Río Yaqui. He permits some outsiders to enter the Río Yaqui for purposes of trade.

And he creates a system to tax this trade. There is one other new tariff. Any captain who brings his ship to the Yaqui port must haul guns and ammunition on each and every trip. Travelers on foot have to donate their weapons to the growing Yaqui arsenal. Deserters from the Mexican army must also give the natives their guns. Rich ranchers are kidnapped and their ransoms flow into the Yaqui treasury.

To increase food production, Cajeme takes a cue from the practices of the early Jesuits. Each Yaqui pueblo has to set aside a field of a certain size, assign men to cultivate it, and donate most of the harvest to a system of community granaries. He begins the manufacture of gunpowder on the Río Yaqui. And he reorganizes the people into a government. The governors of the Yaqui towns function as Cajeme's aides. Beneath them he selects captains of war, and each captain is charged with maintaining a certain number of men who will be trained, armed, and ready to move on short notice. For the religious matters of the people, he reactivates a role that had fallen almost into disuse since the mission days, that of *temastían* or sacristan. These ministers attended to a special cargo, the faith and culture of the Yaqui people. Cajeme brings to the forefront the tribal councils, forums open to every adult Yaqui, men and women together.

An unseen force seems to course through the veins of Sonora. There are many stories. *Vaqueros* disappear from the herds of the Mexican ranchers and reappear on the Río Yaqui as cavalry. Hands leave the mines and become sappers tunneling under Mexican fortifications. A prosperous Mexican goes to bed at night and discovers his Indian maid has left in the night and taken all his gold south to the treasury on the Río Yaqui. Dark-skinned sailors, it is said, rise up and kill their captains and sail to the war on the river.

Cajeme becomes a shadow that the Mexicans can barely glimpse within the fabric of the Yaqui world. He is the enemy, but their troops cannot even find him. He is the captain general of the Yaqui people but he professes simply to be a servant of councils and an instrument for enforcing their decisions. He dabbles in foreign policy by making a key alliance with the equally numerous Mayos to the south. What is happening on the Río Yaqui is being mirrored in Mexico as a whole. As

Cajeme forges an independent nation out of the traditional anarchy of the eight sacred towns, Porfirio Díaz makes much the same moves. For the first time since Mexico declared its independence from Spain, it begins to get the structure and central control of a real state. After twice being amputated by the United States in the mid-nineteenth century, Díaz creates a Mexico with real, permanent borders, one immune to the schemes of adventurers and of imperial nations. The various regional warlords either swear allegiance to Díaz or are picked off one by one. Ramón Corral swears his allegiance. Once Díaz has power firmly in his hands, his mind turns to dreams of developing the nation's resources. And once his mind focuses on this matter, his finger moves across the map and pauses at the rich lands and abundant waters of the undeveloped Yaqui Valley. The two great consolidators of late-nineteenth-century Mexico, Cajeme and Díaz (who is also an Indian), base their plans on the same piece of ground.

In Sonora railroads boom, mines reopen, government grows daily stronger. By 1879 José T. Otero, the vice governor of Sonora, emphasizes the importance of colonizing the Río Yaqui. "The government under my charge," he explains, "has decided to appeal to that of the Union [meaning Díaz], requesting its help in organizing these tribes civilly, reducing them to the obedience of the authorities, dividing the land of their pueblos in a manner convenient to the support of life by means of work and forcing them to enter at once onto the road of civilization."

Everything is over now. The past is finally past for good. The struggles between the various ideas have ended. The markets tell us this and we repeat what the markets say. History has become a hobby for buffs or a technical wasteland for mandarins. But it has ceased to be considered visceral and living. We like the old photographs to be sepia so as to shout their otherness, their half-life spent across some great divide that separates them from us.

In September 1882, the Mexicans send a thousand soldiers into the Mayo country. On the night of October 15, Cajeme moves into position with two thousand troops. The battle lasts two and a half hours, and then Cajeme and his forces melt away. The Mexicans are spooked. They are used to facing Indian warriors but they have caught a glimpse of something new: an Indian army. And then even this glimpse disappears. Cajeme has no imperial goals. He seeks to defend the traditional landholdings of the Yaquis. He does not take the war to the Mexicans but waits for them to bring the war to him. An odd armed peace falls over Sonora, and to the casual outside observer, nothing seems amiss. An American hardware salesman travels about and gives his report to the *Los Angles Times*, an article published as "Seductive Sonora." The visitor praises the peace of the state and is excited by the many business opportunities. He ends by noting that he anticipates "to see Sonora an American state within five years if the present influx of Americans continues."

The government decides to murder Cajeme. In January 1885 a party of thirty men goes to Cajeme's home in Guamúchil. When they find him gone, they burn the house down and deal roughly with his family. Cajeme rushes back, seizes all the ships in the harbor, and fines them. He demands the Mexican government turn over the attackers to his government for punishment. The Governor promises to see justice done according to Mexican law but refuses to turn over the men. Cajeme acts. Massive blows are struck against ranches, against railway stations. The twenty-one ships detained in the harbor are burned.

A Mexican army invades the Río Yaqui on May 8, 1885. They find stout forts that Cajeme has erected throughout the Yaqui country. On May 16 six hundred Mexican troops attack one of Cajeme's forts at a place called El Añil. The Yaquis kill twenty soldiers, wound fifty-seven, and when the Mexicans break off the battle, seize their cannon. In June they attack the fort once more with fourteen hundred men and fail again. The Mexicans are managing to lose a war and yet hardly ever see a Yaqui. The forest is so dense along the river that it is almost impenetrable. They find abandoned camps, they are fired upon by unseen enemies. And then in July the rains come and they retire from the field. The war goes on and finally El Añil falls.

The peace talks come that December and the Mexican representatives must face the governors and the councils of the eight towns.

Cajeme is a figure barely seen on the edge of the meeting, a lean man off in the distance watching. When the time comes to sign an agreement hammered out with the councils, Cajeme finally speaks. He says, "My word is worth as much as my signature, and the people have always made peace without signing any piece of paper." The talks collapse with that statement.

Cajeme is there in the background, a figure flickering through the forest. Corral writes, "He seemed to be an imaginary being, invisible, a myth created by the fantasy of his people." He cannot matter. He does not compute.

I wonder if this symbol thing gets in my way. If my interest in Cajeme is that he stands for resistance to authority and thwarts the power of markets and banks and machines. I wonder if he is just a toy to push around on a page and make some points with about now as opposed to then.

But I feel that he existed and in some form still exists. I feel he is walking around speaking strange tongues in distant cities on distant continents. He seems like a wolf to me that came in from the cold and sat by the fire. But would not stay or become tame.

Now he is barely a name, but for me, he cannot ever be a symbol. He did these things and they echo in my mind.

The generals decide the only solution is to kill all of them. They send out their troops into the mountains and into the forests and the troops kill anyone they meet. The cattle and food are also taken. No one sees Cajeme—they say he "vanished like a shadow." A message comes from him. He will surrender if all Mexican troops are removed from Yaqui ground immediately. Otherwise, he notes, he will fight on to the end.

No crops are planted for a year. The soldiers are everywhere and killing everything. Four thousand Yaquis surrender, two thousand Mayos come in. But not Cajeme. He is rumored to be out there somewhere with eight hundred men. Three Mexican garrisons are stationed along the Río Yaqui. Corral wants Cajeme dead and issues a description of the man he has not yet met: "regular height, rather fat, big eyes, thick lips, beardless, much black hair. Special markings: missing half the index finger on his right hand. Speaks good Spanish and his speech is measured."

On April 12, 1887, Cajeme is arrested in a private house in the Guaymas area. A Yaqui girl has betrayed him to save her brother's life. Corral comes south to see the invisible man. Cajeme is taken to Guaymas proper. He sails on the ship *Democrata*.

It is 1935 and time to burn a witch. It is the *Dia de San Juan*, and a fiesta is held each June 24 in Cócorit to beg the rains to come. When the ceremonies end, some of the men go over to the railroad station and drink mescal. One dies and another man is accused of bewitching him. They bind the accused witch's arms and take him to the Yaqui guardhouse in Cócorit. For three days and three nights he is denied food and water. His arms remain bound. Six men cut the wood and pile it up a half mile out of the pueblo. Then they tie the man's feet and throw him on the pile. He never makes a sound.

Rosalio Moisés writes all this down in the spiral notebooks that record his life. He is there watching the burning. His notebooks periodically blaze with burnings. A man named Juan, he writes, lived with his two daughters and treated them like wives. Other men were kept from them and when he found one daughter in bed with a man, he became angry. Eventually, the girl had a baby. Juan took the baby three days after its birth and burned him up. The girl took sick with pneumonia and died.

Moisés never mentions the smell of the burning flesh. He is very reticent about many matters. He does not touch on his fear when in the late thirties he visits Yaqui rebels who are still holding out in the sierra. The chief of the band was born in the mountains in 1874 and has never left the sierra or the fight. He is an arc of anger that reaches back to when Cajeme organized the wild broncos of the mountains and declared the Río Yaqui an independent nation. Mainly what Moisés remembers is being hungry, always being hungry. He notes how sometimes during the hard times he would have to walk a mile or more away from the village to find a rat. When the rains came and there were crops, he could fetch himself up a rat closer at hand.

Sometimes I think Darwin was wrong, that we can influence our DNA, that we can acquire traits and pass them on. There is no proof for this feeling and it stands naked and defenseless facing an army of evidence to the contrary. But I feel it in my bones. Cajeme lives and dies and it matters. His name disappears, his actions are erased or blurred by memory into myth and fraud. But his hand can still touch the shoulder. A man went to a river and removed the cloak of his training, became something else and refused to bend to the long words about industrialism or the long guns of the state. True, he died and became no more. But he does not go away. Even when forgotten. This I feel and cannot justify.

But I cannot shake the belief.

They try him at a secret court-martial and neglect to tell him of either the trial or of his sentence. Perhaps he is too busy to care. Corral asks him question after question and eventually writes a memoir of Cajeme almost two hundred pages long. The Mexican is of course struck by Cajeme's valor and, after witnessing the captain general rip the very guts out of Sonora for a decade, cannot deny his leadership abilities. But most of all he is captivated by Cajeme's manner. Corral finds a civilized and well-spoken man who has devoted hard years to rending asunder everything Corral has tried to create and passionately believed in. Corral is the man who dreams railroads to tie the fabric of his society together. Cajeme is the man who sends men to rob the trains on a regular basis. And yet, most painfully for Corral, Cajeme cannot be dismissed out of hand. He has lived the very essence of patriotism. He took up arms against the French, he stood on the field when Maximilian was executed by a firing squad. He has seen more of his nation than probably ninety-five percent of the population. And he knows of the United States also.

If Corral were to sketch a Yaqui who could share the industrial modern future, he would have drawn the portrait of a person remarkably like Cajeme when he was sent to the river to be the Mexican official ruling the Río Yaqui in the mid-seventies. In fact, Cajeme insists during their interviews that he has always been a "patriotic Mexican." He recalls the time a North American came to him to ask the cooperation of the Yaquis in building a railroad to aid in the exploitation of the Yaqui carbon fields. He dismissed the man abruptly, he informs Corral, telling the gringo, "We Mexicans do not need foreigners to come and take us by the hand and bless us." And yet it has all turned into a disaster. The valorous Mexican officer named José María Leyva has mutated like some *fantasma* into the savage called Cajeme. What is worse, this savage named Cajeme has created on the Río Yaqui the rudiments of a nation and a kind of democracy that has constantly eluded each and every ruler of Mexico. Try as he might, Corral cannot simply discard Cajeme as a backward savage—not after noting the town governments he created, the tax system, the public granaries and arsenals and fortifications. He reviews the various battles with him, seeking clues to the source of the ferocity and dedication that motivated Cajeme's troops. Corral cannot believe Cajeme's tally of his forces at various engagements. Surely there were more Yaquis than that when they chewed up Mexican armies. Cajeme's face reveals a slight smile and he says, "When Indians are behind a gun, they become many."

Like a Victorian novel, Corral's history must have redemptive qualities and end in a sound and soothing moral. And so he records that Cajeme now realizes that the Yaquis are beaten and must learn to submit to the government and meld into the promised modern world. Corral quotes Cajeme as saying, "Before we were enemies and we fought; now all this is over and we are all friends."

As the interviews go on, Yaquis crowd around the house where Cajeme is held prisoner, straining to catch one last glimpse of their doomed leader. Leaving is not easy for Corral since he knows the reality of the secret sentence. He is one of the three men that run Sonora and the fate of Cajeme is in his hands. But Corral also knows the future and this dreamed-of and golden future cannot come into being until all the Cajemes are struck down. When Corral finally leaves, he notes, "I was filled with a profound sense of liking for this Indian, so intelligent and so brave."

They put Cajeme on a ship on April 21 and sail to the mouth of the river. His guards are very upset and do not like the task they now face. They reassure their prisoner that everything will be fine. Cajeme looks at them and says, "Do not waste your jokes on a man who is about to die." The Mexicans march him through each of the eight sacred towns and arrive on the twenty-fifth at Cócorit. An American happens to be in the area and later he files a newspaper report in the United States. He says Cajeme was taken into a deep woods, put up against a tree and shot. There was also a deep saber gash across his face. His body is thrown over a mule and given to the people in the pueblo. When the American visits this tree shortly after the execution, he finds the bloody hat of the dead man nailed to it. A redwood cross is also pinned against the tree and inscribed I.N.R./HERE FELL GENERAL CAJEME, and then the date and also the exact time of the killing, 11:05 in the morning. At the foot of the cross, the Mexicans had tacked up a further message: "With five bullets he paid for the evil he did. Pardon. Pardon. Pardon."

The Mexicans breathe easier and feel their problem is solved. They have killed the indispensable leader and without his cunning the people will fall back into their docile ways.

Corral argues in his biography that Cajeme will be the last Yaqui leader. "The sacrifice of Cajeme," he allows, "was very painful, but it would give the effect of securing the peace in the [Yaqui and Mayo] rivers, the basis and beginning of a period of civilization for the tribes."

The moon rides full and golden in the burning sky. Summer is now days away and there is no containing the heat in this desert. The cereus are blooming, big and obscene white flowers that are laced with perfume to bring on the sphinx moths and nectar bats for pollination. In the mountains the storms begin to build. The sky is not safe after midday.

This is because of the serpent called a *bakot* in the language of the Yaquis and the Mayos. These creatures are black and horned and huge. The *bakots* live in mountain springs and for this reason the high springs never go dry. Sometimes the serpents leave the mountains and go down onto hot desert flats. That is when the floods come. The only way to stop the floods effectively is through the services of a fat dwarf called Suawaka. The Yaquis believe the thunder is the twang of the dwarf's bowstring as he slays the serpent. The Mayos contend it is the crack of his rifle.

Men get power by visiting a serpent in his cave. The huge snake twines around them and licks them with a hideous tongue. If they show fear, they are fated to become animals. If they are brave, they receive power in whatever field they prefer. I sit in my yard, watching the big cactus flowers beckon in the night, and listen for the licking of the serpent in the mountains of the growing storms. Surely there are men up there at this very instant seeking power.

In Mexico City everyone is seeking power. A criminologist suggests a fifty percent boom in crime this year. He blames all this energy on *la crisis*, the economic collapse of the nation. He says we are now watching a society pulverize itself. Apparently, the record books hold only three known examples of crime surges of more than thirty percent in a year. One such boom occurred in Tokyo right after World War II. A second was in Denmark when the Nazis slaughtered most of the nation's cops. And there was a similar upsurge of mayhem in Spain when the dictator Francisco Franco finally managed to die. I flip to a Mexican paper: fire eaters are back on the streets in Sonora. There is a photograph of a youth with a plume of flame extending out from his mouth. Usually, the fire eaters are at intersections and do their act for small change. Inevitably they swallow too much petroleum over time and their brains deteriorate into a general idiocy. In Mexico City, there is a kind of rehabilitation center packed with nothing but former fire eaters who have spit one flame too many and gone soft in the head. What kind of a life makes it seem reasonable to do a stunt on a street corner for small change when you know you will end up a gibbering fool?

Of course, crime booms and the appearance of fire-eating idiots do not mean the fabric of society is unraveling but simply that the fabric is being rewoven by new and unbeckoned hands. If there is no work, crime offers self-employment. If there is no adequate way to redistribute wealth, crime offers a way to reslice the economic pie. Crime is the ultimate form of laissez-faire with constant job retraining, no taxation, no social security or perks, little or no regulation and limited liability. Crime, at least initially, is ultimate capitalism. True, over time it, like all human efforts, becomes organized, regulated and less competitive. But at the start, and we are living at the start right this moment, it is straight out of the books of theorists who fantasize an economy free of the death grip of the state. Like all true competitive situations, unregulated crime is a little messy. But it is at this very instant redistributing wealth with far greater efficiency than the state, and for this reason, it is growing.

I can hear a voice whispering, a voice saying do not waste your jokes on a man who is about to die. Mexican authorities seize nineteen thousand cartridges of various calibers at the line. The ammunition was heading to Guerrero, a largely Indian state far in the south where the guerrillas have been up in the hills for decades and where the rich go to rest in Acapulco. It is a small item, a tiny blip on the big screen of the information flow. Much more space is taken up by the United States' request to hold a world bankruptcy meeting to set in the necessary safeguards so that there will be no more bumps in the road of global progress.

I can feel Cajeme looking over my shoulder. I turn and he has a faint smile on his face. He's been dead over a century, but contrary to the hopes of the authorities, he keeps hanging around. There is a statue of him down along the Río Yaqui. He is holding a gun. I don't say a word to him but go back to my reading. I don't think he would tell me much anyway. He is cordial and well spoken but still he is reticent. Corral for all his interviewing—and he was flabbergasted by Cajeme's total recall of battles and dates and tiny snippets of fact—could never find out why he went to Río Yaqui in the mid-seventies as a loyal Mexican and a notorious traitor to his race and then instantly led a revolt. In fact, historians for a century have worried over this big hole in their understanding of Cajeme. When I finish with the paper, I toss it on the floor and Cajeme snatches it up. He scans the pages like a starving wolf, his lips slowly moving as he silently mouths the words. Apparently, his English is getting rusty.

Worms are still feasting on Cajeme's flesh when the Yaquis rise again. The structure he put in place survives his death and a new man appears to rally the people, a man called Tetabiate, which in Yaqui means "Rolling Stone." He is the leader who takes the people to the very bottom of their deepest agony. He moves with four hundred Yaquis to the highest peaks of the Bacatetes, places with names like Buatachive, Mazocoba, La Gloria, Aguilas del Chino, Mazatán, and La Pasión. They move into the forts and trenches created under the direction of Cajeme. The Yaquis sweep down and once more set Sonora aflame. Their tracks are sometimes found but almost no one ever sees a Yaqui warrior in the flesh and lives to report the event. During the long war under Cajeme, the Yaquis had dispersed to various mines, ranches and farms throughout Sonora, seeking shelter from the bloody storm. Since they are working fools, they have no trouble finding jobs. The basic yardstick in Sonora is that a Yaqui will do the work of two Mexicans for half the wage. Ramón Corral, vice governor of Sonora in 1887 when Cajeme is killed, salutes the Yaqui Diaspora. He is sure the experience will help the Yaquis in "forming a common mass with the rest of the population." Also, he believes, "contact with the white people would extinguish little by little their racial hatred, civilize them and create certain necessities which they could not obtain otherwise except by means of work within the confines of society." Corral is preaching the faith of consumerism, a religion still bleating just outside my door. What he gets is a fifth column. The raiders spreading fire and death from the peaks in the Bacatetes feed off the Yaqui laborers for money, guns, bullets, food, and from time to time manpower. Sonorans wind up giving wages to people who use the wages to kill Sonorans.

Americans show up once again with schemes to develop the Río Yaqui. They write brochures, float stock company scams, and fail totally. It is not safe for strangers on the Río Yaqui. When the Mexican army presses hard, Tetabiate and his people offer to discuss peace terms. And then after a lull the fire flares up again. In 1897 one of these lulls occurs and comes to be called the Peace of Ortiz. All the Sonoran dignitaries are there, including Ramón Corral, who is at the moment serving as governor. It is the fifteenth of May. The Mexican accounts speak of a procession of four hundred warriors carrying white flags of peace. Documents are signed that are supposed to end the conflict forever. Yaqui accounts report events at Ortiz that the Mexican chronicles missed. It seems the Archangel Michael was there and he hovered over the platform as the documents were signed. The Mexican general looked up, saw the heavenly figure, and shit his pants in fright. For two years, there is a kind of armed peace and the government showers the Yaquis with promises and supplies. Outsiders began to drift into the Río Yaqui. The eight towns send a letter to the Mexican general explaining that they had only signed the Peace of Ortiz because they thought the agreement meant whites and soldiers would leave their land. This has not come to pass, they continue, and therefore "we have no blame for all the misfortunes that there are." Soon Tetabiate is back in the mountains with his warriors and fresh supplies. Attacks against Mexicans resume.

It all comes to a head at a mesa called Mazocoba. It is January 1900 and Mexicans pour all their forces into the Bacatetes. The Yaquis take up position at a fortress they have constructed, a small peak surrounded by cliffs with only few narrow defiles permitting access. Come morning on the eighteenth, one thousand soldiers hit the citadel. Hand-to-hand combat ensues. Many Yaquis leap from the cliffs rather than surrender. Four hundred dead litter the battlefield, and more than one thousand are taken prisoner. Only 834 of this number survive the march out of the sierra. The government recovers only forty guns. And Tetabiate escapes.

Now the years blur. The government reaches for a solution to this vexing matter of people who will not accept the inevitability of the modern world. The solution is elegant in its simplicity: kill them all. You are walking down the street and you are taken. You are herding cattle on a ranch and you are taken. You come out of a mine shaft after a hard shift underground and you are taken. You are a child sitting in the dust of your yard and you are taken. All over Sonora, Yaqui Indians are disappearing. Sometimes you are shot down like a dog but more often you wind up for a while in the prison in Hermosillo. The governor is said to come by and sit in a chair while you line up for his inspection. Nearby are masked Yaqui traitors and they nod and gesture to signal their opinions to the governor. He lines you up eventually in three formations. One formation goes back to work, another is shot, and the third is sent to the port at Guaymas. Here you are pitched onto some old tubs and begin your voyage. You travel to Yucatán, where the big growers need strong backs for their henequen plantations. The fiber is one of Mexico's key exports and, as in any soundly managed and developing economy, exports are crucial in keeping up the balance of payments that decide who is going to live and who is going to die in the international trade. The aging dictator in the capital is caught in a process that dictates to him: to make the books look right he has to gut Sonora of its key labor force, you and your friends, and send you to Yucatán, where you almost all die within a year. Partly you die because the work is murderously hard. Partly you die because the tropics with their new diseases and conditions overwhelm you. And partly you die of a broken heart. Through the endless wars of the nineteenth century, through the slaughters in the sierra, through the havoc that swept constantly through the eight towns of the Río Yaqui, one thing has persisted and seemed to keep you alive: the family. And now in Yucatán the family breaks up—the man sold here, the child there, the woman somewhere else. Something snaps deep within and then you die. By 1910 a quarter of you, maybe half of you are dead. The rest are scattered in refugee communities from Yucatán to Los Angeles.

You are wayfarers, afraid to admit your real identity, cautious about observing your religious rites, stateless trash floating across the burning ground of this place. You are part of an audition for the century called the twentieth. You are the out-of-town tryout for the new fashion, genocide. You are an early mock-up for a new and growing breed, the DP—the displaced person. You are a pariah and soon the world will provide you with many brothers and sisters as the killing machines fire up. There is only one thing that keeps you from vanishing into oblivion. You never give up. You never stop fighting. You never stop dancing. You never stop believing. How you persist in your faith is a mystery as the year 1910 rolls around and remains a mystery to this day. Scholars of various stripes pick at the carcass of your people and ask questions about your rituals and beliefs. They do this decade after decade and yet they never quite come up with an answer as to why you survive and others do not. You remain baffling, remote and apparently indestructible. Once in a while you catch on fire and earn salvation with a match and a few moments of agony. You live in the poorest barrios, do the most miserable and difficult work, go hungry often and live hand to mouth. Yet somehow you breed, keep your language alive, and transmit your culture to generation after generation.

There is an image from those hard years in the first decade of the twentieth century that neatly captures your life then. The governor of Sonora decides that his policies, while sound, are not quite enough to satisfy his appetite for real results. So he mounts an expedition to Tiburón, the largest island in Mexico, floating like a desert dream just off the coast of Sonora. It is the homeland of a few hundred Seri Indians, a native group that in the eyes of Mexicans almost falls off the scale of what they consider human. He tells the Seris that if they are sheltering any Yaquis on their ground, they will suffer greatly. A few days later the Seris come back and give the governor five severed hands of Yaqui men, and five braids off the heads of Yaqui women. He is satisfied at this recognition of the authority of the state and returns with his trophies to Hermosillo. The Yaquis take to calling the governor *el segundo dios*, the second God.

In the end, the Yaquis are not saved by the first God or the second God but by something familiar. War. In 1910 the Mexican nation crumbles and falls into a civil war that rages for ten years. And now everyone wants Yaquis for troops. Álvaro Obregón comes and offers them their land forever if they will fight under him. The people form a battalion and become the terror of the campaigns. The killing is something they are seasoned in. They are the guns for hire. They fight against Pancho Villa. They fight for Pancho Villa. Their arms appear under many banners but their conditions are always the same. When they win, they insist on the return of all their lands along the Río Yaqui and to be left alone on these lands until the end of time. The generals always agree to the Yaqui terms.

They make us all look like cowards and this is not a good feeling. They have survived everything and yet still live at the edges of our towns in the shacks and hovels. The century is winding down and the Yaquis stumble along with their strange dances, their desperate lives and the occasional flashy suicide. They take jobs, learn some of our customs, fiddle with their own rites, and yet seem never to fundamentally change. They are an affront to every government, social worker, priest and scholar that bumps into them. So generally they are forgotten and, if remembered at all, seen as a curio on the edge of the real world. At Easter some people come to watch their dances and that is about it.

They are prime evidence of the river of blood, a river without banks, without its name on any map, a river coursing almost secretly across ground claimed by others. Within the Yaquis the living and the dead are both alive and moving, and they are moving toward each other, stumbling across the ground into each other's arms where they are forming a new and unforeseen entity, a people who fail to meet the ordinary definitions of citizenship or territory, a refuse that flourishes and yet is almost unrecognizable. They are an early spring feeding into the river of blood. They have faced the serpent, felt its hot licks on their faces, and obtained power. This power is at first difficult for others to recognize. It is a power that does not hold high office or command armies and navies, nor is it a power that takes over industries or meets in boardrooms. It is the power of the indestructible and the despised. The burned ones. The people who have learned the reality behind the reality, the visitors to the world they have imagined, which is the real world, a world stronger than any currency, more durable than any bond, and more far-reaching than any economic summit. It is the past refusing to go away.

The river is rising. All over the planet the floods come often and the structures we build to contain them prove more ineffectual. It does not matter what kind of dikes we build. We can throw up massive security forces and still the drugs move at will. We can build big steel walls and still the people cross and move and mock the walls. We can create quarantines and still the plagues migrate to new ground and flesh. The world we think we believe in is ending before our eyes and no amount of meetings or discussions will come up with enough sandbags to stop the flow. Our fathers and mothers placed their faith in the new high dams. We sense the rivers cannot really be tamed.

What has been, cannot continue. What is coming, cannot be stopped. The river of blood has been building for a long time and global plans cannot dam its flow and webs of computers cannot in the end protect anyone from its flood stage. We can survive or we cannot survive. Still the river rises.

I spent weeks trying to find out more about the man who climbed on a mesquite limb, doused himself with gasoline, placed a noose around his neck, drank a can of lye, struck a match and then fired a pistol. He still exists as a shadow in the memory of the town. But no one seems quite able to recall his name, and no one is certain of the year in which he found the purity of the fire. My friend Arturo, the old cop, racks his brain but the name remains just out of reach, floating out there like the smoke coming off the burning mesquite tree. So he exists and yet he does not exist. He is recalled but no one can make his face come into focus or his mouth speak words of explanation. He is a pioneer whose message still is trapped in a code we have not yet broken. I know he is one of us, I can tell by his actions, but I must learn more before his wisdom flows into me like lava. He is one of us because he could see the future and realized there was no place for him in this future. That is why he is not simply a grotesque suicide. And that is why we can neither totally forget him nor consciously remember him. He saw too clearly what we do not want to know.

Rosalio Moisés keeps scribbling in his notebooks. He stays at this work for more than a decade, and when he dies, he still has not finished. But he leaves us a vision. In the late forties he is bewitched and takes to his bed in a delirium. Eventually angels come and he flies with them on his sickbed and wends his way high up in the sierra. There he is introduced to Jesus Christ. Jesus treats him in a kindly manner. He says, "Now I will show you what it is like if you truly follow me." They walk around in a church and suddenly the world falls apart, black clouds boil, lightning sears the sky, a great wind comes up. Rosalio looks up and sees the air full of rocks, sand, big timbers, chunks of metal. And nothing hits and nothing hurts him while he is with Jesus and keeps his faith. Then Christ says, "We will now see the war." And so they walk over to the war. Rosalio sees a great battle, bombs go off, smoke drifts across a bloody field, clouds of gas float full of death, bullets scream. Christ then says, "Now we will go this way." They come to thousands and thousands of candles, each burning and each taper the measure of the length of an individual human life. Next they go to a place of cool streams and many flowers and there are millions of people there, all dressed in white, and Christ explains that these are the good people.

Then they enter a desert plain and it is hot and sultry. Mirages ride the waves of heat and everywhere the ground is covered with thorns and cacti. There is no water and the millions of people here look ugly, and their faces are twisted by some inner agony. They can hardly be recognized as humans, some with the heads of birds, some horned like bulls, some hopping around like frogs. Rosalio sniffs and what he smells is like the vapors off a pulque vat.

Christ says, "These are the condemned people. They are here of their own choice. They are here just what they made of themselves on the earth."

After this experience, Rosalio recovers his health and joins a sacred group that participates in the Yaqui Easter celebration. He makes a mask each year and dances for days and does not eat. He has seen the future, smelled the poison gas, dipped his hand into the clear mountain stream, walked the hell of the desert flat. He writes this all in his spiral notebook. He writes it years before I enter the mountains of bone, face the furnace heat of the deserts of flesh.

I have no sacred group to join. Christ has not flown me into the kingdom and shown me my candle or the winds of war or the clean white sheets worn by the saved. And yet I am not without my resources. I do not have to visit the past because the past comes to me. I do not have to visit the future because it is swirling outside my door. I am moving into the river. The flow carries me along and my will is not at issue.

The man is swinging from the tree and the tree is burning and the tree is mesquite. The river of blood swirls around my feet and is rising. The deep roots are sucking and we are all being pulled up and transmuted and now we will finally face the sun. We are of the wood. Twisted, gnarly, but of the wood.

There is really only one thing left for me if I am to have anything at all.

Dip my hand into this river of blood.

Touch my face. Feel the burning.

Bone, mountains of bone.

Flesh, deserts of flesh.

There is not enough pure water. This is important. In the city of New York no one drinks the water. So we must get bottled water for the opening. I have come here fresh from the union gathering, Los Angeles to New York, and we all know there is nothing in between that matters. But down here in Chelsea for the opening, Paul's opening in a sense, they need bottled water to go with the jugs of cheap wine and the tray of soft cheeses, and so off I go into the wilderness of the city. A drunk sleeps rolled in cardboard, the gallery windows glow with treasures and three blocks away at the grocery, I bag some quarts of precious water and stare with envy at the vegetables. Fat shallots at a fair price, two kinds of endive, a bin of radicchio, good chilies, the first wave of winter squash. The greens explode in the gray of the city and the rough texture of the squash begs my hand. I touch them and then am off back into the streets with dusk falling and the chill finding our bones.

Scent flows off the pretty women, drifts out of doorways where the cook fires glow, licks my face from the river, storms out of garbage cans, the sweat off the bums, whiskey breath off a man in a suit fleeing his money on Wall Street, the steam of vegetables and small dogs out the open window of a Vietnamese restaurant, city of smells, stenches, scents, everything but the poison flower of gasoline that chokes most towns in my country. New York is for the nose, everyone gets close, no room on the sidewalk and you can smell the hot lingerie, the bad deal coming out of his eyes, the cigars rod hard in the mouths. I frequent cheese shops, look through glass at the slabs of slaughtered animals, taste the blue air of saloons. A small park stabs my face with grass and leaves falling gold on the ground, dog shit at the curb, urine wafting out of the alley, the raw red wine slapping the face just when the cork gives way. The subways especially, the tunnels of scent and then the crowded cars with bodies speaking to each other in the invisible tongue. Clutching my bottles of water, I'd give anything for a joint, just one little hit off a good stick, anything. I look down at the dog on the leash, the black nose wet in the dusk, a co-religionist.

The gallery is hardwood floors, bright lights spotlighting the walls, white everywhere, a Swiss notion of neutrality, people gathering. Then the table with piles of copies of the little book of photos and memoirs that now is part of Paul's body. I slow.

I walk over to a white wall and look at one of Paul's drawings: "Empirical Rhetoric." A track of lights, bright lights nestled in their tulip-shaped fixtures, wave at me with goosenecks. Barbara is busy fussing at the table with the cheeses and wine. Everything must be right. The table with the little books beckons, each and every volume safe inside its shrink-wrap.

Friends of Paul's drift in and talk about knowing Paul. There is a whiff of studio and lofts in the air, the faint shadow of bohemia on the floor. A portrait of Paul glowers from the wall—he seems to have abandoned smiling forever. He is the serious man who has spun beyond the trammels of everyday life and plunged headlong into the *is*ness of things, the molecular structure of iron, the caress of rust, the polymers hooting and hollering from a sheet of plastic, the importance of stucco and the even greater importance of the decay of stucco. Sometimes Paul writes with the atomic density of lead. He comments on one of his earlier shows, "It is about the grammars of material, about complexity, saturation, editing and formation . . . How we read objects through other objects or through fields, where the breaks occur and do not occur."

Barbara bustles about the gallery, smiling at one of Paul's old girl-friends, pumping his friends for clues about her dead boy, fussing over the hanging of his drawings, gliding like an ice skater across the polished wooden floors. I drink. That's it. I drink. I know what I cannot do and I cannot pretend he is alive and I cannot deny her the right to her pain. Pain keeps him alive for her.

Paul writes: " 'Illusion' is understood to be body based, abstraction as it goes with artifice is always the language necessitated in these issues when images, or words, or thinking, is the work. Effects, images, and all the various 'readings' carry as much weight and meaning as anything else."

I guzzle my drink and say, no, Paul. I am the man with the pick hacking through the floor toward the healing dirt below. I am the denier of the surfaces, the enemy of the gestalt. Not the true believer but the endless appetite. I hate words like *illusion*, like *style*, like *lifestyle*. I refuse to believe scent is perfume, something manufactured in a lab to grab me by the nose and make me follow her into the café. I live in a world where her scent wells up from within and grabs me by the strands of my DNA.

But this is a lover's quarrel. Paul is not a dead man for me but a boy rifling through the trash of alleys and fondling objects as form and color and texture. He is a fiend for the *is*ness of things, as I am a fiend for the *is*ness of flesh and dirt and the unblinking eye of a serpent. He is not a collector of things, I think, but a devourer of materials. He is a giant maw swallowing whole the textures and densities of my world, a mad scientist in his lab in Brooklyn fashioning the lonesome effluvia of my world into some pattern that is called Art. And he is beyond being remembered and demands to be felt, to have us touch surfaces and then bite into iron.

Now people drift in from the streets of Chelsea, the gallery goers out for a bit of culture in the evening. They drift in clutching guides of some sort and take in the walls and the room and then drift out.

Barbara looks busy with this and that. People are gathering in the back room of the gallery now and talking about art and New York and now and again Paul. I go out the door and sit on the stoop of the old brick building and watch art lovers and bums walk past. The cold feels good on my skin. The wine in my mouth is not enough. I want a grape full of sun and dirt, a giant bowling ball of a fruit filling my mouth and drenching my cells in alcohol.

Blues, and before the blues the shout, the holler of slaves chopping cotton under a southern sun, the chant working its way down the rows and then finding a guitar and slipping and sliding in the juke joints, migrating to the whorehouses of Storyville and becoming jazz, which never can stop since its only definition is becoming, becoming, becoming. That is what I want: to shout.

Then as I sit on the stoop in front of the gallery in the cool night air swallowing wine, I hear of the demon machine. The demon machine moves across the earth and eats it and spews out black glass. The artist is considering a commission in Israel, where he will devour a designated hill. I think of the Trinity site in New Mexico.

I rise and go back into the gallery and Barbara is busy being the den mother to her son's book opening with cheap wine, bottled water and soft cheeses. He's up on the wall, glowering. On most of the walls are huge canvases by an artist, the backgrounds blazing pinks and blues, the foreground cutouts from color photographs of a guy on the floor with his young child.

I catch Barbara's eye across the room and she looks like a wounded deer. She knows and no one wants to know what she knows.

Her eyes are post-nothing. Her eyes are as old as sight.

Ten blocks away I find a bistro on a side street. The bar top is zinc, the barkeep a woman. She pours me a big glass of red and I sit at an outside table in the cold and drink and close my eyes and light the cigarette.

Nothing stops the rock from crushing the bone.

And the smacking of the lips.

6

I feel the hunger. The dark green flesh of the cactus glows with life by the ash and ground bone. I've come to depend upon the garden and so I stare at the Madagascar palms, their thorny trunks bristling under the canopy of the mesquite tree. Red wine swirls against my tongue because this bone gardening, this wall of green flesh, has all become hopelessly oral with me. I eat, therefore I am. I appreciate nothing, devour everything. I remember Arturo, sitting down here in a chair on that Sunday in January, the last day he left home under his own power. He could barely walk then, his chunky body dwindling as the cancer snacked on various organs, and his skin was yellow from the jaundice. He held on to my arm as we crept through the garden, down from the upper bench, past the bed of trichocereus, under the thin arms of the selenicereus snaking through the tree overhead. He looked over by the notocactus with their dark green columns, their tawny rows of bristles and small bubbles of white down on their crowns where the yellow flowers would finally emerge, and he said brightly, "Hi, Dick."

We sat in plastic chairs surrounded by garden walls that were purple, yellow and pink, colors to fight back all the nights. He knew he'd be dead in two or three weeks, and he was. He knew he'd never see this spring, just as Dick had never made it to the previous fall. And five months before Dick had been Paul. And five months after Art came Chris.

The day was warm for January, at least for this year when cold and rain had come far too often, and we sat in the sun looking up at the trees and cactus and shrubs and herbs, into a jungle din of green and hard stone. I'd built a grotto with the Virgin of Guadalupe, a tortoise, an elephant, a red wax figure of a naked woman bought from a *curandero* (I was told by the holy man, "Think of a woman, light it, and she will come to your bed"), and nearby under a desert honeysuckle, the plaster head of Jesus Malverde, the *santo* of *narco-traficantes*.

Art says to me, "At least you've got him facing the right way."

I turn to him with a puzzled look.

"South," he snorts.

Summer air rich with scents hangs in the soft light of dawn. The coffee in my hand is black and steaming, the smell jolting me along toward the day. I look up and see the spent blossom of a giant flower drooping like a claw in the tree. I've been gone, never noticed the bud, which had to have reached a foot in length, never caught a glimpse of the growth as it shot out an inch or two or three each day toward the end, living some kind of oblivion as the rank organ of the tropical cactus grew, bloomed in the night and then collapsed from the frenzy of it all. *Selenicereus pteranthus*.

Rich black coffee, fresh ground, tiny espresso cup, the bitter flavor on my tongue, the drooping flower. It is very brief and unimportant. I have two *talavera* candlesticks, handmade by Mexicans with all the rough differences that come from such a making, and they are blue bottomed and then green leaves surge upward and white calla lilies float above the leaves, and when I light the candles and see them, I am back with the giant cactus flower and the black coffee steaming in my hand. And I believe also in wine and flesh and the facts of the bone garden.

I love the feel of red wine on my tongue. I live to drink and smell and lick and see and rub my fingers over rough bark. I believe that life is not balance. I believe life is sensation. I'm not sure what death is, but life is about things like peas.

In 1696 Madame de Maintenon, Louis XIV's longtime mistress, feels "impatience to eat [peas], the pleasure of having eaten them, and the anticipation of eating them again are the three subjects I have heard very thoroughly dealt with . . . Some women, having supped, and supped well at the King's table, have peas waiting for them in their rooms before going to bed."

Peas, green peas that is, are new to the French court and all those lascivious mouths and expert tongues are anxious for this new sensation. I applaud this pea frenzy. Who would want a Stoic as a cook?

Madame de Maintenon, sixty-one years old, now secretly wed to the king, stalwart of court etiquette, she likes her pea pods dipped in a sauce and then she licks them.

I instantly miss the sunlight going up the stairs. Outside Brooklyn in January is brilliant and the sea is in the air. The stairs feel narrow and dim and cold and dank and it is like leaving childhood behind for the grave. Up above, somewhere, is the studio that has lived for years in my imagination. The place where Paul works to create art. His mother's told me that that's what she put on his tombstone: *Artist*. And I think it was the right thing to do. So for a long time, I've tried to imagine this place, to connect a blond boyish face with a studio in Brooklyn, New York. I always failed because I could never imagine light in such a place, not a beam of it.

Now my eyes drift over the gloom and my skin feels the chill. I keep loose, hum to myself, paste a half smile on my face because I dread what I might find. Not the place where he killed himself. That is a necessary part of being here. But I dread stumbling into the terrain of a crabbed life, discovery of a space of retreat and fear and loss of appetite. I don't want that for the boy I know.

In my memory, he is a child, permanently around the age of, say, ten. I've seen his later photographs in driver's licenses, and the face seems gaunt, the eyes hollow. I can feel the needle in the eyes.

There are things that are true and then there are things that should be true. Alexandre Dumas, the French novelist and confidant of the count of Monte Cristo, is said to have had this dream of a recipe. I have no confidence that he ever cooked it, but I wish to believe that he did. Take a pitted olive, and stuff it with an anchovy filet. Now put that stuffed olive inside a black bird. Now put that black bird inside a quail and put the quail inside a pheasant. Then the pheasant goes into a turkey, and the turkey, by God, is placed inside a pig. We need a roaring fire, of course, a huge roaring fire. The pig is roasted over this fire. Perhaps we sit there with Dumas and the count sipping rare vintages and relishing the fire and the roasting flesh.

When all is done, eat the olive. That is all. Just eat the stuffed olive.

I want this story to be true.

Art basks in the sun, half dozing, and smiles at his little joke about Malverde. Probably he savors that time when we visited the shrine in Culiacán years ago and young drug guys would come and nervously make offerings and old men would act like lay priests and the whole thing was in a hut right downtown near the state capitol. Across from the shrine was a dirty vacant lot, and that had been where they'd hung Malverde in 1909 for banditry. And then an old blind woman, they say, hobbled near the tree and her sight returned. I can look over at this instant and see all that in the dull glaze of Art's dying eyes, the smell and magic of death and poverty and belief in Mexico gleaming amid his yellow flesh.

The January yard throbs with life—the holdover hummingbirds that live off our feeders, the cape honeysuckle, paloverde, bush hackberry, and *Caesalpina mexicana* that all hold their leaves, the salvia starting to swell with the promise of spring. The birds mob the seed tray and Art likes looking at them. When I set up a feeder for him at his place and sparrows and finches and doves descended by the dozens, he'd stand out there beaming and say, "Look at my birds! Look at my birds!" The justicia is still green and that reminds him of his apartment where I planted a bunch of it and that reminds him of sitting in his yard with a beer, the hummingbirds swooshing around and that reminds him of when he was alive.

And thinking of all this makes me want to mash my face into the pulp of the cactus and smear the wet and sticky flesh all over my body and suck deeply the raw smells of the earth. I don't want to be a plant, I don't want to understand plants, I don't want to own plants. I want to vanish into them, disappear into the hum, the keening sound, that pervades any garden. This is not a theory. This is a basic appetite, like drinking blood and ripping asunder raw flesh. I have only recently become so aware of this plant hunger, only since all the dying came. I cannot easily explain it except by ticking off what it is not. It is not grief. It is not fear of death. It is not depression. It is some kind of love, the kind the poets don't know but the chemicals and hormones swirling through our bodies announce. I am about that kind of gardening. And I am about it because of death.

That is what I know so far.

He never seemed short, never. I stand about six four and he made maybe five six, but he never seemed short. We partnered for years and every once in a while there would be a photo of the two of us together, and I'd be taken aback to discover I looked like Ichabod Crane, and he seemed the size of one of the seven dwarfs.

That's why the suicide bars made perfect sense. He wasn't short, he was thirsty. Dick couldn't control his thirst for the bottle and spent his life in and out of drunk tanks and then, the last fifteen years or so, in and out of detox centers. Years ago, when we first met at the newspaper, we'd leave work every few months and find some tough bar, the kind of place where they open at six a.m. and all day it is a shot and a beer, and we'd head into these places and drink for hours and hours until we could no longer feel the anger that filled us and were at last free to be drunk and go home and sleep.

He'd get aggressive when he drank and sometimes pick fights. He always lost the fights and never cared. He just had to swing out at things. The rest of the time he was mellow, thoughtful, the kind of guy women felt was sensitive. He believed in family, Little League coaching, all that stuff.

But he had to have those suicide bars.

And so did I.

That's why I didn't figure on him really dying. He never had, you know. I'm supposed to say that the drinking, the coke bingeing, the hell raising were all about fearing life or hating life or wanting to die or something like that. I don't think that is true. I think he couldn't control his drinking. And then, that last year or two, he couldn't control his depression.

He'd look at my cactus and say he had one in his yard, out by the pool, a big one that had huge white flowers. It was a *Cereus peruvianus*, I'd seen it many times. He'd bring it up because even with the blackness of the depression, he was still clinging to the flowers.

She has the gift of writing exactly the way she speaks and speaking exactly the way she thinks. For years I have gotten letters from Barbara and they are always fresh and clear and without any of the filters we generally use to guard our hearts. When she writes of her son's death, it is the same. Paul was not a surprise to her. She is an artist, her father was an artist, his father was an artist. There is a lineage here. And it has never been easy, art is not made by the easy, but it has been in the house for generations and felt as a part of life.

At first she was very angry. Not at Paul, at least not in a way she was ready to say, but at the people around him who introduced him to heroin and then did nothing as the drug took over his soul. Shouldn't they have done something? Didn't they realize what they had unleashed? Aren't they responsible? And of course, the questions were sound and the answers were deserved and Paul was still dead.

Barbara is too honest to ignore this fact. So she writes, "There are ways we use to cope. To stay alive because others need us. Actually, in my case I stay alive because my dead son needs me. I figure I had to carry him for nine months and shepherd him through his childhood. Then he was independent for some years. Now he needs me to orchestrate and promote his career in art, albeit posthumously. It's not that, as some people say, 'Paul would have wanted this or that.' Paul is dead, and what he wants isn't a real question. I do this for some basic reason. I am still his mother, and it is my job. If he needs it, I do it."

She is grateful about November. She always hated November, as do I. Then Paul told her she was wrong. Look, he insisted, the leaves are gone, now you can see the structure of the trees. He told her that if she could learn to love November, months like July would seem glutted and excessive. November, he kept going, is Japanese, July is seventeenth-century Italian. And the light. My god, look at a November sky. Blue gray, a beautiful blue gray. So she is grateful.

About November.

I went to the restaurant because a woman from Perth, Australia, told me I must. Of course, I was supposed to have a thick Florentine T-bone, but I did not. Florence was not Texas for me. No, I went to Cibreo because it is famous (Cibreo number two is in Tokyo) for classic Tuscan food and I wanted to chew and savor and swallow the bench-mark. The place is small and maybe six or eight blocks from Dante's house. The night air was cool and flavored with the roasting chestnuts of street vendors.

The place has an open kitchen, low-key help and high prices. The wine ran fifty a bottle, dinner for two passed two hundred. It was about yellow pepper soup. Mince some celery, onion and carrots—this is the good part, the slow part, with just a constant chop, chop, chop and the feel and color of vegetables. Now put them into the kettle with two tablespoons of good olive oil and stir them over a moderate heat for maybe ten minutes, until they get soft. Earlier you've grilled, say, half a dozen yellow bell peppers, skinned and seeded them, then cut them into strips. Add the peppers and let them flavor everything for four or five minutes, then put in a couple of peeled and diced average-sized potatoes. Next a quart of water and a couple of cups of good chicken stock you've made in the by and by. Now let it all simmer for about twenty-five minutes, until the potatoes are soft. Puree it all and then you might add some bay leaves and milk to knock down any acidity. Or you might let well enough alone since either way it hits your system like a megavitamin. Get it to the consistency you want, then eat it. It is a very simple dish, most things that matter are. Certainly that is true of flowers, smells, colors and the fresh breath of sky. At Cibreo they were insistent that you should never cut up the onions with a machine. I believe them. I paid two hundred bucks to taste a simple, very simple soup. I have swallowed the $E = mc^2$ of cooking.

By the time I got to the restaurant that night, everybody had died on me. And I carried this fact around with me like a stone. But it did not hurt my appetite. It was not that kind of dying. It was cooking and gardening and dying.

There was no fear. I think that mattered. My neighborhood is a street three blocks long and I just had a notice jammed in my door from the local vigilantes. They tell me not to leave the house without my cell phone so I can call the cops pronto. And dammit, look out the window and keep an eye peeled for bad guys. For our three blocks of one-story, single-family homes, my neighbors are putting up a Web site so that we can be constantly in touch and never have to see one another or talk to each other. I have been provided with the voicemail address of the local beat cop (make that geobased police officer). I don't think I can live this way even though two guys pulled a gun on folks and robbed them three blocks away. And I know I can't cook like this.

What I can do is get four yellow bell peppers, some potatoes, milk, onions, carrots, celery and cook them and then puree them and heat the soup.

Rossini, the great opera composer, could recall only two moments of real grief in his life. Once when his mother died. And the second time was out on a boat when a roasted chicken stuffed with truffles fell into the water and was lost.

The cooking began earlier, like the gardening, but both take hold around this time. I walk to the market, come home and flip through books for recipes, and then begin. While the sauce simmers, I open a bottle of red wine. There is never enough red wine. I always cook from

Italian recipes because they are simple and bold and I love the colors, the red of the tomatoes and the green skin of the zucchini, and because I like peeling garlic and chopping onions and tearing basil. The oil matters also, the thought of olives, and I prefer the stronger, cheaper oils with their strong tastes and smell.

The cooking slips into a manic phase at the same time that my appetite fades. Something about death makes bubbling pans on the stove essential.

The garden also goes out of control. I put in five or six tons of rock. Truckloads of soil. I build low terraces and plant cactus and herbs. I have no plan, and the thing grows like a weed. It begins to get out of hand when Dick dies, or maybe it is Paul? I can't remember. I sit in the yard surrounded by the rock, a dark sandstone quarried in the northern part of my state by Mexican laborers. Each wooden pallet has a man's name written on it. The rock has a wonderful lichen growth, and when the sky is overcast, the lichen glows like a banked green fire.

I begin to doubt the word *death* as they die all around me. Not deny the reality of a boy hanging from a pipe, a friend with a bashed head hemorrhaging to death on the floor, an old man turning yellow and weak as the cancer eats him, or Chris standing in the velvet summer night air as the reek of tropical blooms floods the garden and hiccuping uncontrollably from the radiation treatments. I see these things, smell them, feel them. I do not doubt them at all. Nor do I have any knowledge or belief in an afterlife. I simply doubt the word *death*, the black shroud it draws through the air when uttered, the canned, predictable reactions to its passage through a room.

Maybe it is the scent. Some years ago I am living on the ranch, Miles Davis is blaring from the speakers, August heat bakes the valley and Chris is in the kitchen roasting chilies on the gas jets. I am drinking wine, the smell of burning chilies floats through the air. Chris is dead now and his ashes are scattered on the flanks of a peak but I can still smell the roasting chilies sweetly coating the August air.

Food smells good, very good, even if I do not care to eat much. On a sunny winter afternoon, I visit Art. He talks less as the cancer reaches his lungs. I go home and brown a pork roast that I have studded with garlic and rosemary. Then I simmer it in white wine for an hour or two. It comes out tender and juicy with a browned crust, suffused with flavor and fragrance from the garlic and the rosemary Art gave me to keep evil away. I let the roast cool a few moments, slice it and pour on the wine sauce.

About two weeks before he dies, I go over on a Sunday afternoon to sit with him alone. Light floods the living room and for the first time in all the years he has known me, he speaks of his father, who died when he was two or three.

The family was Anglo and came out here from Ohio because the old man had tuberculosis. They put him in the lunger ward of the hospital and his son went to work at the mortuary, where he met Art's mother and married her. Each day he would go to the hospital and visit his father, who scribbled children's stories about the mice that grazed near his feet as he sat out in the desert sun.

The son was twenty-two and came down with tuberculosis and died. The old man rallied and lived on for decades.

When Art finishes this tale, he laughs, the rumble cracking as he gasps with his collapsing lungs.

She won't let go and there is nothing I can do about it. The months slide by, then a year, and the first anniversary is past and I think maybe it will heal. But she knows better, she tells me these kinds of things never heal, that you just get used to the pain. She is the mother and Paul is the son and he is dead and she is alive and this violates the natural order of things. So she won't let go. She works, she organizes his papers, letters, his artwork. She pitches in to have a show mounted. She is active. The pain stays.

She revisits the studio. She writes me, "Found out Paul hung over eight or nine hours. That would not have happened had I been there. Eight or nine hours AFTER he was found. Fuck the criminal codes. My baby hung by his neck for as long as fourteen hours. I didn't think there could be more pain."

I don't really like opera but I am willing to learn. When Rossini got a decoration from the duke of Modena, he was angry. He wrote back, "I asked for salami, not decorations. These I can have anytime, anywhere. Salami, on the other hand, is your specialty."

When he was composing *La Gazza Ladra*, he plunged into debt buying oysters.

He died leaving us a bunch of music and at least seven new dishes.

We'd been drinking for hours and cooking and eating and I don't remember why. It was warm, real warm out and the moon smeared all over the desert at the ranch and so we decided to make a little turn round midnight, head down and check the pond with the ducks, then cut over to Oro Blanco wash and stagger along in the sand and feel the night moves course across the desert. Everything went okay, no one was fatally injured storming through the desert in the night. But what I remember is Chris stepping off like a drum major, a bottle in one hand and his spectacles balanced nicely on his nose, as if the brush and mesquite and rock and cactus were no bother at all. He strode through the land like he belonged there.

We heard the owls calling as we made our way.

Art sits there yellow from the jaundice. We're down in the lower garden, I have to have a garden, and I listen to him and feel the life ebbing out of him and I want to lean over, there, lean over there in the part of the garden with the bone and ash, and take up that notocactus and mash it in my face and smear the wet green pulp all over my body. Green and blue. The light is golden.

Homer wrote that no part of us is more like a dog than the "brazen belly, crying to be remembered." By the twentieth century there were fifty or sixty thousand codified recipes in Italian cooking alone. By the mid-twentieth century, Italians were eating seven hundred different pasta shapes and a single sauce, Bolognese, had spawned hundreds of variations.

What can death mean in the face of this drive? What can death say at this table? I'll tell you: Art calls up when things have gotten pretty bad and says he has this craving for strawberry Jell-O.

There must be something about the mouth, about the sucking and the licking and the chewing and the sweet and the sour. The pepper also, and the salt. An English cookbook of 1660 suggests a cake recipe that consumes a half bushel of flour, three pounds of butter, fourteen pounds of currants, two pounds of sugar and three quarts of cream. There is the leg of mutton smeared with almond paste and a pound of sugar and then garnished with chickens, pigeons, capons, cinnamon and naturally, more sugar. You chew and savor and then what?

There were times, before he took sick, that I'd go over to help Art cook. I'm down on my knees in the patio and Art is sitting in a chair with a beer. He has grilled steaks to a cinder and caught the juice. And now I pound the meat with a claw hammer until it's infused with cloves of garlic and peppercorns. Then I shred it with my fingers, put it all in a pot with the saved juice and herbs, and simmer it. This is *machaca* according to his late wife's recipe, and it takes hours, and this is life or the best part of it, he believes, as he sits in the chair while I bend and pound to spare his battered old joints. Once we make it out at the ranch, and Chris brings his tools so that we can choose just the right hammer for the pounding.

This time we are outside the old downtown barrio while I pound in the desert sun and nearby is the justicia with flaming orange flowers and the chuparosa with the buzz of hummingbirds and the nicotiana reaching up twelve, fourteen feet, the pale green leaves, the spikes of yellow flowers, the costa hummingbirds with purple gorgets that seem to favor it and Art beams and says, "My birds, my plants."

He takes another swig of beer and beads of cold moisture fleck the can. Maybe it is the mouth, I think, as I sit down in the garden swirling red wine in my mouth, dry wine, the kind that reaches back toward the throat and lasts for maybe half a minute on the tongue.

Anyway, when we made the *machaca*, it was the mouth. And the eyes. And the scent. Also, the green of the plants. Art was alive then and being alive is gardening and cooking and birds and green and blue, at the very least. He finishes that beer and then goes into his galley kitchen, I can see him in silhouette, and he pulls down a bottle of Seagram 7, takes a swig and puts it back on the shelf. I pound, the garlic and pepper and grilled flesh hang in the air.

The beef is tender, the chilies hot but not too hot, just enough to excite the tongue and the seasonings bite, the garlic licks the taste buds and I begin to float on the sensations as Art drinks his Seagram and the plants grow and stir, the hummingbirds whiz overhead and then hover before my face, my tongue rubs against the roof of my mouth and it is all a swirl of sensation as I remember that summer day cooking.

When my father was dying, my mother checked about health insurance, made sure her coverage would not vanish with his death. And then she told him as he was dying not to worry, that she would be okay "when he was gone." He opened his eyes and asked, "Just where do you think I am going?"

I must tell you about this flower. It only opens in the dark and it slams shut at the very earliest probes of gray light. When it blooms, no one can be alone at night, it is not possible, nor can anyone fear the night, not in the slightest. This flower touches your face, it kisses your ear, its tongue slides across your crotch. The flower is shameless, absolutely shameless. When it opens its white jaws, the petals span a foot and lust pours out into the night, a lust as heavy as syrup and everything is coated by the carnality of the plant. It opens only on the hottest nights of the year, black evenings when the air is warmer than your body and you cannot tell where your flesh ends and the world begins.

A month, maybe a month and a half before Chris died, he came over in the evening. He could not control his hiccuping by then, and he found it better to stand in his weakness than to sit. He wore a hat because his hair was falling out. We were out in the darkness, him hiccuping, and no longer drinking, and the flower opened and flooded the yard with that lust, the petals gaping open shamelessly and we watched it unfold and felt the lust caress us and he hiccuped and took it all in.

The voice has changed, he is no longer a child, and I can hear in it that his face has grown angular. I do not yet know the haunted eyes. He is calling from Brooklyn and wants to know about the Navajo/Hopi land dispute. I have not seen Paul since he was a boy running along the beach by the Michigan shore. Up above, the farms had gone to hell or to the banks, the old orchards were half feral and when I walked in the woods, I sometimes found low-lying clumps of prickly pear and would be amazed that they could be so far from home. But then I was far from my desert home also, standing there swatting mosquitoes in the Michigan woods. The sky is often cloudy, the rain comes often and everything is very green except the lake, which broods with a kind of faint green or gray tone most of the time. The air is always wet.

He found out about the cancer right after Thanksgiving. I called right after his checkup and he said, "The good news is that the colon cancer didn't come back. The bad news is that I have liver cancer."

Art lived ten or twelve weeks more.

The cancer was everywhere, of course, by then. I took him over some marijuana brownies and that evening he took two, and then spent half the night in the kitchen—frying steaks and potatoes, whipping up this and that, gorging at all hours. And after that he refused to ever take another brownie. He said they upset his stomach.

But Lord, that one night, he came alive and tasted deeply.

They take away the mints because the case is metal. They scrutinize the carton of cigarettes also, and then I'm allowed on the ward. Dick is puzzled by the shower, why the head is buried up some kind of funnel in the ceiling. It takes him weeks to figure out they are trying to prevent him from hanging himself. Of course, he cannot think clearly what with the steady dose of electroshock treatments. He checked himself in after the suicide attempt failed. He had saved up his Valiums, taken what he figured to be a massive dose, and then, goddamn it, still woke up Monday morning when by any decent standard he ought to be dead. It was the depression, he tells me, the endless blackness. He could handle the booze, and when he was rolling that was a quart or two of vodka a night, plus coke, of course, to stay alert for the vodka.

There was that time he'd checked into detox with blood oozing from his eyes and ears and ass. But he could handle that. He was working on the smoking, didn't light up in the house.

But he couldn't take the depression, never tasted blackness like that. We sit outside in the walled yard, kind of like a prison, and for two days I try to get him to pitch horseshoes. Finally, on the third night, he tries but can't make the distance between the two pits. The shoes, of course, are plastic, lest the patients hurt each other. But we worked on it, and he gets to tossing okay.

We've been friends for a good long time, business partners once, and we've survived being in business together, so we must really be friends and he's always been like me, riding a little roughshod over the way life is supposed to be lived, but he'd kept his spirits up. Not now.

When he gets out, I go over to take him to the store. He cannot move. I walk him from the car into the market, and then walk with him up and down the aisles. He cannot connect with food. I buy him bananas because his potassium is low, and lots of green vegetables. He can't abide this, he tells me he's never eaten anything green since he was five. Then I take him through the checkout and home. The place is a wreck. One day I show him how to clean off one square foot of the kitchen counter. He watches me do it. I say, look, you do a foot a day and if you don't do a damn thing else, you'll feel like you did something.

I bring him over and cook dinner and make him eat it. Then we sit in the yard, he stares out at the cactus and trees and his eyes glaze at the twisting paths and clouds of birds. He can hardly speak. The blackness, he says by way of explaining.

My huge Argentine mesquite arcs over the yard. Nobody believes I've planted it myself, dug the hole and everything and that when I'd put it in the ground, it did not come up to my knee.

I keep trying to get Dick to plant trees. But it is like the horseshoes. It comes hard.

The machinery standing in the gray light of the big room comforts me. I have stumbled into a surviving pocket of the nineteenth century, that time when people still believed they could throw themselves at problems and wrestle with materials and fabricate solutions. The morning bleeds through the large windows and glows against the shrink-wrap machine. He had a thing about shrink-wrap—the more you stressed it, the stronger it became. I soak up the room and feel at peace. This is a proper shop for a craftsman and his craft. His craft was pretty simple: he was going to be the best fucking artist in the world and show that all the other stuff was shit. He was going to cut through the fakery and the fashion and get to the ground floor, the killing floor, the factory floor. He was not about tricks or frills or style. He was brutally simple and industrial strength. I can feel him here, his mouth a firm line, his hair carelessly framing his face, his body bent over slightly as he tinkers with some project, oblivious to everything including himself, pushing on relentlessly toward mastering a riddle that only he sees or feels or can solve. He's forgotten to eat for a day, the dog watches him silently from a corner of the big room, a stillness hangs over everything and is only slightly broken by the careful movements he makes as he constructs and alters and reaches carefully for the place he wishes to be.

Over in a corner of the shop is the apartment he carved out of the vast cavern of the old factory, and sketched on the door is an arrow pointing down to the floor and a message to slide the mail under here. It has the look of something a twelve-year-old would do. And enjoy doing. There is a feeling of grime everywhere, an oil-based grime that has come off machines as they inhaled and exhaled in the clangor of their work. I stand over a work table and open a cigar box of crayons and carefully pluck two for myself, a blue and a red. I ask Paul's friend a question and he visibly tightens and says suddenly that he can't stay in here anymore. So I go alone and look down the narrow hallway to the door and then I glance up at the stout pipe, it looks to be six or eight inches in diameter. And coming back to the factory room I see a piece of a black doormat that Paul had nailed to the wall. It says GET HOME.

I think, well shit, so this is where he hung himself.

King Solomon's palace was probably one warm home. He lived with seven hundred wives and three hundred girlfriends and somehow everybody tore through ten oxen a day, plus chunks of gazelles and hartebeests. The Bible says the wise old king had twelve thousand horsemen charging around the countryside scaring up chow for the meals back home.

Money does not replace the lust for food. Or the flesh. Nothing replaces it, nothing. Sometimes it dies, this appetite, sometimes it just vanishes in people. But it is never replaced. In 1803 one restaurant in Paris had kept its stockpot bubbling twenty-four hours a day for eighty-five years. Three hundred thousand capons had gone into the pot over the decades. This is what we like to call a meaningless statistic. Until we open our mouths. Or catch the scent of a woman. Or lean over into a bloom raging in the night.

She cannot deny her feelings, she is too honest for such lies. Barbara is astounded by the anger inside her. "Recently," she notices, "I fly into rages at the dumbest things. I do understand why I scream when I hit my head on the cupboard. It is like the final insult—I can't tolerate one more pin-prick of pain."

He'd come out to the ranch, a remaining fragment of the fifty to eighty square miles that once wore his family's brand and he'd sit on the porch and have a beer. Chris worked as a carpenter and enjoyed life. He knew every plant and rock for miles around. He didn't seem to give a damn about being born into money and now living without it. I never heard him say a word about it. He cared about when one of his cows was going to calf. And he liked not owning a horse, he prided himself on getting along without one and in wearing sensible boots instead of narrow, high-heeled cowboy boots like every other person in a western city.

He'd show me things. The foundations of a settler's cabin down the hill. The little collapsed house where he and his first wife lived along the arroyo. An old Indian village.

I remember the village clearly. We walked for an hour or two or more and then hit a steep incline under the palisades. Chris paused and pointed out the hawk and falcon nesting sites. Then his legs went uphill at a steady gait, like pistons. At the top, we slid through a narrow chute and were upon a small village on a mesa. At the entrance was a low wall and piles of rocks for throwing at invaders. This was clearly a fort people fled to in some time of trouble five hundred years or more ago, in the drought time of the cannibals.

Chris said he'd been coming here since he was a boy. The place, like almost everything else in the area, was his secret. We sat up there in the sunshine swallowing a couple hundred square miles of scenery and saying little. I hardly ever heard him complain. Things are. And if you look around, they're pretty good. Have a cold beer, a warm meal. And take in the countryside.

In the first century, Apicius put together a manuscript that lets us visit the lust of the Roman palette. The empire made all things possible— Apicius once outfitted a ship because he'd heard some good-sized shrimp were being caught off North Africa. The emperor Vitellius, said to be somewhat of a pig at table, favored a dish of pike liver, pheasant brains, peacock brains, flamingo tongues and lamprey roe. Apicius is supposed to have killed himself when he was down to his last couple of million bucks because he could not bear to lower his standard of living at table. Before there was a language of words on paper there must have been a language of food. Speech begins with the fire and the kettle. I am sure of this.

We had sat in the yard and watched the woodpecker eat insects in the throb of the August air. His speech was very slow and nothing ever seemed to lift, nothing. Dick had been fired, the drinking had come back, the electroshock didn't seem to do much good and the gambling dug in deep until he had about a hundred thousand on the credit cards. So we'd sit in the yard and I'd explain that you can't beat a slot machine, that you can't win. He'd say, that's it, that's it, you can't win.

So when I left for the memorial mass in a distant city, I felt ill at ease. It was a rough time. Across the river in Mexico that day they strangled three or four doctors and then piled them up like cordwood down by the line. Out at the cemetery, we stood around the grave drinking beer and talking, and then we went back to the house in the barrio for dinner, one cousin looking down at the grave and saying, hey, see you back at the house.

The next day when I came through the door, the phone was ringing. They'd found the body. Dick had been dead two days. He died clean, nothing in his body. He'd accidentally tripped on the rug, hit his head on the dining room table, that was it. He'd been working on a book about the drinking life.

Dick had always had one terror: that he would die drunk.

So God smiled on him.

I feel surprisingly at peace. Walking the few blocks from the subway, I took in the Brooklyn street, warming to its resemblance to the endless warrens of houses and factories I knew in Chicago. Behind the factory building stands a Russian church thrown up in the twenties by those determined to keep the lamp of faith lit on a distant shore. Across from that is a small park with beaten grass, the kind of sliver of light our city planners have always tossed to the inmates of our great cities. And the workspace itself, with its patina of machine grime, its workman's bench, its monastic sense of craft, and diligence, recalls the various places Paul toiled as a boy—his room, the cellar, the corner of some cottage in the country. I think to myself, Paul, you kept the faith.

I got up before dawn to go over the letters I've brought with me and the bank statements, all the while sipping coffee in a mid-Manhattan hotel. The numbers on the statements blurred as I sat amid businessmen studying CNN on the lounge television, and I felt as if I were watching the spinning of a slot machine, only this machine always came up with the same result: a hundred dollars a day. December, January, February, the steady withdrawals are punctual and exact. I thought to myself, Paul, you create order even in your disorder. So later when I stood in the big room where he tore at the limits of what he called art and plunged into some place he hoped was behind that name, when I touched his row of tools on the workbench and admired his shrink-wrap machine, whirring in my head was this blur of numbers as he swallowed his earnings in a grim, orderly fashion. I looked over at the wall, the one punctured by the hallway leading to the doorway and the stout pipe against the ceiling and read once more the doormat still whispering GET HOME. I reach up and rip it from the wall. This one I am taking home.

He kind of scowls and comes limping across the kitchen at me saying no, no. He takes the knife, and says, here, see, you gotta do this rocking motion and with that he chops the hell out of the cilantro. Art will be dead in three weeks and this is his last hurrah, teaching me how to make salsa cruda. He's real yellow now, wheezing all the time, and beneath the yellow is the color of ash. He is a dead man walking. A week or two before, when I talked with him about something we had to do, he said, "We should have done that when I was alive." Now we are putting salsa in quart jars as outside the sun pours down.

He's got these papers to straighten out, and we go over them. He's going to do a bit of writing and so I bring the office chair and computer. But then he can't sit up anymore and we try and jerry-rig something in the easy chair. And then that's too much and the damn fluid is building in his body, he's all bloated and distended, and by God, he tells the nurse who comes to the house each day, he's gotta get the swelling drained at the hospital. And she says, that won't do any good, you're not sick, you're dying. He listens without so much as a blink, I'm sitting right there, and then he pads down the hall to his bedroom and lies down and sleeps. In twenty-four hours, he goes into a coma. The next day he's dead after a night of family praying and shouting over him—ancient aunts hollering messages in his ear for other family members who have gone to the boneyard ahead of him. His cousin, the monsignor, says the funeral mass.

To make salsa, the salsa he learned from his wife, Josie, who learned from her parents and back into the brown web of time, like everything that matters to the tongue, is simple. Put five or six sixteen-ounce cans of whole tomatoes into a big pot, reserving the liquid. Coarse-grind the tomatoes in a food processor, a short pulse so they come out chunks and not puree. Now add them to the reserved juice. Cut up two or three bunches of green onion, very thin slices so that you come out with tiny circles. Now very finely cut up a bunch of cilantro. Add five cans of diced green chilies, a teaspoon of garlic powder, the onion and the cilantro to the tomatoes and their juice. Sprinkle a teaspoon or two of oregano. Taste and adjust seasoning. Now start crushing chiltepins (*Capsicum annum* var. *aviculare*), and add to taste. Add salt. Taste again. Keeping crushing chiltepins until it is right for your tongue.

That was the last time I really saw him move. He was yellow and hardly eating anything, but he knew some things can't be allowed to end.

I'll admit I was angry at first. His mother had been worried for months, sensed something was wrong and I'd said there is nothing you can do. Or I'd said there is nothing to worry about. So when I found out, it was like a slap in my face. And I was angry at Paul. You goddamn fool, I thought. I was at the moment buried in the senseless wind of the Great Plains at a spot under Pine Ridge not far from where the U.S. government murdered Crazy Horse when they realized he would never listen to their reason.

Ten months later I am standing in Paul's space in Brooklyn looking at the tools he used to deconstruct art and reconstruct art. I plunder the odd piles of stuff in an effort to bag his drawings and ephemera. But mainly I just take it in. That's when I finally get rid of the anger. I still don't agree with him. But I find peace in the workmanlike air of the place.

Despite the stout pipe, despite the blur of numbers on his bank statement, I feel calm in the big room.

The bottom line is always simple and the way to this line is to get rid of things. I can stand at a hot stove and make risotto, a rice dish of the Italian north. Melt some butter in the oil, then sauté some chopped onion, toss in the rice and coat it with the oil, add the liquid (make the first ladle white wine, then go with broth) a half cup at a time, constantly stirring. In twenty minutes, the rice is ready, the center of each kernel a little resistant to the tooth, but ready. Each grain is saturated with the broth and onion and oil flavor. Then spread the rice on the plate to cool, and eat from the edge inward. Pick a brilliant plate with rich color—I like intense blues and greens, you know—to play off the white. Some mix in a half cup or so of Parmesan, but I just sprinkle some on top, usually Romano for the bite. That is your choice. The rest is not. After all, we are in Paul's workshop, a thing to be kept clean and simple and direct.

The kid worked. Like most products of the Midwest, I can't abide people who fuck off and don't do things. I can remember my father sitting at a kitchen table in Chicago with his quart of beer telling me with a snarl that in Chicago we make things but in New York they just sell things. Paul kept the faith—I can tell by the bench and the honest tools.

I look up at the torn drywall. When Paul didn't answer the phone, his uncle flew from Chicago to New York and took a cab over here to Brooklyn. Clawed his way through the drywall—I look up at the hole he made—and found Paul swinging from the big pipe. He'd left a note and neat accounts on the table, plus his checkbook so everyone would be properly paid off.

Paul was a piece of work.

It got so he couldn't do much. One day his ex-wife Mary stopped by the ranch to check on him and he was sprawled in the doorway half in the house and half out surrounded by the dogs and cats.

She asked him, "What do they think you're doing?"

Chris said, "They think I'm nuts."

So Mary took him into town. He'd been busy at the ranch despite his weakness as the cancer ate. He'd been building check dams to cure a century of erosion, he planted a garden, put the boots to the cattle and let the hills come back. He said ranching was over and it was time for the earth to get some other kind of deal. I'd run into him a week or so before at the feed mill and he was chipper. His hair had just about all fallen out because of the radiation but he said he felt good. He was in town to get a part for the pump.

He was real lean by then and when I went down to see him at Mary's place, he was stretched out in bed. He wanted to talk Mexico, the people, the plants, the cattle, the way the air felt at night. I brought down some pictures and we hung them around the room. He was having some kind of magic tar shipped down from Colorado that was supposed to do the trick and beat back the cancer and he was tracking the pennant race also. People would drop by at all hours to see him since the word was out that he was a goner. He'd smoke a joint with them, and talk about this and that, especially Mexico, which he knew was color and sound and smell and taste and a wood fire with a kettle on the coals. Some of the time he lived down there in a shack with a campesino family. When he fell down in the doorway at the ranch, half in and half out, he was pretty much set to go back to Mexico. Of course, that was on hold at the moment as he tackled dying.

He lasted about a week. I went over one day, and he was propped up in bed so that the tumor blocking his throat didn't pester him too much. He said, "Chuck, I got some great news. We just got two inches of rain at the ranch."

Yes. I can smell the sweet grass as the clouds lift.

She is at war with herself, at war with the life within her fighting the death without her. And she knows this. And she writes me this. She says, "So after I talked to you, I went out to the cemetery. The sun was out here, and it was a beautiful day. Snow in patches hugging the earth in lovely patterns making me realize the earth has temperatures of variation, like a body. I had not realized that before. Then as I drove back a rage overtook me, and I raped and pillaged. I went to where I used to live along the beach and cut branches from bushes I know will bloom (not in obvious places or where it would hurt the bush or tree). Many many branches that filled up the trunk of the car and the back-seat. It took an hour and a half to get them all recut and into water all over my house and closed porch. I've been cutting forsythia and 'forcing' it but haven't tried these others—redbud, cherry, baby's breath, flowering almond, weigela (probably too late a bloomer) lilac (doubt this one will work)."

As she writes this to me, it is March, a month when boys hang themselves, a month when winter has stayed too long. A month when spring is near and force may be applied.

I don't trust the answers or the people who give me the answers. I believe in dirt and bone and flowers and fresh pasta and salsa cruda and red wine. I do not believe in white wine, I insist on color. I think death is a word and life is a fact, just as food is a fact and cactus is a fact. Last night more leaves fell from the hackberry tree as winter sank its claws deeper into the desert.

There is apparently a conspiracy to try to choke me with these words. There are these steps to death—is it seven or twelve or what? fuck, I can't remember—and then you arrive at acceptance. Go toward the light. Our Father who art in heaven. Whosoever shall believe in me shall not perish. Too many words choking me, clutching at my throat until they strangle any bad words I might say. Death isn't the problem. The words are, the lies are. I have sat now with something broken inside me for months, and the words—*death, grief, fear*—don't touch my wounds.

I have crawled back from some place where it was difficult to taste food and the flowers flashing their crotches in my face all but lacked scent. My wounds kept me alive, my wounds, I now realize, were life. I have drunk a strong drug and my body is ravaged by all the love and caring and the colors and forms and the body growing still in the new silence of the room as someone I knew and loved ceased breathing.

I stand in the room with Art's warm corpse and I wonder what has changed now, what it is that just took place. And I realize that I have advanced not an inch from where I stood as a boy when I held my dying dog and watched life wash off his face with a shudder. I do not regret this inability to grow into wisdom.

Almost every great dish in Italian cooking has fewer than eight ingredients. Get rid of things or food will be complex and false. In the garden, there is no subtlety. A flower is in your face. Be careful of the words, go into the bone garden and taste desire. So it has taken months, and it is still a matter of the tongue and of lust. And if you go toward that light and find it, piss on it for me.

I would believe in the words of solace if they included fresh polenta with a thickened brown sauce of shiitake and porcini mushrooms. The corn must be coarse-ground and simmered and stirred for at least forty minutes, then spread flat on a board about an inch thick and cooled in a rich yellow sheet. The sauce, a brew of vegetable broth, white wine, pepper, salt, some olive oil and minced garlic, is rich like the fine old wood of a beloved and scarred table. When you are ready, grill a slab of the polenta, having first lightly brushed it with olive oil, then ladle on some sauce. And eat. The dish is brutally simple. But it skirts the lie of the words of solace, it does not deny desire.

Never deny desire. Not once. Always go to the garden and the kitchen. Whatever death means, the large white cactus flower still opens in the evening and floods the air with lust and hot wet loins. The mushroom sauce on the corn mush will calm no one either.

That is why they are better than the words.

As I sit here, Chris is to the south, Art is to the west, Paul is back east and Dick is in the backyard by the fierce green flesh of the cactus. These things I know. The answers I don't know, nor am I interested. That is why food is important and plants are important. Because they are not words and the answers people offer me are just things they fashion out of words. A simple veal *ragú* is scent and texture and color and soft on the tongue. It is important to cut onions by hand. The power of the flower at night is frightening, the lust floods the air and destroys all hope of virtue.

There will be more blooms this spring, the cactus grew at least ten feet last year. They will open around nine in the evening and then close at dawn. I'll sit out there with a glass of red wine and the lights out.

When I tell people about the blooms, about how they open around nine and close before sunrise and do this just for one night, they always ask, "Is that all?"

Yes. That's all.

There is something beneath the style, concepts and flutter of words. This something exists on the same plane as pain. And it is called pleasure. I am across from St. Mark's in the East Village on a fall day. The sun is warm, the bistro doors are open, and here is a white plate of prosciutto, mozzarella, ripe tomato, foccacia, and a small bowl of olive oil with freshly torn basil leaves. The sidewalks pulse with people, and I can taste the hog in the aged ham, feel the sun in the tomato, taste in the mild, tangy cheese the grass of some distant hillside. The grain lives in the bread as I dip and chew and dip again. The red of the tomato explodes on the plate. Everything I know or will ever learn is simply a twist on this plate of food. There is no concept on this plate, it is the plane from which the concepts come, and to which the concepts finally return.

Barbara is across the river, sorting through a warehouse of the pieces that he used to configure his installations. The artist who had been his mentor and friend told us Paul had been seduced by materials. I look down at my plate again.

I think that Paul lived above the plate, analyzing it, or beneath the plate examining its molecular structure. And that I always want to eat the plate and not wonder why. I want to look deeply into the face and swallow the life but not fix or file the life. I live in flight from intellect and Paul lived in flight from what I am.

The salt and rose color and sharp taste of the prosciutto floods my mouth and I become a tongue flapping by the open door on the busy street. I don't want to understand taste, I want to taste. I don't want to understand art, ever. I want art to find that part of me beyond my thinking and understanding, to make me feel and by that feeling make me finally be. I want a world where everything is food, books are food, photographs are food, harbors are food, music is food, women are food. The night is food. The sunrise also.

And not food for thought but food for what thought keeps seeking and cannot seem to find.

The extra virgin olive oil hits my tongue and I want her for the first time. Again.

A woman walks past. She is very tall and has light brown skin, her kinky hair is dyed blond and plastered against her skull with some kind of material that looks like mortar, her body sheathed in a tight dress, her hips swinging as she wobbles past on her platform shoes, the sun dancing on her face, the eyes blank and wide, the hips studied and trained, my god, all of her so tall, towering above the others, gold hair brown skin gray sheath black shoes wide eyes and tomato on my tongue.

A woman walks past, she is in her sixties but has not been told, her bare midriff of flab spills over red slacks, her short hair electric with orange, high heels, stiletto heels, the lips a smear of red, she wobbles and seems like one a.m. in a cheap bar full of blue air, her eyes intent, locked on someplace straight ahead, and the eyes center and steady her as she wobbles along on those gigantic heels.

They come and go like that for an hour as I sop up the olive oil, sip a glass of red wine, tear at the bread, inhale the cheese, prosciutto and tomato.

I look once again at the note from Barbara in her big loopy hand-writing: "My life is *so hard* I can hardly stand it. But I will of course. Last thing my mother said to me was 'Barbara, you're so . . .' and I waited, hoping for 'pretty' or 'smart,' but she said, 'dependable.' It's true. I feel like the Little Mermaid who walks on knives so that she can stay on land and love the Prince."

The artist told me about a bridge he built in Germany. It has some kind of suspension design and its webbing holds glass. As cars drive across it, the glass shatters and grinds and crumbles and alters, the glass is remade and redesigned by the traffic, and this changes the play of light, it is being destroyed and it is being created by people all wound up with driving their cars and talking over their cell phones and thinking about their next appointments or love affairs or bad divorces or maybe, if they are truly blessed, their next meals. They are driving and creating and destroying even if they do not realize it, he said. I wanted to ask him, what happens to the bridge at night, when the light is gone? When the plate is empty? And still the rock swings and crushes the bone. What then?

He also told me that he called Paul, and Paul said, hey, I can't talk right now, I'm in the shower, I'll be back at you in a few minutes. But he didn't call. He carefully knotted a rope.

She is sitting on my bed with her back against the wall in the tiny hotel room. The bed is the width of a cot and I have the window open and the curtain hangs out and flaps against the brick wall. The light is very weak, the window opens onto an air space sucking down the sky over New York City. We have spent a day or so making sure we were not alone. It was safer that way and besides, we both knew the time would come soon enough. It is morning and I have been up for hours sitting on the cot smoking cigarettes and drinking coffee from a deli on Lexington. I am waiting for the bar to open downstairs so that I can drink fine reds from someplace in France and bathe in the studied cool of the waitress who thinks chic and feels cold under her careful hair and thin painted lips. I think she has begun to warm beneath her scorn for me, begun to wish I would eat something when I drank and learn to dress better and buy some good shoes, she is especially concerned about the shoes and that I should groom myself and savor wine instead of swiftly downing it. Yes, I sense a warmth slowly building beneath her sullen efficiency. Maybe if I did something about the coat, the cheap blazer that never wrinkles and that hangs like sheet iron off my frame, maybe if I traded up to fine fabric, perhaps a tasty wool clipped from a precious sheep in the highlands and then woven by a crofter in a cottage where the air sags from burning peat and all the lassies have blue eyes and rosy cheeks and fornicate all week and repent on Sunday in the doldrums of Calvinism, fucked one of those lassies also, but more importantly bought the fabric, found a good tailor, had myself measured and fitted and then, in good shoes of course, came down and waited impatiently for the bar to open, yes, she would tolerate my impatience and early hour, if I just paid some attention to these matters that matter, then, I have no doubt, the warmth behind her gray eyes and sullen expression would grow and grow, a bellow of desire would blow upon this warmth and flames would lick her body, lick deep into her vagina, her heart would begin to beat and she would pour that glass of wine with a smile. Of course, after this rehab, I would cease to guzzle it, I would twirl the glass and catch the scent and delicately taste the new bottle and then nod yes, nod ever so gracefully, rather than the way I behaved yesterday, when she poured oh so little into the fine stemmed glass and waited for my sampling and I looked at her sharply and said, pour and fill the damn thing, and went back to staring at the cold tabletop in the morning light.

Barbara sits up squarely on the narrow bed, back against the wall, body at attention. I eye the room one more time. I can stand and reach out and touch both walls. The ceiling also. The television is blank, I have never turned it on. The bed is six feet long and I am six feet and four inches. The sheets are thin and coarse, the pillow tiny. There is a chair, a small table for a phone, a lamp, and a carpet patterned to hide the vomit and the spills. The bathroom is a phone booth with shower. A tub is down the hall. In the morning, I bump into a man in his seventies exiting the room with the tub, do this each and every morning as I descend to the French tough love of the bar, and the old man is dressed in blue trousers, white starched shirt, red necktie and his skin as pale as the moon. He nods and moves off with a faint hint of cologne marking his passage. He has the solidity and dignity of a banker as he exits the tub room down the hall. His glasses are thin wire frames, his face unsmiling and sure of something. His skin looks powdered like a baby's bottom. He glances with disapproval at my sheet-iron blazer and seems to lift his nose ever so slightly. He is my wake-up call for the French waitress waiting to give me my lesson in wine etiquette.

Barbara's face is round, round with that swelling that comes from weeping, and she wakes now each and every morning with her eyes open and tears pouring out. She wants no more of therapists and the pills. The weeping keeps her clean and pure. Her hair is gray, the eyes dulled by tears, the mouth either a straight line or a downward turn. She folds her hands before her and clutches her purse to her side.

There is no beginning, no preamble. We go into it without fanfare. There was a woman at the book opening and Barbara caught her from the corner of her eye, caught this glimpse of her from across the room and buzz of talk and gleam off the polished wood floors and for the entire evening she avoided her.

"Because she knew," she explains as she sits on the bed. And I do not ask what constitutes this knowing. The light in the room is gray, a pallor seeping in from the air space.

"I knew if I looked at her, or talked with her, I would disintegrate. I wouldn't be able to help it. Because she knew."

I say nothing because I know what she knew. I know she has been to the dark country I have only peered into from the edges, the place where the food sits flat and empty on the tongue, where the dead never die but neither do they ever really live, the place where sensation becomes electroshock, where morning never begins a new day. A place worse than the room of the blue mist, a place blocked off from the river of blood, a bone garden without desire, and there is no torch song or memory of such a time. I have never been to this place, not once, not for an hour. Stars always dance across the blackness of my skies and the scent of a woman wafts on the air of my tombs.

The woman had a boyfriend and the boyfriend had a mother and the woman felt very close to the older woman, the mother, and then the mother died by her own hand. No one spoke of her, she ceased to exist and then the dead woman invaded and lived inside the living younger woman. Which Barbara caught out of the corner of her eye and fled.

I say nothing.

She says, "I know you are still angry with Paul."

I nod. I slow my heart, slow my tongue. There is no need for hurry since we are already there.

She says, "I just want to check out of here."

Then she looks at me and almost smiles at my obstinance in the face of her desire. And it is true, I am here to stop her from exercising her own free will. Not because I think she is crazy and not because I question her right to kill herself. But because I have decided to no longer permit it.

I hear birds singing as I sit in the small silent room, feel the sunshine, think of the bitter fruit of red wine coursing across my tongue. I am helpless in the face of my senses. The birds sound golden, the notes rich and sustained, the quivering inside their song narcotic. Then my eye shifts to the limb and on the limb the leaves, green lush leaves, veins in the leaves like rivers choked with life, a slight breeze, the leaves flutter and splash sun on my face. I am a fool for such things. The taste of spring water, the sharp stab of thorn into my bare foot as I scamper about on the desert floor, the scream of a hawk—the very phrase "a kettle of hawks" can elevate my heartbeat—the steam coming through a grate on a winter's night, the hot grease clawing through a restaurant vent, the beads of moisture on the glass holding a cold drink, the makeup designing a woman's face. The taste of fresh bread. In a cave, in that place of total darkness, you can see the blood vessels in your eyes.

Barbara's eyes are wide open and she is weeping and tears do not flow but seep, a wet sheen cascading down her face. The thing about the darkness of the cave, the thing that I always miss is sound. Last year I coaxed Barbara into feeding birds. When the ice came, she got a heater for her birdbath. But I know she cannot hear the song.

In the third century Wang Bi wrote, "The Image is what brings out concept; the language is what clarifies the Image. Nothing can equal Image in giving the fullness of concept; nothing can equal language in giving fullness of Image."

But what if it is not Image and language? What if it is Barbara weeping in a small hotel room with her back against the wall?

There is a point on Cape Cod where once scientists counted twelve million songbirds migrating overhead on one dark night. But almost no one else knew they were up there, hardly a soul, and so for them it did not happen. And Paul is dead and Barbara is sitting like a statue in the small hotel room and it is only the three of us now and none of us can reach up at the moment and grasp the strands of life passing overhead.

I light a cigarette, inhale and then slowly let the smoke fall out of my mouth. My back is to the window. It is not time to reach out. She is talking now, she talks on and on and it all makes perfect sense and is cleanly and tightly said. And I say not a word. I listen to the birds like I always do.

"You have to understand," she begins again. "You have to understand, I'm a person of roots, I belong to something, I'm part of a tree.

"And I always wanted to have a child, and then I had Paul, and he was an artist and then he too was part of this tree. And when he died, he killed the tree. And I died too."

Then comes silence. Then the touching. I can feel the roots gliding, probing, going down. The rot, the wet stench, the darkness of the ground.

The weeping does not stop but the eyes remain wide open.

The curtain flutters ever so softly against the bricks of the air shaft. I put out the cigarette. Everything has been devoured, chewed and digested. The boy running on the beach in Michigan, stooping down to find stones full of fossils, and in each stone the imprint of some squiggly thing from long ago. Paul had an eye for the fossils and always found the most. I can see him now in the glare of the sand, the lake spreading gray or blue depending upon the day, his tow head hunched over as he seeks his treasures, things from a few million years ago that go into his pocket wet and will be recycled. Up on the bluff, Barbara is hanging laundry on the line. Across the river in Brooklyn, the work sleeps in a warehouse slowly crumbling and revealing both its skin and its internal structure and the living tissue and decay hidden behind the word *art*.

I go downstairs and face my French waitress. I have come to love elevators, the closeness to others, the safety from everything else, the calm feel of falling. The door swishes open into the lobby, then a left to the street, a quick right and the tables are already out in front of the bistro.

The glass is in front of me. I study the faces of the people walking past on the street and I find them good, harried, haughty, relaxed, tense, no matter, I find their faces to be good. I am not ready to eat yet but it is coming near. For the moment, the faces are enough.

The French waitress is at my elbow asking if I want to eat. Not yet. But it is coming near.

I drink and my fingers tear at the shrink-wrap as pretty women walk past, the Mylar film distorting them but still I can tell they are lookers. I tear and tear at the shrink-wrap and finally the sound roars through, full, unfiltered.

The form comforts with its government type and little rectangles of order. It is modernism taken to the max, the place that obliterates the cage of figurative art, denies the cheap pleasures of the decorative, demands that we see anew.

The piece is called *Medical Certificate of Death* and is done in a bold black and white. Paul is signed on as the artist, the work apparently completed March 09, 1997, at 9:51 a.m. in the borough of Brooklyn, NEW YORK CITY. It was, the work states, done at Home. The style was Asphyxia, and this was accomplished "Due to or as a consequence of Hanging." There is a poetry to the elementary style of the composition. For example, consider the brushstroke after "HOW INJURY OCCURRED: Hanged Self. USUAL OCCUPATION *(Kind of work done most of working lifetime. Do not enter retired)*: Self-employed."

"KIND OF BUSINESS OR INDUSTRY: Artist."

There is a note from Barbara attached to the work. This one is typed and has the black and white clarity of the work itself. She says, and truly she is saying this since I can hear her voice coming off the page, "On another matter—sort of. Do you have any connections with the NY police department? I've thought about this. There must have been some photographs made of Paul hanging. Do I want to see them? Maybe I do . . . I think it's like The Stations of the Cross. I want to travel the path. As much as it hurts, I want to be with him. And death shall have no dominion. And time is round."

One night a few years ago I sat with a connoisseur of human lone-liness, a man who wandered the black hours with his video camera collecting bad deaths like coupons. He had a floor-to-ceiling book-case of tapes from his wanderings and we watched them streaming past on the monitor. I remember one hanging, where the man swung himself from a tree limb by stepping off a bucket. By morning when they cut him down, his feet touched the ground. There is this friend of mine, a border man, who also knows the hanging. One of his kin caught a border killer out in the hills and put a noose around his neck, tossed the rope over a limb and left him there on his tiptoes as he rode off to check fence. Came back a day later, and the man's feet were planted firmly on the ground and all the life had been choked out of him.

When I read Barbara's note, I think only of one thing: will the photo-graphs be black and white or have they switched to Polaroid? High contrast or the two-dimensional color that makes everything a decal? And did they use a flash?

I will not mention this to her. The cops will never give up the photo-graphs to the grieving mother. They know where art ends and life begins even when the life is ending. Time is not that round and that moment will stay in the past and in the files.

Of course, the files do breathe life into Paul. He is a deadbeat now. The mail comes regularly demanding that he get out of his midwestern grave and hightail it to New York City and pay his parking tickets, plus interest. The letter begins,

Dear PAUL H DICKERSON:
You have failed to respond to our previous notice concern-ing your unpaid New York City Parking Violation judg-ment(s). THE CURRENT JUDGMENT AMOUNT DUE IS: $2,256.50
The Office of the Sheriff is authorized to take the following enforcement actions where applicable by law:
- GARNISHMENT OF YOUR NON-EXEMPT WAGES
- SEIZURE OF YOUR BANK ACCOUNT(S)

- SEIZURE AND SALE AT PUBLIC AUCTION OF
  YOUR MOTOR VEHICLE(S) AND OTHER NON-
  EXEMPT PERSONAL AND REAL PROPERTY

Then the official note rattles on with numbers to call if you don't agree with the City of New York or places to pay if you do. A self-addressed legal-sized envelope is thoughtfully enclosed.

Barbara toys with doing something about the bill, but there is a part of her that likes the mail that keeps coming demanding money from her dead son. She is gladdened that the sheriff still counts him among the living. Once the smoke alarm goes nuts for several minutes and there is no smoke. Another time she hears Paul's name on television. There are clusters of these things and they are not to be denied or pondered. But they can be savored. Besides, the City of New York refuses to give up on Paul. She sent them death certificate after death certificate but they apparently scoffed at this ploy. Then the demand letters ceased for a while. But now they've reactivated their minions and are back on the trail.

Paul never stops, he is in the studio, the pale light of the city seeping through the slabs of glass, the south wall a long bench with tools carefully arranged, his face intense with dreams of materials and the gloss of skins, his eyes focused on someplace within himself. Scattered about are the abandoned machines he has found and brought home for their final work in the cannibal kitchen. The hand moves, the iron is adjusted, a puddle of mercury is poured into a small bowl. Step back, take it in, sense the proportions, wander in the process beneath the words, touch the plaster of Paris, bend the wire, now the light hits the mercury and it glows like a dead eye in the arrangement, arc, right angle, rough, smooth, rod, carpet, pale light, shrink-wrap, here, here, just a slight twist is called for, yes, that is it.

Outside the city sleeps, the throb has died. No one knows what is going on in here, no one cares about the studio, the warehouse, the orphaned machines. The cyberspace world does not register here, nor do the markets and global flows of capital and the screams of brokers on the trading floor and the mayors cutting ribbons. Or the museums hanging the bones of earlier light and form. Paul is alone in his laboratory, he stands on the final beach reaching down for the wet stone holding the fossil, the stone only he can see. His head is full of theories of light and form and artifice, things he has noticed and taught himself, taught himself so thoroughly that he has had to forge his own language to write it and talk it and here in the old factory he clutches his real vocabulary, the things you and I have shunned, have cast off as trash. He is the dreamer of the unloved and misunderstood, the flow and rumble and rage of things beneath the surface, the anger of the internal structure, the inexorable march of the materials and the light. And hardly anyone seems to know this fact except himself, and when you realize that kind of solitude, it can be exhilarating, just as climbing a cliff without a rope is exhilarating, just as spinning into three a.m. alone with a bottle can be exhilarating, just as tearing through the shrink-wrap . . .

No, no, that projection is the wrong angle, a twist, and then the mercury shimmers as it vibrates from this touch, the lethal, beautiful puddle of mercury, metal made liquid made light made weight, the secret of the word *density*, of the word *mass* now freed to flow between the fingers. There is something missing, a piece of the engine of process beneath the word *art*, there, in the corner, that gear lying in the dust, pick it up, ah, put it here. The thing . . . locks in. A wall suddenly goes up. Nothing more can enter. It is a finished thing, beyond the words but within feeling. A nation unto itself made from the rubble of the nation. An answer to a question not yet asked but one that will someday be on all lips. Here, stand back, a deep breath, a feeling of peace.

The tree in my yard continues to come back. The huge severed root made the leaves drop and limbs stand like bones against the summer sky and for a while it seemed dead. But finally buds appeared, new shoots broke through the bark, the whole mass seems to stagger. Light licks the tree, and in the dark of the night, there is a faint murmuring and then in the hours when the city sleeps deeply and noise vanishes, a faint sucking sound rumbles up from the ground. The weather menaces globally now, too much rain here, drought there, and in my desert world this means warmer weather and a long chance for the mutilated roots to heal and then regroup and plunge once again into the depths of the soil. It has taken months for this healing. At first I was impatient and plied the tree with chemicals and floods of water. Now I accept its rhythms and watch as day by day it sucks itself back into life. At night I sit out in the dark and watch it eat the dirt slowly created by its own litter.

Sometimes I walk over and rub the bark to reassure myself that it is still rough.

I am walking along, the night is cool but not cold, and I have just trotted out of Little Italy and am marching north into the street numbers. The sidewalks are full with Friday night and everyone wants love and no one knows exactly how to look for it and how it looks but still we want it, and we walk along smelling the city, my god, the wonderful smell of exhaust and perfume and sweat and cooling and booze on the breath of the men swinging past. Barbara is talking art, lots of art, and I half listen in my ignorance of color and form and density and structure. Paul did this painting, and it hangs in her house, and he called it *Ship to Shore*, and she cannot quite describe it to me but I feel the yearning of the paint slapped on the canvas. Or should it be *Shore to Ship*? Does the direction matter since it is always a question of reach, and desire? I believe in this painting I have never seen, believe because I believe in Paul, the kid, he's down there on the beach right now, down below the bluff, he's finding small smooth stones with fossils gleaming up out of the hard skin, but he knows, he knows the skins and he can learn from the fossils, the once-squiggly things, he can learn the structure. Barbara walks and talks and she says, "His work is inexorable."

I like the ring of that, like it for the same reason I like the roots of mesquite plunging downward, seeking and hungering and never giving up. My anger slips away, at least for a while. Paul was about something, about connections and things living beneath things that create the things we wish to see and be.

There is a window full of masks, the delicate, fancy masks they sell in Venice for Carnival, the kind of stuff you imagine Lord Byron wore as he reclined in the gondola on a fine night and then rolled over and banged some countess as a bridge passed overhead and sighed. We stop and look in the window and our wide-open eyes scan it and we suddenly have the faces of children.

Down the street a ways, two white guys sprawl on the sidewalk with a hat in front of them for coins and bills. They have a cardboard sign between them that says DESPERATE MOTHERFUCKERS.

I wish I had written that.

What I am looking for is a fine grocery, one that sells precious things, expensive meats from pampered slaughtered beasts, light oils and strong spices, fresh herbs, stout pots and pans, dark rich coffees. There is a sauce, a kind of chutney in Italy, *mostarda de Cremona*, which is a mix of mustard and fruits in a syrup. The best comes in tins and is excellent with roast pork. I cannot find it easily, nor is it offered on the Internet. The only samples I have tasted I brought home in my luggage from Florence. And then the needle grabbed me and I was an addict. The pork, of course, is boneless loin cut from the center and wrapped with string. The flesh is pierced and pocked with slivers of garlic and snippets of rosemary. Browned in a cast iron pan, then the wine is poured on and the whole thing simmers until barely cooked—just a hint of rose-colored flesh in the center. The roast rests, ten or fifteen minutes on the board, is cut thick and while it rests, the wine is reduced to almost a syrup and this reduction is poured on the slices. For this roast, I want the *mostarda*.

I never find it. The city does not offer me much time. Art, you know, the reduction of life to form. The shrink-wrap. The cannibals around me block my way. But now, weeks later, I think of the *mostarda* and can taste the sweetness cut through with the mustard.

The mail comes through the slot in the door. I stoop and pick up a card. It is from Barbara and the writing is not in a loopy hand but in strong block letters.

The card says,

LOVE IS STRONGER THAN DEATH.

Exit Wound

Come, we all know the way. We were all born after midnight but it has taken us years to come into this knowing. There have been false starts and we mark these mistakes in our ritual of carving out decades and eras and giving each a name lest we forget or ever understand. But the real issue is not the names or the idea of blocks of time with little names. The real issues await.

Consider the shrink-wrapped machine Paul cherished in his studio. The equipment has not been idle since Paul tied that noose. All the social programs are shrink-wrapped. All of them. All of the policies. The treaties, also. The drugs deny us the sensation of the transparent material clinging to our bodies. We must shake off the drugs in order to realize our condition. Feel the plastic tighten on the loins, the constriction at the throat, the lips struggling to move, the words strangled, the breath short. Now, a vast shudder.

Come, we will go to the ground. Over there, in the bosque of mesquite where the sweet shadows splash on the ground. And then after a few moments' rest, when we feel strong enough, when we feel ready, we will go out into the white heat of the flat.

I am in that room, that sterile American room warehoused in a motel by the interstate, a room very much like the one where we first met. The room is down the line, hundreds of miles west of that earlier one but still it is the same room with the same digital clock and the same television offering fifty-five identical channels. This time it is about a thousand yards from the line and that point where the mesquite begins to give way to oak and elderberry. When I lived at the ranch outside Chorizo, Chris was appalled by my enthusiasm for elderberry. I noticed it held its leaves until around Thanksgiving and then rested briefly and sprouted green again in February. The ranch house stood on a small knoll and the wind would howl for days. To the west, Chris had planted junipers years before but with the scant water they had barely grown. So I went downslope, just a little, and for days dug a hole in the rock with a steel bar. Then I walked to the wash where I had eyed a young elderberry, a small sapling maybe six feet high. The day was oddly still and as I dug out the sapling, I looked up for some reason and saw a golden eagle riding a thermal over my head. And then seemingly out of nowhere a red-tailed hawk appeared and started to dive on the eagle bashing against the tail again and again, all this done in apparently a perfect fury. It was a day of singular calm, the kind where I could hear the trees talk and understood every word, a sky overhead of aching blue, and then suddenly this aerial war. The hawk won, and the huge golden eagle wheeled and disappeared over a ridge where three deer browsed, one buck and two does. That was the day I dug up the elderberry, much to Chris's amusement. And I planted it as a bet on the future, the only wager worth making.

Now I am back to the same ground, quartered in this bleak room maybe twenty miles west, at least for an eagle, from the ranch itself. I do not go there now—the ground around the house sings too much of Chris and his voice pains me.

The mesquite remains strong around my room, bosques clog the bottoms and trees lord it over the hills but the edge is near, the oaks are probing, the elderberry gleams. This is the right place and I know it in my bones. The rivers, they are many here. Below me runs the river of the Holy Cross. All around me flows the Río de la Sangre, the River of Blood. And I am lodged in the Río Rico, the Rich River. It is a resort waiting for the guests to discover its existence. I have been here before and always have come for the same reason: the silence of the vast loneliness that grips the resort in a death hold. The air conditioner roars by

my ear, outside the summer rains slowly build, and clouds float overhead taunting every living thing, but the sky refuses to weep. The
mesquite knows and abides. I live in torment, anxious for the blessing
of the rains. For years, they have hardly visited. Just to my south in
Sonora, the past year has been dry with only eight percent of normal
rainfall. The beasts die, the desert writhes, and my own kind, the men,
women and children, struggle and parch. Yes, they parch with huge
cracks shattering their faces, seizures twisting their limbs, the eyes
empty sockets, the hair dead and limp off the ghastly skulls. The cattle
are beyond hope. The fields empty. For the first time in this century,
there is no planting in the Rio Yaqui valley. The burning trees will
appear soon, I can feel it, taste it. The flames will lick the wood, men
dangle once more and suffer the infernos of their imaginations.

I have come here at the order of the mesquite. I listen and obey.
This is the place to settle accounts. And I am not alone. The torch song
echoes off the walls, this song clings to me like a garter. Then there are
those voices in the next room at 3:18 a.m., those familiar voices, they
draw near. And talk and I listen.

Riding, he remembers, riding. I can feel the whispers play across my
skin. He has these scraps of names, events, memories and deals, and as
we sit in the semidarkened room, voices tear at the silence. Often the
voices speak Spanish. Arturo feels the cancer now as it eats his liver, his
colon, his lungs and most certainly other organs. He tends not to give
in to things. When he was a boy, his grandfather paid other kids a
nickel to fight him so that he would become tough. But now his ankles
swell, his skin goes yellow from jaundice, the belly grows from edema,
the flesh flees his increasingly scrawny neck and arms, his voice becomes
raspy as the lungs fill with fluid. But his mind stays alert. He is living
the end time, and at this point everything is equidistant, fifty years ago,
today, tomorrow, all the same. All a new kind of now.

The dying came slowly but clearly. First came the bellyache, and
then he finally went to the doctor and they cut out part of the colon.
Then the best part of a year to chemotherapy and he laid off the bottle

completely. But with the fall, he began to slip back to where he had been, back to darkness and anger and a refusal to taste life. He quit watching cooking shows, then quit cooking, then took to take-out burgers and whiskey. He had shut off people, let the threads of a lifetime drift away. I said nothing, let him act out his desires. But I noticed. Now he is in an Indian summer, a short season of lucidity before all comes down.

That is when the ride comes up, a tale boiling out of his failing body and taking him to the days when he was young and hungry in the fifties. Rancho Diablo rests just west of the city on a flat pan of desert. The Purple Gang out of Detroit colonized the site long ago and used it for members who had to lie low or who needed a rest from their arduous toils. This is all known and of no account. The city and the gangsters had struck a deal long before and the terms were no dirty work here and no problems with the authorities. What mattered was the blooded stock, the fine horses kept at Rancho Diablo. Someone rustled the horses and Art was handed the problem. So his lungs full of fluid, his voice raspy, his skin now yellow, he saddles up one more time. Now he rides.

He has always had a thing for horses. As a boy, he jockeyed in match races down by the dry river. Once he tumbled head over heels into a mesquite, came up bloody but unbroken. Art squats by the corral, sees the tracks heading south, follows them on foot. The tracks just keep going south. So he gets a horse, mounts and rides.

Suddenly, Art is animated, his failing voice gains vigor and is somehow young once again. He feels the horse under him, smells the sweat, squints his eyes into the harsh desert light, and slowly plods south on the trail. The way follows a valley tending uphill, the mesquite and saguaro and cholla ever so slowly give way to grasslands and hints of oaks. Fifty miles south he hits the line at Sasabe, twin hamlets straddling the border and devoted to the making of adobes. He plows ahead into the next nation. Then it is days to the capital of Hermosillo. He rides past ancestral ground, places where his kinfolk persist, through the town where the government put his great-grandfather up against a mud wall for his execution and then spared his life when a huge bribe was delivered. His great-grandfather came north, swearing he would never set foot in Mexico again. He rides through all of this and then the land tilts down again and hits hard desert with tree ocotillo, ironwood and pockets of *guayacan*. There is much heat and little water. And few people.

The tracks bear south, ever south, and Art rides through white light and dust and sleeps on the ground and stays the course. That is the memory flooding out of the dying man, the memory of sound horse-flesh, dry winds and relentless riding. On the edge of the capital, the tracks lead to a set of buildings. Art dismounts and enters. It is a slaughterhouse and he is too late to save the blooded stock.

He manages a gasping laugh about the slaughterhouse. But the ride was a wonder, a movement from Rancho Diablo into the great desert of our flesh.

The huge lettered message on the prison watchtower all but shouted: SECURITY IS NOT CONVENIENT. The tower looked down on well-tended roses. Surely, Mr. Poland understood this thought. After all, his stock in trade was planning, constant vigilance, control. He was made for the world being born all around me, a true child of it and, for those interested in literature, a foreshadowing element. He was the rootless man, the refugee always wandering, the thief in the night taking from those who own the things. Too bad he had to leave, just when things were looking up for him and his ways. We must remember the message SECURITY IS NOT CONVENIENT, as I sit close by the rampart of our newest gated community, the United States of America. The fence is close at hand, the savage fence that can lop off the fingers of an unwary climber, the fence now backed with military might, aided by ground sensors and aircraft, the fence now viewed through infrared when the night comes down.

We are not about much anymore, but clearly we are about being safe. The federal government has pasted forty death sentences on our fore-heads, a tally worthy of eighteenth-century England, when a pilfered egg could fetch up the noose. There is a man out there, right this moment, and he is becoming legend. I am certain of this fact, this legend business. He will be a *leyenda* and men will sing of him when after midnight they are drunk and deep in their sorrow. This man is like me, a creature of the edge. But he has gone over it, done the very thing that terrifies me. Gone over it and now he wanders spreading his message. He kills. Here, there, possibly everywhere. He is a Mexican man, the authorities assure us of this fact, and they have listed thirty aliases he commonly uses. He first visited the United States in 1976 and has stayed at times for long stretches, usually in our prisons. He cannot see very well and must have his glasses, a trait shared with Mr. Poland, who was blind as a bat without his spectacles. But this handicap does not apparently interfere with the work. The man, the one I am speaking of, that man, rides the rails in the United States. And wherever he travels, he leaves death. The authorities believe he hops off the trains, slaughters people, and then hops back on. He is a linear man, you can see that, and thus he is not at all like me. Except for this matter of the edge, for being a child of the edge. I admit we share this blood tie. But I pull back, always, just in time, pull back because I become afraid. He is fearless and rides through our nights, penetrating our gated community. At least two hundred people now do nothing, absolutely nothing, but try and keep up with him. He has become an obsession for a nation of more than a quarter billion souls. Imagine that, a human ant colony struck numb by one fellow riding the rails. Perhaps he sings Woody Guthrie songs as he is hurled through our entrails. Listen, can you hear "This land is your land, this land is my land"? They say he has taken to leaving messages over his kills. They will not share these messages with us—security, after all, is not convenient—but I think the messages are unnecessary for our understanding.

He has come from the river of blood. I have been waiting for him, waiting oh so many years. Wait, I will open the door, the sliding glass door, there, I have done it. Now I can hear the mesquite just outside, hear the sucking sound of the roots. This helps, yes, it helps. This rootedness. It keeps things at bay. But he is riding, killing, and I know where he came from. He is the future, yes, indeed.

Years ago, almost thirty now, I was riding the El in Chicago when I thought I was having a heart attack. What was killing me, though, was not my heart but myself. I will explain. I had taken a job teaching in a university, a good job with few hours and fine pay. I had money, leisure, status. At the Newberry Library, a renowned archive of Americana, I had my own carrel where I could retire and think big thoughts. The library was a warehouse of Native American materials. I could walk the stacks and hear the captive tribes whispering on the shelves. The unruly matter of pre-Columbian culture had here been reduced to order. The chants, the murders, the sacrifices, the holy buffalo skulls, the wampum, the fetishes, everything had been made neat for contemplation. I was a creature of this contemplation, a scholar.

I began to slip into strong drink. One day I sat in my apartment for half a day drinking and listening to the same album over and over. My big Newfoundland dog stared at me with horror. Then I got in my truck and drove to the center where driving tests were administered. They included a behind-the-wheel exam on a special roadway. I careened through the course, my reactions were vastly impaired and from time to time I jumped curbs, blew corners, and ran through signs. I passed. My examiner was drunk also, a perfect stranger to me, but clearly a soul mate, dead drunk and sipping from a pint as the exam was in progress. After my graduation and certificate, I drove back to the apartment and the giant dog and listened to the same album for most of the night, until finally the alcohol brought me to the floor.

The sense of a coronary on the El came a bit later. My chest tightened, my breathing grew rapid and it took all my power not to hurl myself from the train. I got off at the stop and sat on a bench and realized something was terribly wrong with my life. I walked over to the Newberry and sat once again in the square facing it. I did not enter, not that day, not ever again. The tightening in my chest left, never to return.

I quit teaching, walked out on a three-year contract. The department head, the world's authority on Andrew Jackson, thought me insane for leaving. I have no quarrel with his conclusion. But I left. Drove the perimeter of the United States with punches deep into Canada. Then down the West Coast, restlessly looking, a beer in my hand at all times. It is mainly a blur, a convenient blur, the enemy no doubt of security. I came to rest in the great desert and have never left. I cannot seem to get out.

I had been trained to be a historian and I decided to do just that. I would be the historian of my world. For a year I did manual labor. Then I began to write. Slowly I fell into my work, always under some disguise as a reporter, or editor, or contributing editor.

My world, the one I appointed myself the official historian of, was the edge. I decided in those moments of tension and panic by the El track that the essence, the raw, bleeding, throbbing heart of my time was to be found on the edge, not in the center. The middle ground strangles the voices and they can hardly be heard. But at the edge they scream, and the edge I picked, this place of the great desert, was where the world of hunger we call the Third rubs against the world of silence and property we call the First. So I came to ground on the banks of the River of Blood.

And now this man appears, this rider of rails, this dispenser of death, this messenger from the edge.

A woman asks, "What did his face look like?" There are many questions about the execution, all circling back to one: What was it like?

I do not know.

I can't possibly know.

But the face was very pale, very pale. And the lips pulled back ever so slightly. Into a sneer, if you wish. Or perhaps the lips revealed nothing more than a brief recognition of finally knowing. Arturo when he was a young man worked as a mortician and pointed out to me that the lips of a corpse always pull back after a few hours and morticians for generations were trained to do delicate stitchery to keep them closed. Now, he cackled, everyone uses Krazy Glue. But in Poland's case, the face was very pale, and the lips for whatever reason pulled back ever so slightly.

The money must have been colorful. The English pounds and Irish pounds and Scottish pounds with their odd sizes and faces and inks. All this money neatly stacked on a kitchen table in Phoenix, the wives and the brothers sorting it out, the heat a beast just out the door. The pound notes had traveled so far, across the ocean deep, and they fell into a vast abyss where they had no value and became wastepaper.

The face is a more certain thing, very pale. Of course, this could be the result of the lighting, the fluorescent tubes with the mutilated spectrum playing down on the hospital-like room, splashing weakly against the clean gray tiles and the black eye of the one-way window. Once the side door to the witness chamber, which was dark and lit only by the glow coming off the death room, came open, and I saw the prison guards standing in a knot in the white light of the Arizona afternoon. A blond woman stared in, her lips thin and firm, her face tanned yet blank, her body ill served by the uniform of khaki and dark browns. Then the door closed again, the sun disappeared and all that remained was the gurney, the man, the fluorescent light. There was silence, just the strained breathing of the witnesses, all of them struggling not to gasp.

The face was very pale.

I have hungered for the deep, that vast blue eye floating out past the edge and far from shore. I have always wanted to make things and have usually failed. I lack the talent for much besides brute labor. I can recognize talent—pick the painter, the architect, the landscape wizard, the furniture maker—but my plastic sense, my feel for three dimensions, is flawed and I know. When I was a boy on the farm, we'd raid cucumbers from the garden—not that anyone cared, since we took the big ones that had hidden under a leaf and gotten away from everyone and grown massive and seedy—and cut them up to make boats. We'd float these ships in the round metal cow tank, and I can smell the sweet green water and hear the buzz of the flies in the July light of the Midwest. The tank is never clear and the water is more like slimy soup. I stand there and watch it run off the snouts of the cows after they drink. It is always mud around the tank, from cows pissing and shitting and just slopping water. We'd go to the east side of the barn, next to the double door leading to the milking stalls and the little room with the separator.

There is no light when we go to the barn before dawn and find the cows milling, waiting to enter and be milked. The air is sweet with the smell of hay and straw and cows. Kittens twine around my feet waiting for the milking and then the cows come in and go to their stalls. Some are touchy and have to be hobbled, most are gentled, and we hook up the machines and you hear the motors start and it is before dawn on the prairie and the scent of hot milk floods the air. I watch out for the tails swishing and dream of building barns and cupolas and hen houses, and plowing fields and planting gardens, orchards and vineyards, all these things and more, all dreams of sketching my heart onto something solid, something apart from myself. I want to build and I never look out a car window at buildings without thinking of throwing up my own design. I can smell the wood, feel the swish of the brush as I paint the siding. I will enclose space and create a world.

The farm brought this to my skin, the sense of random buildings that had all poured out of someone's mind—the wood granary with its worn flooring, the hog barn, the chicken coop, the pump house, the machine sheds, the small factory feel of the place with everything painted that flat red with white trim. The floor plans made no sense, the rooms and nooks and crannies were everywhere, the staircases seemed to erupt for no apparent reason and then straggle upward. Besides the buildings, there were the various slices of the ground, the yard and outside of that, past the white picket fence, was the orchard, and wrapped around all this was the grove to stop the winds that came off the plains and raked the land.

My aunt thought about none of these things, she thought of card games, of the burying ground across the road where she planned for herself and her husband to be planted, she thought of ice cream, and when the truck came every week she was right out there in the yard with a cigarette dangling and picking out her flavors, and she thought of the news, was never shy about current events and knew damn well how things should be done.

When my aunt was a young woman in the twenties and early thirties, she lived in Los Angeles and we never asked about that time when streetcars ran and L.A. was some kind of paradise by the sea with no rules, just a bunch of midwesterners running amok. And then somewhere in there she ran a speakeasy down by the river. I can see the old photographs with their odd brown tones and they beckon like a lost world, a place that looks comforting and full of black coffee and cigarette smoke and the butter is kept on the windowsill with the eggs to stay cool. Always, the coffee is bitter and in thick mugs.

And yet I know this seeing—this safe world of red barns and heavy mugs and little boats we'd carve out of cucumbers and float in the stock tanks, the cows standing there with drool and blank eyes, this world of horseflies, apples rotting on the ground under the trees, the raw smell of mown hay in the meadows—is counterfeit for me, a trick played against my eyes, to get me to believe in straight streets and church choirs. There is a truth missing and it's on the floor of the speakeasy by the river, in the scent of cheap perfume coming off a woman's neck, in the wild habits of the barnyard and the surly stenches coming off the pens and fields.

I cut the cucumber, the form emerges, a skiff perhaps, it is nothing like what I saw in my mind, I have failed once again. But the hungers stay, the desire to shape things and taste them.

I can remember becoming obsessed with killing crows, practicing for hours with a call, crawling through the brush of the grove to get close, studying the mysteries of the variable choke on my bolt action twenty-gauge shotgun. I would dream of pheasants, the feathers flying as I scored a clean hit. I would look for them in the red clover and I always missed.

So you see, I came originally from the center. I tried to stay. But the edge beckoned. I should have recognized the cucumber boats for what they were, a child's effort to find a way out into the deep, the blue eye past the edge. Always I carved boats. Never a train. The boats were not very good but the thought was clearly there.

Maybe the problem is the shrink-wrap. After all, Paul fell in love with the stuff, even got his own machine.

I think he was onto something. I feel the world slowly strangling in the shrink-wrap of dead ideas, of treaties, of policies that pretend everything is contained and will remain contained. This world will not admit the existence of a man on a train, and then when despite this vast new faith, the man appears riding the rails, this world hunts him down in defense of its idea. Security is not convenient. No, certainly not. Ike Morgan is off in the crazy place in Austin, smothered by decades of state incarceration, look, see him over there at that table on the lawn? See, he's doing yet another George Washington with a black face. Or maybe he's drawing Lyndon, the man who is climbing out of his tomb. The thousands are crossing the line, clawing at the gates of the community. The shrink-wrap just won't hold.

Listen. Hear that train whistle blow?

Four selenicereus bloom in one night, the huge flowers white against the dark bark of the mesquite. Each day the tree puts on more leaves, each day the severed roots heal. I glance at the blooms in the gray light of dawn as they begin to close. They belong to the night. They seek love after midnight. The flowers look to be ten inches across, a falling off from normal and a sign I think of the great drought gripping the desert. In Sonora, just to the south, rainfall is, as I have noted, way off. Here it is off thirty or forty percent. The desert licks against the city and I feel its tongue in my backyard.

Nothing seems to give security. I know security is never convenient but they forgot to tell us that it would be altogether absent. We do not have closely watched trains.

The edge is growing and spreading toward the center the same way the red fingers of an infection splay out and race across the flesh.

Kentucky, my old Kentucky home. Bluegrass. The heart of the heart of the center, yes, indeed. The train slows, he hops off. Two students walk by the tracks. A man and a woman.

He comes out of the bushes and he has a knife. He sticks the knife in the side of the man and wants money. They are hungry, they are ravenous in the river of blood. But the man and the woman have no money. They are students. So he ties them up. He kills the man. Then he comes for the woman. He rapes her. He beats her. He breaks her jaw, cuts her up good. She passes out.

She awakens covered with shrubs. In my great desert, a lion covers its kill with shrubs. She lives to tell.

But that was a while back. And he still rides the rails.

She tells me that Christmas Day they took a walk through the brown hills around Chorizo. They do this every year, a kind of custom, and when they do this walk, they insist on an absolutely straight line to see what might turn up. It was cool but sunny this particular Christmas and they walked off their straight line and came upon a kilo of marijuana out in the middle of nowhere. How it got there is anyone's guess. Bounced out of a truck? Tossed from a plane? Silently slipped out of a pack as a caravan trudged through in the night?

No matter. The question is how to peddle it. It must be worth quite a bit. So that is the question brought back from the annual Christmas Day walk through the hills.

These things never get asked and the answers never get into biographies. For that matter, there is less and less talk about walking straight lines, especially on Christmas Day. But it does happen, it did happen, and then, how do you sell it and for how much?

I never walk a straight line. I at least take that precaution.

I'm always coming up from Lost City—it's out there, way out there, but I'm not telling where—coming up through the creosote flats and the sun is good on my shoulders as my feet give way with each step in the soft dirt, and coming up, always, from Lost City. It's a trail, an ancient trail I'm on, and I can see pottery fragments at my feet now and then, and seashells, yes seashells, dropped here far from shore by someone in a hurry a long time ago, someone busting ass back then before Columbus raised sail and hit this hemisphere with his heavy jones. And always I'm plodding along with a ridge to my east, palisaded rock, and falcons nest up there, and sometimes I can see them up high, trying to hide in the sun as they survey the universe and line up for a kill. The creosote dominates, and every once in a great while a barrel cactus, but very few of them, maybe one every so many miles, mainly just the crunch of the dirt under my running shoes. Each hour after noon, I stop and light the stove and fire up a brew half coffee and half cocoa, the coffee instant and black and bitter as hell. I can taste that bitter against my tongue and it is sweet like honey to me because it snaps me alert and says, you are alive and tingling and drink this down and you can throw this pack back up on your shoulders and walk some more.

Let's just have it that way: I'm coming up from Lost City. The coffee is bitter, damn fine in its bitterness, the falcons nest just over there to the east and that is how I remember and taste and feel. Questions don't bring me there, the feel does.

I go to ground. That helps. But less and less. A scientist has been studying the death of silence in the United States. He notes that now even the most remote deserts shudder with the vibration of our thunder. He does not mention the river of blood, perhaps he is holding that back for another paper. But he is right about the shudder. I can feel it shaking my body.

I hear the singing of the rails. Everywhere. The torch song also.

Near Lost City, I sit under a mesquite. It is the best that I can do.

I have always needed dirt. I need the smell, the feel of it in my hands, the color, the texture. I have much less need of grass. Dirt is coarse and savory, grass is merely something that hides the vital world of dirt. That is why deserts have been essential, since they are the kingdom of the dirt.

They face us in their nakedness. We cannot mistake their meaning. So we turn away. But the deserts keep growing, yes they do, even our scientists notice this fact. They are thriving. They feed off that river of blood.

Come, we all read it, there, posted on the Sheetrock of our souls. This will not take long, we have no need of long manifestos. We are past universities and think tanks and focus groups. We have left the meeting room and the talk of postcolonial this, postmodern that, and more importantly, the postponed world. We are of the tree and listen to the wood. We have no truck with theory. We seek no alternatives. We are now of the grain.

Mr. Poland, lunch will be served after the event.

But first, a brief announcement from underground.

The Mesquite Manifesto states that we must:

Eat.
Lust.
Caress.
Fight.
Swallow.

Now, choke it down.

First, three fried eggs sunny side up with four slices of bacon on the side and one order of hash browns. Also, two slices of whole wheat toast and two pats of butter. Two servings of Raisin Bran cereal would be nice too. A whole carton of orange juice, two cartons of milk, and please two cups of Taster's Choice coffee.

Got it?

"I understand," the document rattles on, "that my last meal shall be reviewed in conjunction with food items which are readily available, either in the prison food inventory or which can be obtained locally from a grocery store. The quantity of food afforded to me shall be in reasonable portions that normally would be consumed at a meal and which could be eaten within a thirty (30) minute period.

"This is my last and final meal request. I will not resubmit my request."

The thing is signed in a clear, graceful hand, Mike Poland.

The river of blood rises, breaks through to the surface, and courses boldly through the desert. This happens more and more frequently now but little remark is made of the fact. I check the news, listen eagerly to the weather, yet never hear mention of this new turbulent river. I find oblique items about trade and illegal immigration that glance against the rage of flow. But the thing itself is ignored and yet I find myself forced to wade the flow without warning. I go to the blood.

I get a call, I won't tell you from whom. The caller has a tip about the man riding the rails. I listen closely since the caller is well connected and his tips often turn out to be true. He has heard a rumor from the FBI, a rumor about the man riding the rails. The caller says the agency thinks the man riding the rails may have killed a dozen women in Juárez. The man riding the rails has a mother and the mother lives in Juárez. He also has kinfolk in the Midwest. And in New Mexico. And in Vermont. And in Mexico.

He travels, you know. He glides with ease in and out of the gated community. He knows all our ways, has mastered our language. He has studied us. Of course, he has gone too far. His photograph is everywhere now. Or I should say his photographs, since a good-sized set belches forth from our prisons and jails. He is said to be a master of disguise, he could look like just about any man with brown skin. And he goes wherever our trains go and they lance through the vibrant flesh of the nation willy-nilly. They are the great monument to our early days of power, the fruit left us by the robber barons.

Just down the hill from my room, the train tracks slice north. They come from Mexico, are essential to commerce and the new order being busily wrapped around the world. Perhaps he is riding by right now and only the roar of the air conditioner is keeping me from hearing the train.

There is an inside there but no outside there, not ever, not in one line of those endless letters I read by Michael Poland. There is one fleeting reference to canning vegetables when he and Sally Ann lived in Oregon, that's it. The world becomes a vast fluorescent-lit room with stale air and endless pawing over details and massive defenses of behavior. The world becomes a closet or a storage locker.

This, I believe, can be fatal. When the Poland boys dumped the bodies off Bonelli's landing, tossed them weighted with rocks in stout canvas bags, they felt the dead men had left the real world forever. Less than a month later, they bobbed to the surface 5.7 miles north of the landing in a place called Debbie's Cove. The six-foot bags were now only four or five feet and badly frayed at the end where the rocks had rubbed and rubbed and torn the hell out of the material. The third bag holds the police gear and guns—this failed also, and the cord used to strangle the guards was recovered. In a color photograph taken at the time, Russell Dempsey is face-down on the beach, his head covered by what's left of a bag, his body swollen but intact, his jeans soaked, his skin very white. He is perfectly preserved, down to the identification in his pocket.

Out there had come in here. The lake had kept the dead men close and the cool waters had saved their flesh. But the shallow shelf had betrayed everything. A simple chart used by any boater would have made plain the problem. A week after Michael Poland was lethally injected, two ships appeared on the sea bottom of the Mediterranean off Israel. They had set sail in 756 B.C. with a cargo of wine. They were perfectly intact, preserved by the cold bottom waters. The salvage operators noted that deep cold waters can suspend history, stop time itself.

Gardening could have helped or bird watching or nature walks or some fishing. Almost anything would have restored a slight connection with out there. Of course, a talk with any mesquite would have been a major step. Out there. Or die in here.

He alarms no one. He is very quiet. He does not go to the cantina. No, not when he is at home. They have traced the man on the train to his lair. He hails from Durango. I have loved Durango since my fifteenth year. You have seen it—Sam Peckinpah shot *The Wild Bunch* in Durango, a great American tribute to the importance of loyalty, a tribute smeared with gore. When I was fifteen, my father and I parked our bread van in the capital of Durango on a city street. The van served as a camper with a gas stove and two bunks. I remember a knocking on the door, my father opening it and seeing urchins standing there in the twilight. He said nothing. Then reached into his storage shelves and started handing out cans of food, one after another. All this happening silently.

Afterward he rolled a cigarette, smoked and said, "Jesus." We never talked of the matter that I can recall. He saw something in those faces and I think what he saw was himself, that hungry urchin he had once been. After that I returned to Durango several times on my own. It is a big state full of desert and on its western flank it climbs into the Sierra Madre. In this high ground, it hosts a family famous in drug circles for heroin and marijuana. The family is a vast gang more than three thousand strong with tendrils of drugs reaching into the American Midwest. The authorities find this web of kinship all but impenetrable and for decades the family has thrived. They visit to the north constantly. A few months ago they were in my own city looking for an informant so they could kill him. In this they failed, at least for the moment, but in their work they are almost always successful. They are a legend in the drug world and their legend floods others with fear.

The wolf is rumored to persist in the sierras of Durango, a village is reported to host a shrine to the animal. The wolf marks a line in the flesh between the north and the south. The mountain lion is notorious for its fear of canines, sometimes being treed by small dogs. The jaguar, the cat of the south, holds no such fear and rips dogs asunder that pursue it during the hunt. This is sometimes explained by the fact that the jaguar, *el tigre* in Mexico, evolved below the range of the wolf, while the lion came into the country with wolves competing for the turf and the kill. Durango is a place of both and a hoped-for last bastion in the Sierra Madre of the wolf, a finger of the northern fangs into the south. It is truly a hard country.

This is the Durango from which the man first took to the rails so many years ago. He lives, it is said, in a town called Rodeo. He is, as I have noted, very quiet and does not carouse. His fellow citizens see him gliding by on a bicycle but know little of him. His favorite route takes him past the local police station. He is called Angel when at home.

He comes back, they say, to visit his wife and infant daughter. He is not perfect, of course, the records show he has been given one parking ticket. His wife describes him as a model husband. She herself works in a lab at the town health center. As for Angel, there is not much to be said. He never talks to anyone, just comes and goes.

He is bilingual, they all note that fact, and a few years back he taught English at the private school next to the police station. He has degrees also.

In the United States, he is wanted for eight killings. At home, he is hardly noticed. He does seem gone a lot. His work entails travel. And messages. And shrubs carefully placed on the kills. Of course, we will hunt him down and kill him. That is obvious. But what if he then re-appears? Again and again and again. He is the basic product, the one being manufactured globally far faster than we can throw up gates around our communities. We all know this in our bones.

That is why we lust for the execution chamber, for the lethal injection. It seems to answer a need. It seems to keep the gates functional. This gesture is theater, nothing more, but who has a right to scorn theater? The play is essential for us, and after all, everything can't be Old Vic. We love our theater. It is scripted, we can hold the program in our hand. I remember the deputy warden diligently studying the protocol sheet for the killing of Michael Poland. The carefully typed sheet gave off a comforting sense of order as he leaned over it and ate a chocolate chip cookie as the clock slowly moved toward three p.m. He also carefully sipped from a bottle of mineral water. He was the picture of perfect ease, a man who had the situation under control. That is the very thing I have always lacked. I am drawn to the flowers that bloom without warning, there high in the mesquite, the giant cactus flowers lasting but a few hours of one night, lusting after midnight in the velvet of the blackness. I crave the root of the mesquite but go toward the explosion in the night. Safe in my garden, there where Dick's ashes form a paste in the soil, yes, there where Arturo made his last visit as the cancer tolled inside his body, there I try to remain. But fail. It is a sanctuary but it offers no security. My office beckons, the building painted La Purple and Canario, two colors duplicated from an old Mexican flip book of colors. The pigments are dense and violent, the purple obscene, the yellow a shout. This is my cocoon, a shimmering place. I never believe in security, I am on red alert, always.

I keep an eye peeled for the burning mesquite. It will come. There is no stopping it. I am resigned to all this, I have come to the edge with my eyes open. The purple, the yellow, they are comforts, but they cannot stay the fire. The tribesmen refuse to stay in those archival boxes in the Newberry Library. The lines we draw in the dirt fail and are scorned. The man strikes the match, dangles, fires the gun, the flames lick the wise old tree. The sucking sound dies off in the inferno. Paul's shrink-wrap bursts into flame and is gone in an instant. Chris shouts, great news, rain at the ranch, but the downpour vaporizes before my eyes. Arturo rides in, dismounts, approaches, but a brown hand stops him and his measuring, points to the white line on the ground and nods no, no. The bone garden of desire glows in the flickering light. Dick puts another dollar in the machine and tries to believe he can beat it. The torch song slithers through the air.

Been waiting for this train, long time coming, my ear to the rails keen for the first vibration announcing the report. Now it is coming, he is riding the rails. His legs dangle out of the open boxcar, he is singing a torch song as the locomotive—wonderful word—hurls him into our safe centers. He is, of course, a madman, a berserk fellow who does not appreciate our largesse and generosity. In the big scheme of things, he means nothing, he is a mere trifle. The global markets purr on and take no notice.

How can he be blocked? How can we ever pull ourselves back from the edge? That is what I want to know. We lack the wisdom of the mesquite. We are the sworn enemies of all roots. We sever them at will, turn a deaf ear to their sucking sounds, deny their ways with our ways.

Security is not convenient.

I make a brine of salt, sugar, cloves, bay leaves, peppercorns and a stick of cinnamon. I place two chops in the brine for twelve hours. Then I make noodles and a pesto of two kinds of basils, garlic and a tomato. I sauté apples and onions as a sauce for the chops. I place them in a skillet of hot oil and cook each about five minutes on a side. I use a digital thermometer to catch them at exactly 137 degrees, the point at which trichinosis perishes in the flesh. I open a good cabernet from Chile and eat.

It helps not at all.

I open another bottle and drink it.

It is too late for my remedies.

If the mesquite crosses the line, and the Yaquis cross the line, and the Mexicans cross the line, and the drugs cross the line, and the trains cross the line, how can I hold the line? God knows I want to. I want the line to be marked by a white picket fence and I will dwell on my side with a lilac bush by the door. The mesquite I will murder, cut it down and stop the terrible sucking sound. I will wreak havoc in my march toward order. My fury will burn the blue mist from the air, my hands will strangle the torch song. I will plow under the bone garden. I will get off the rails forever, they are not to be trusted.

I look out the window of my room. The mesquite licks against the oak. The line is going. The fences are coming down. I must go down to the sea again.

Can't you hear that train whistle blow? Quick, light a hundred-dollar bill. We will cleanse the ground with fire. First, we will burn the trees, all of them. Get a rope, now. We are ready. Touch the shrink-wrap with the flame.

The railroad man roams. The authorities say that he was sexually abused as a child. And gang-raped in a U.S. prison. They think he is now having sex with corpses.

To the south the sky is black. The rains are near. I can all but taste them. Lightning stabs at the mountains, thunder claps out hope from afar.

But I cannot wait. The flames lick the bark, the burning tree goes up in flames, the river of blood flows around the trunk and ignites. From the glow I see the desert of flesh stretching before me, endless and blazing with heat. This is my ground and in time it will be your ground also. The maps deny this fact. They are useless now. The line is gone for good. But the trains still run on time, we have that at least.

After the event Mr. Poland wishes lunch. He is really hungry. The canvas bags are gone now, worn away by the rocking of the waters. Replaced by a thin, tightening film. The money's no good now, the pound notes flutter in the wind, the heehaw of wild spending is over. We can look right through the shrink-wrap, maybe take a shot, for a few seconds, at pretending it is not there. Come with me and we will sink into our pleasures. No, we won't do a line or have a toke or open that bottle. Those things are nice but they never go far enough.

Come, we will walk toward the blue waters and leave the sucking roots behind. Here, by the beach, grow stands of *cardón,* a massive cactus that thrives where the desert tastes the moist breath of the sea. I love *cardón*. They are creatures of the edge, towering fat things framing the waters just beyond. Imagine, smell the sea air, imagine out there. Blue mist in the air. We will violate all the lines. Just off the shore, the reef reaches out and forms a rough bottom at the end of a forty-foot free dive. It is time for the dive. The waters will put out the fire, this must be true, it is a matter of faith.

Kick, kick hard, kick the legs, down, down toward the bottom. The waters grow cooler, the cold is layered like a cake and the body blades through one layer after another, the dark bottom comes nearer and nearer. Pull with the arms, kick the legs, down, yet farther down. The lungs scream but are ignored, the dive has become everything. The feet come to rest on the rock, the head pivots around and stares. The cold penetrates and has weight, a cold that feels like Jell-O and encases the body. The fire is gone, doused by the sea. A matter of faith. Silence, finally silence. The vast shudder ceases. The surface is an idea without substance, there is nothing now but an eternity here beneath the waves.

Put out of mind the frantic need for air. Believe. Now look up, yes, up, there, look, *mira, mira*, there floating far above, the cold eye of a yellow disk, the sun rests lightly on the waters and has no heat.

A mere kick of the legs, a pull by the arms, the body will rise, yes, rise, this is certain. Bubbles trickle out the lips, the salt stings the eyes, panic comes through in waves, yet still the body does not move. Fish glide by, reef fish acrylic in the brilliance of their color, and there close by the foot a moray eel, green with an obscene intensity, extends out of its shelter, the face voracious and surrounded by an avocado glow of flesh, the mouth sensuous and yet made for tearing meat from the bone. A shark glides by just above, a serene creature always on the lookout. The cold steel of the water presses against the face, a bone-chilling cold, and the water is a cement setting, an imprisoning thing. Just kick, use the arms, it is that near, then will come the rising, the escape back to what has been fled, a kick, a pull, a gasp, the promise of breaking through a gray lid, tearing at the shrink-wrap that chains the body and denies it freedom.

This is the moment.

Always the moment.

Undertow licks at the legs, tugging the body seaward, taking it out there away from the shore, far into the blue away from the edge and the memory of the *cardón* fat and green and massive on the shore.

Come back to life.

But how to come back unless there is a life to choose?

Arturo lying there all yellow, the breath rasping, shudders coursing through the body, the sound of a horse's hooves in his head. Dick refusing to eat anything green, shoulders slumped, the eyes glazed, the soul very rough and pocked with craters, the head downcast, Dick refusing to look up at a bird on the limb, denying the flat disk floating on the surface, and saying, as he pulls the handle of the machine in the casino, "You can't win." Chris, Jesus, he's excited, rain at the ranch goddammit, inches of rain tearing down the hills, flooding the wash, a roar rising from the valley, a tongue of foaming brown water yearning for the sea, rain by God, his hollow eyes gleaming, his white lips mouthing some words, it is all about weather, you know. And Paul, he's right over there, eyes cold, eyes anxious, eyes hungry, eyes searching, his hands resting on the shrink-wrap machine, gonna make everyone notice, gonna make'm finally see, the rope swaying in the cold waters, the machine purring and spewing out shrink-wrap, a tongue of transparent film lashes out and hunts prey.

This is always the moment.

Find a life to choose. Don't look at the mail or be swept away by the vast driftnet of cyberspace. Go to ground. Tear away the film. Eyes open now, there are no secrets with eyes open. They are promising major dates, millennia, eras, golden shores. Magic surgery, special pills. Fiduciary statements. These are all lies, there can be no room service. Take it, don't ask for it. Probe deeply, lick the soil, turn out the lights and feel the night sky. Security is not, security is over. Back there, yes, there on the land, the river rises, foaming red across the earth, building toward flood level, and the river will not recede within safe banks in our lifetime. This cannot be helped, too late for that, but must be faced. Turn down the music, listen, hear that train whistle blow.

I tell you there is wisdom in the mesquite, things we must reckon with if we are to be more than numbers or pie charts. The money is simply not enough, nor are the medicines, though I truly love the potions in my darker hours. But there must be an act, a willingness to taste and feel. The rains draw near on the desert, I can feel them close by. The trees yearn and wait. They do not know how to surrender. Jesus, don't you think I'd like to quit? But such a thing would be a grievous sin and to hell with God, still a grievous sin. There is no way out of here. The gated community is closed until further notice. Soon the torch songs will render them ash. The train will come hurtling through. The blue mist will spread like a message from the Lord. Burning trees, also.

Confused? I'll spell it out. Be for a place and then you can have a place and then you can finally be someone. Or the shrink-wrap will see you now. Here, lie down on this gurney. Never mind the needles. Ladies and gentlemen, the main event.

Rise, yes, rise, now, kick the legs, pull the arms, upward toward the sun, claw at the shrink-wrap, the lungs scream, rise. Blood orchids await on the shore, there high in the trees, the petals open for a monstrous feeding. The mesquite, a bosque of mesquite, the deep roots, sucking sounds. At the water's edge, there on the lip of the deep, *cardón*, huge, burly in strength, towers framing the blue waters just beyond. *Cardón*, feel the word licking the tongue. The edge will reveal the center. The edge will reveal ourselves. But we must not go over, not fall into the abyss. Do not listen to the train whistle. Still, the edge must be dealt with or it will come to us in its fury. Lunch will be served after the event. First, the singing of some torch songs. The tree will burn. A walk through the bone garden of desire. Then the blue mist. A river of blood.

Come, we will do these things.

Rise now, kick the legs, ignore the screaming of the lungs. Back to shore.

Eat.

Lust.

Caress.

Fight.

Swallow.

The salt taste bites the tongue.

I think a woman is part of the answer but then, I am a man.

Barbara remembers and in the memory sees flicking patterns. But more often feels the warmth.

So she remembers, "I separated when Paul was about eighteen months and divorced when he was two and a half. At that time I sent him to the Institute for Juvenile Research at the University of Chicago for a psychological evaluation—in case I needed to watch for anything. They said he was completely normal (whatever that means) but that I should be sure to set boundaries for him. Implying that either he needed them or without them he would push beyond boundaries. I didn't know how to do that, so I didn't worry about it.

"He was considered a 'failure' at Montessori school. He wouldn't put the square peg in the square hole, but turned it into a train, or a plane, or something."

The sound of harpists, musicians, flutists, and trumpeters shall not be heard in you anymore. No craftsman of any craft shall be found in you anymore, and the sound of the millstone shall not be heard in you anymore.

The light of the lamp shall not shine in you anymore, and the voice of the bridegroom and bride shall not be heard in you anymore. For your merchants were the great men of the earth, for by your sorcery all the nations were deceived.

—Revelation 18:22–23

Acknowledgments

I feel like I'm closing the barn door after the horses have fled. I owe more people than I can properly remember or thank for their help in writing this book. First, I'll tip my hat to people and publications that printed some things that are part of this book, generally in a different form. So thank you Clara Jeffrey at *Harper's*, Melissa Harris at *Aperture*, Scott Norris at Stone Ladder Press, David Granger and Mark Warren at *Esquire*. Basically, the origin of the book has nothing to do with publications, but I tend out of emotional or economic need to park versions of what I am working on with magazines. I write for magazines so I can pour the loot into the black hole of books.

My memory fails me when it comes to the hundreds of people who were kind and thoughtful in helping me to understand things, people such as Barbara Houlberg and Meg Keoppen, Roy Elson and Tom Shook and, hell, hundreds more. For example, I wandered into an execution because Barry Graham got me invited and I learned the culture of killing people because Dale Baich was my guide. And almost everything I do depends on the kindness of strangers and entails the pleasure of meeting and knowing a lot of people. I like people and so my life tends to get crowded with them and when I write, well, they all matter and make a difference.

And then there are the folks that helped me with the writing: my agent, Kathy Anderson; my editor, Becky Saletan; and my witch, Mary Martha Miles. They have all forced me to do better, and in such lonely work as writing, this help is a lifesaver.